Examining Physical Education for AQA A

Second edition

Kirk Bizley

To my dearest, patient wife, Louise.

Heinemann Educational Publishers
Halley Court, Jordan Hill, Oxford OX2 8EJ
a division of Reed Educational & Professional Publishing Ltd

OXFORD MELBOURNE AUCKLAND JOHANNESBURG
BLANTYRE GABORONTE IBADAN PORTSMOUTH
(NH) USA CHICAGO

Heinemann is a registered trademark of Reed Educational
& Professional Publishing Ltd

Text © Kirk Bizley, 1996, 2000, 2001

First published 1996
This edition published 2001

05 04 03 02 01
10 9 8 7 6 5 4 3 2 1

British Library Cataloguing in Publication Data
A catalogue record for this book is available from
the British Library

ISBN 0 435 506757

Designed by Dennis Fairey & Associates
This edition produced by Wendi Watson Design
Printed and bound in Spain by Edelvives

Acknowledgements
The author would like to thank the following for
their help during the writing and production of this
book: the Central Council for Physical Recreation, Alistair
Christie, Alison Clements, Dave Elston, Jennifer Johnson,
Gareth Key, Chris Pike, Bob Rees, Leigh Robinson, Liz
Breadmore, Rob Bircher, Sue Walton and Jan Winton.

The publishers would like to thank the following for
permission to reproduce photographs:

Action Images pp. 54, 56, 65, 127, 129, 130, 174;
Allsport pp. 39, 55; Aqualisa Ltd p. 34; The *Birmingham
Evening Post* p. 128; Gareth Boden pp. 9, 21, 25, 26, 27,
28, 50, 76, 117, 184; Chris Brown/Action-Plus pp. 18,
44; Clive Brunskill p.119; BSIP, Krassovsky/Science Photo
Library p. 105; J Allan Cash Ltd pp. 132, 149; Casio
Electronics Ltd pp. 101; Trevor Clifford pp. 165, 171;
Coloursport pp. 59, 158; Mike Cooper/Allsport p. 49;
Kevork Djansezian/Associated Press p. 109; Andy Lyons/
Allsport p. 19; Patrick Eagar p. 91; Alan Edwards pp.75,
92, 97, 123, 134; Empics p. 14; John Evans/Camera Press
p. 111; Stu Forster/Allsport p. 16; Stuart Franklin/
Magnum Photos p. 182; Melanie Friend/Format p. 31;
Sally and Richard Greenhill pp. 103; Otto Greule/Allsport
p. 113; Robert Harding Picture Library pp. 32, 108; Tony
Henshaw/Action-Plus p. 87; Mike Hewitt/Allsport pp.126,
127; Tommy Hindley/Professional Sport pp. 57; The
Hulton Deutsch Collection pp. 153, 173; The Hutchinson
Library p. 141; Jed Jacobsohn/Allsport USA pp. 150, 178;
Mike King/Action-Plus p. 13; Glyn Kirk/Action-Plus
pp. 17, 63, 81, 89, 118, 159; Manchester United Football
Club p. 177; Mike McNamee/Science Photo Library
p. 114; Raoul Minsart/Powerstock ZEFA p. 42; Steve
Morton/ Allsport p. 138; National Coaching Foundation
pp. 145, 148; R. Palomba/Retha Pictures Ltd p. 30;
Popperfoto p. 110; Mike Powell/Allsport p. 8; Adam
Pretty/Allsport p.124; Radio 5 Live p. 161; Rex Features
pp. 135, 176, 183; Pascal Rondeau/Allsport p. 146; H.
Rogers/Trip p. 168; Shaun Rotterill/Allsport p. 136; Ross
Setford/ Empics p. 93; Sky Sports pp. 166, 167; Sporting
Pictures pp. 12, 15, 35, 41, 45, 46, 47 (both), 48, 53,
106, 115, 154, 163, 164, 175, 181; Michael Steele/
Empics p. 156; Billy Stickland/Allsport p. 155; Meg
Sullivan pp. 10, 22, 33, 94, 98, 99, 100, 102, 137, 185;
Neil Tingle/Action-Plus p. 157.

The publishers would also like to thank Sally Smith for
picture research, Crystal Palace Football Club for the
brochure reproduced on p. 142, Sport England for the
logo reproduced on p. 144. For permission to reproduce
the cover photographs: Gareth Boden (basketball players);
Sporting Pictures (speed skater and Marcel Desailly with
World Cup). The publishers have made every effort to
trace copyright holders. However, if any material has
been incorrectly acknowledged, we would be pleased to
correct this at the earliest opportunity.

Tel: 01865 888058 www.heinemann.co.uk

Contents

3 Factors affecting individual performance and participation *and* Social and cultural factors affecting participation

The Student Book

This book has been written for secondary aged students (particularly Key Stage 4) and especially those who will sit the GCSE Physical Education examination/Games examination. The book is designed to meet the needs of students following AQA Specification A, but the information is also relevant if you are following one of the other examination board specifications.

The book has three sections.

1 Physical activities

This section is closely linked with the practical coursework component of your course and covers Assessment Objectives 1, 2 and 3, plus section A(9.1) and B(9.2) of the subject content (for the written paper).

The units in this section of the book are designed to help you to prepare and perform practical activities more effectively, while increasing your knowledge about the ways in which you can improve your skills and make full use of the types of guidance that may be available to you.

Various units in this section consider the different roles you may have to adopt during your course, and information from many of the units can be used for non-performers adopting a different role. All students are required to perform the practical aspect of the course but if you are unable to perform in a practical session then you may be able to take on one of the other roles such as coach, trainer, observer, assessor, analyst or leader.

Several of the units also cover skill areas A, B, C, D and E of the specification. They will enable you to prepare yourself better for the assessment your teacher must make of your work in these five areas.

Unit 7 particularly matches the criteria in skill area D to show evidence of the abilty to analyse and take action to improve your own and others'

performance. The final unit in this first section covers the requirements to show the effective performance and analysis of physical activities.

Tasks are set throughout the units. These can be used:

- as practical tasks to be performed during the practical lessons
- for homework topics
- for longer-term coursework projects.

2 Health, fitness and factors affecting performance and Principles of training

This section covers Assessment Objectives 2 and 3 of the overall examination outline, concentrating on sections A(9.1) and B(9.2) of the written paper theory work – which accounts for 60 per cent of the total theory marks.

In this new edition of *Examining Physical Education* these units have been revised and updated to cover sections A(9.1) and B(9.2) of the specification. The units relating to training (units 28–30) also directly support the practical component requirements on planning, performing, monitoring and evaluating a health-related exercise/training programme including leading a warm-up/warm-down session. These units may be used at the beginning of your course to prepare you for this aspect of the practical assessment.

The information contained in these units provides all of the basic theory information that will be necessary in order to comply with the requirements of this section of the specification. They also have the added benefit of providing information that can be used by all core Physical Education students to satisfy this requirement under the amended orders for Curriculum 2000.

There are tasks sets throughout this section and many of them take the form of extra work topics. These can be used:

- as homework topics to reinforce the information from the unit which has been covered

- for group work or whole-class discussions

- as practical activities, in the case of tasks that lend themselves to being performed in a practical way.

Wherever possible, you will be using the units in this section in as practical a way as possible. This may include using the textbook as an extra teaching aid while you are in the sports hall, training gym or even taking part in an outdoor game.

3 Factors affecting individual performance and participation and Social and cultural factors affecting participation

This section covers Assessment Objective 3(a) – 'factors affecting participation and performance in physical activity' – of the overall examination outline; sections C(9.3) and D(9.4) of the written paper theory work. This accounts for 40 per cent of the total theory marks.

Again, in this edition of *Examining Physical Education,* these units have been revised and updated to cover the areas in sections C(9.3) and D(9.4) of the specification. Likewise, topics have now been removed from the syllabus, have been removed from this edition of *Examining Physical Education.*

All of the units contain information that is as up to date as possible at the time of going to print (June 2001). However, this section reflects trends in society and, as a result, this area is subject to much change and development. The tasks set in this section make allowance for this and suggest ways in which you can keep up to date with change

and/or check on the latest information or developments.

An extremely effective way of making sure that you are up to date with the topics covered in this section is to keep newspaper and magazine cuttings and to check other forms of the media regularly – for example, television and the Internet.

The Teacher's Resource Pack

As well as this student book there is also a photocopiable Teacher's Resource Pack which has been produced as a complimentary publication and which supplements the content of the student book.

Most of the worksheets in the Teacher's Resource Pack start with a 'key understanding' section. This identifies the main points you should know about and understand after completing that particular unit in the student textbook. The worksheets also contain 'key questions', which can be answered using the student book. Sample answers to all the 'key questions' are given in an answers section at the back of the pack. Where relevant, there are also practical tasks which you may be given, often in a practical lesson or session.

Other resources

Further publications are also available by the same author, which can be used in conjunction with *Examining Physical Education.*

PE Matters 11–14 and *PE Matters 14–16* look at practical activities in detail and give information about all of the major sporting activities. *Revise for PE GCSE: AQA* is a revision guidebook that is based on *Examining Physical Education.* It has all the necessary information condensed into a concise form.

SECTION I

Physical activities

This section looks at what physical activities consist of and the ways in which they are affected or assisted. Physical Education is a practical subject and this section emphasizes the practical nature of PE and the influences upon it. Many of the tasks are of a practical nature and can be completed in practical sessions or practical blocks of work. In essence, this section is about the theory behind the actual practical activity because it should make you think more carefully and deeply about the ways in which you participate in practical activities.

Much of the information will also help you to fulfil the criteria required for all of the five skill areas in the practical component. Knowing how skills are acquired and then developed; being able to identify what qualities are needed in a performance to make it good (or better); understanding the need for and role of rules and conventions; knowing what the different roles are which you might be able to adopt, and developing the skills needed to be able to observe and analyse, are all important and require quite a high level of theoretical background to enable you do them properly.

The way you will be assessed in the practical component will not simply be about performing activities, but also about the factors that affect performance and make for a more balanced, effective and well-informed performer. This section will give you specific information to enable you to link together your theory and practical knowledge most effectively.

One of the most important parts of learning or starting a physical activity is the acquisition of skill. The higher the level of skill a performer has, the better they will be at their chosen activity. Also, when either helping someone to acquire skill, or observing his or her skill levels, it is important to understand skill acquisition fully.

What is skill?

Skill is using knowledge or expertise to succeed efficiently and effectively in achieving a particular objective. In PE, skill is the ability to perform activities or movements with **control** and **consistency**, to bring about a desired result – for example, full control of a ball, a bat or of body movements. A skill can be basic or complex, often depending on the type of activity undertaken.

Basic skills

These are usually simple things such as throwing, catching and striking. A key requirement for mastering these basic skills is the control of body movement – **co-ordination**. Performers must be able to fully control their body movements to perform a skill correctly. They must be able to perform basic skills well, before going on to more complicated movements or activities.

Throwing a ball is considered a very basic skill but it is still a very complicated movement. It takes co-ordination between the legs, the arms, the hands and the brain in order to achieve an accurate throw.

TASK I

Which parts of the body do you have to move and control when you throw a ball? Watch someone do it and describe fully the movements you see.

Complex skills

These are skills that take a long time to learn because they involve a high level of co-ordination and control. Athletic field events are good examples of using complex skills. The pole vault, in particular, requires a combination of skilled movements for run up, take off, flight and landing to complete a successful jump.

Nobody could hope to compete in a pole vault competition at even a basic level without gaining a high level of complex skills such as judging the run-up with precise accuracy, carrying and gripping the pole correctly, taking off and rotating in the air, and then landing safely.

All activities have this combination of basic skills leading on to more complex ones and it is the mastery of all of these which leads to a truly skilful performer. Throwing a ball in cricket can be a basic skill but to throw it in from a deep fielding position quickly and accurately to the wicket-keeper behind the stumps is a complex one.

TASK 2

*Choose **three** different sporting activities and for each one name at least one simple and one complex skill which must be learnt.*

A good pole vaulter must master many complex skills

Practice

Skills can only be acquired through **practice**. To make progress and improve in an activity or event, the performer must be prepared to practise repeatedly certain parts or aspects of that activity over a long period of time. There are no short cuts. A performer must be prepared to start at the very beginning when learning an activity or movement. This means that the basic skills must be acquired first before attempting more difficult or complex skills. Even top level performers continue to practise and improve the skills they have learned. This is an important part of their **training**.

In most schools, PE lessons will have an initial **warm-up** session followed by a skills practice related to the particular activity students are about to do.

A group skills practice session

TASK 3

*Name some basic skills for **one** activity. Describe some skills practices that could be used at the start of a lesson.*

Practice sessions

The majority of the skills that are learnt and developed come about through practice sessions and these must be well organized if they are to be useful. A typical practice session would be organized as follows.

1 Warm-up

This is important before the start of any physical activity and it should not be ignored in a practice session. It should include some stretching and **flexibility** exercises as well as some more energetic exercises aimed at increasing the heart rate and body temperature (sometimes known as **pulse raisers**). If the practice session is going to involve one particular part of the body more than another, that part must be fully prepared during the warm-up. If this is not done properly the performer is more likely to be injured.

Top gymnasts, for example, would expect to warm up for between fifteen to thirty minutes before they would be ready to go on to the next stage of their practice session (and gymnasts of all standards always warm up for several minutes).

2 Skills practice

This involves practising the skills particular to the activity. These may be **group skills** (something such as a short corner routine in hockey, which requires a group of players to work together) or **individual skills** (such as a tennis player practising their serve).

If it is a team game activity it would be a good idea to practise both types of skill, to be fully prepared to use them in a game. In netball, for example, the group skill would be practising the centre pass move while the individual skill would be shooting.

TASK 4

*For each of **two** activities give examples of group and individual skill activities that could be practised.*

The skills practice can be made even more useful by having **static opponents** (people who make no attempt to intercept or interfere with another player but who can take up certain positions) and **active opposition** (players who take a full part as opponents and try to tackle or dispossess the others). It is a good idea to use a combination of both of these in a practice session.

3 Game situation

The session should finish with an opportunity to try out the skills that have been practised, in game conditions. This does not have to be an actual game or match because the idea of the session is to improve performance. Instead, a **conditioned game** may be more useful. This is a game or match where some new or adapted rules are introduced which could make it easier to play, or even harder to play! Examples of this include allowing players to serve underarm at tennis to enable the game to get underway more easily, or perhaps only allowing goals to be scored from headers during a soccer game.

The theme of the practice session (i.e. the particular skills that have been practised) can be continued during the game, to help the performers to improve the things they have tried out earlier.

TASK 5

Outline types of conditioned games for **three** *different activities that could be used to improve specific skills required in those activities.*

All practice sessions should be helpful but it is very important that they are organized and well thought out. A coach or a teacher usually takes a practice session with clear ideas of what they want to achieve.

TASK 6

Choose an activity. Work out a practice session a coach could use. Give details of the warm-up, skills practice and the game or match session.

Frequency of practice

As well as being necessary to improve skills, practice is also vital to keep up levels of performance. The amount a person practises will depend on how seriously they take their sport and at what level they play. A **professional** would expect to practise every day, often for several hours at a time. On the other hand, an **amateur** may only practise once or twice a week for a total of a few hours.

Practice does not just consist of taking part in the sport itself. There will have to be some training in order to work on fitness (see unit 14).

A person taking part in an individual activity will probably practise far more than a team player. They have the sole responsibility for their performance and they have to make sure that they are skilful and on **form** (maintaining their standards). It is also far easier to organize one person than it is to organize a whole team, so team training sessions may not be so frequent.

TASK 7

Talk to a team player and an individual performer. Find out how often they practise their chosen activity.

Regular practice is very important

Drills

Team players make more use of **drills** – repeated group practices designed to develop the correct way of doing something. Although they are repetitive they are an essential part of practice. A good example of this is the lay-up drill in basketball, where players continually dribble in, step and shoot at the basket in a group, with one group shooting and another group collecting the ball and then joining the shooting line.

By taking part regularly in drills successful performers can get to a level of **grooved performance** where they have practised something so often they can repeat it almost automatically and consistently correctly.

TASK 8

*Choose a team activity. Describe fully **one** drill that can be performed.*

What should be practised?

The content of a practice session is clearly very important and it will vary between different performers and different activities. A beginner will have to start with the basics while a more experienced performer can work on more advanced skills.

If a skill is constantly practised there will be **reinforcement**, which means that the performer will become better and more consistent at that skill. A performer may experience different effects when skills are being practised. For instance:

- a new skill is learnt quickly, then progress slows down – **negative acceleration**

- learning a skill is difficult at first but then progress quickens – **positive acceleration**

- progress is fairly level and constant – **linear progress**

- possibly the most frustrating effect is known as **plateauing** where a performer appears to

be stuck at a certain level and cannot progress beyond it for some time. When practising a skill a performer may plateau at several points and it may be a long time before progress is made. For this reason, a performer must be prepared to break skills down into stages in a practice session and be prepared to work at them for some time before mastering them. Plateauing is one of the main causes for performers giving up on an activity as they get frustrated by their lack of progress.

Applying skills

It is one thing to learn or acquire a skill, it is quite another to be able to use that skill at the right time and in the right way. Top performers can be selective and consistent in applying their skills – this is what makes them successful.

At the top level in professional tennis there is very little to choose between the top one hundred players in terms of the skills they possess – it is the ways in which they can apply those skills that makes the difference between winning and losing!

Many skills are similar in different activities and a great deal of **transfer of skills** can take place. For example, a performer who is skilful at throwing and fielding in cricket will find that many of the skills are transferable if they decide to take up rounders or softball. So it is important to concentrate on acquiring basic skills, as they can often be useful in more than one activity.

TASK 9

Draw up a list of basic skills and give some examples of activities that may have transferable skills.

Open and closed skills

Some skills are called **open skills**. These show up in situations that are constantly changing. For example, footballers taking part in a match are in a constantly changing environment and may have to change or adapt their skills according to the demands of the game. If a strong wind starts to blow they will have to take this into consideration when passing the ball long distances. Although many situations may arise during the game that are similar in terms of players' positions, passes which could be made or opportunities to shoot, each will be slightly different.

A trampolinist, on the other hand, is performing in an environment that does not change, as the equipment used is always the same and there are set moves, shapes and routines to be used. The skills used here, such as somersaults and twists, are called **closed skills**, as these are skills that have a set pattern.

Not all skills fall neatly into one of these two categories. The skills needed in some activities fall somewhere in between being open or closed – sometimes with an element of each. For example, a tennis player uses many skills that are neither fully open or closed skills.

TASK 10

Give examples of two activities that have closed skills and two that have open skills. List what those skills are.

Trampolining involves closed skills

Feedback

In order to improve in a skill, performers need a way to judge how well they have already performed. This might be as simple as being told by a teacher or a coach if it was good or bad, and ways of improving. Alternatively, performers may be able to judge for themselves how well they performed the skill. Often it is not just whether it was successful or not, but how it was performed which is important.

This information is called **feedback** and there are several types.

- *Continuous feedback* – this is where it is clear to the performer during the performance how well it is going. For example, if a routine is going as it did in practice or if, for some reason, it has broken down.

- *Terminal feedback* – this takes place at the end of a performance.

- *Knowledge of results* – this is a form of terminal feedback at the end of a performance and could be as simple as whether you won or lost.

- *Knowledge of performance* – this concerns how well the performance was done rather than just the end result.

- *Internal/intrinsic feedback* – this is sensed, or felt, by the performer while they are performing.

- *External/extrinsic feedback* – this comes from sources other than the performer, such as sounds or things they can see.

- *Positive feedback* – this is information received regarding successes in the performance.

- *Negative feedback* – this is information about unsuccessful aspects of the performance.

Types of guidance

Most guidance for performers is usually provided either by a teacher (see unit 5) or a coach (see unit 6) and this is one of the main ways in which a performer receives their knowledge of results.

It is very difficult for any performer to actually watch themselves while they are performing to check for any faults or areas for improvement. This is why nearly all top performers have a coach who will work with them all the time, analysing their performance and reporting back to them. This is especially important during the early stages of learning a skill when there will be a great deal for the coach to comment on.

You may find yourself in this guidance/ coaching role as an alternative to performing. It is important to be aware of the responsibilities this role entails and also the amount of useful help you may be able to give.

A coach will work closely with a performer to spot areas for improvement

Goal setting

One of the important reasons for feedback is to use that information for further goal setting for the performer.

Once a performance (or even just a practice session) has taken place, it needs to be analysed and then the targets set for the performer.

These are the points to bear in mind when goal setting:

- Make sure that you are acting on accurate information from the actual performance.

- Be realistic with the goals that you are set and do not expect too much too soon.

- Be aware of the effects of plateauing (see page 11) and be prepared to take your time moving from one stage to another.

- Also be aware that if you do not set yourself goals you are unlikely to make any significant progress.

TASK 11

*Choose **two** different activities. For each activity, give examples of knowledge of results you received. Describe the goals you set yourself as a result.*

Mental rehearsal

Many performers and coaches now treat mental rehearsal as an important part of skill aquisition. It involves the performer spending some time, before actually taking part, going through the performance in their mind. This is a **technique** often used by sprinters before a race. For beginners it can be useful so that there is less wasted effort.

Knowing what you have to do beforehand, and going over it in your mind, makes you better prepared and can also improve your confidence.

Activity	Number of officials
American football	7
Soccer	3
Cricket	2 (3)
Tennis	1 (12)
Gymnastics event	5
Volleyball	7
Discus	5

The table shows how many officials are needed for a small selection of activities. This is just an example of the number of people necessary for a physical activity to take place. In an athletics meeting, there would be considerably more than the five officials for the discus event. All the track and field events together would require a great many officials.

TASK 1

Give reasons why in the table above there are numbers in brackets for cricket and tennis. Who do those numbers refer to?

At most activities many of the officials have organizational roles, as they have to organize the competitors and maintain the smooth running of the tournament or event. Very few officials are actually paid to do their jobs, most of them are volunteers and only receive their travelling expenses for attending the activity.

In professional sports there are more full-time, paid officials at the highest levels. There are two reasons for this.

- The standards and rewards are high and the players and supporters or fans demand the highest standards from officials.

- The sports events earn enough money to be able to pay officials.

In most amateur sports, or activities played at a lower level, officials are not paid. There is simply not enough money available to pay

Many officials are required at some athletics events

them. Often, activities take place with the bare minimum of officials, or with team members or substitutes taking the place of officials. For example, in many soccer matches the substitutes act as the referee's assistants (or **linesmen**) and in cricket matches the players often take turns to umpire. In many activities it is not easy to get officials at all and it can be very difficult to get qualified ones.

It takes quite a long time to qualify as an official in any recognized physical activity, and it usually means going on a course which has to be paid for. It also takes a long time to work up through the different levels as an official, as all officials are expected to be experienced before they can take control of an activity at the highest level.

Being an official can sometimes be a thankless task as it is almost impossible to please everyone, but without an official an activity cannot take place.

TASK 2

*Choose **one** physical activity. Find out the training requirements for an official to become qualified for that activity.*

Responsibilities of officials

The main job of the officials is to organize and control the activity. There are two main types of officials. *Senior officials* include:

- referees
- judges
- umpires

and *minor officials* include:

- referee's assistants
- timekeepers
- scorers.

All of the officials have to work together doing their various jobs to make sure that the activity runs smoothly.

TASK 3

*List **two** activities that need a referee, **two** that need a judge and **two** that need an umpire.*

Other responsibilities can include interpreting the rules, laws or regulations of the activity, checking the equipment to be used, making sure the correct players are taking part and timing the activity. Each activity has its own particular responsibilities.

TASK 4

*Choose **one** activity. Name **three** specific responsibilities of the official in charge.*

Being a tennis umpire can be a very demanding job

Qualities of officials

The qualities which an official must have do not really differ between activities. They may be summarized as follows.

1 A full and thorough knowledge of the rules or regulations of the activity

The officials cannot refer to a rule book halfway through a game so they must be prepared for, and know how to deal with, any incident which might occur. Some activities have very complicated rules and some have so many it is almost impossible to know them all. In golf, for example, there are even local rules which only apply to a particular golf course! When activities have a complicated system such as this the official in charge may need assistance and rulings can take some time to decide.

2 A fair approach to the game

This means that the official does not favour one of the teams or players but is impartial. To make sure of this many activities at the highest level have neutral officials who may even come from a different country.

3 Good physical condition

This may be as simple as having good eyesight or enough speed to keep up with the play. Some activities make their officials take an annual fitness test and some have a maximum age for officials which acts as a retirement age.

4 Firm and decisive

When they are in charge, officials may need to prevent any arguments starting. Their decision is usually final, so they must stick by it.

TASK 5

Choose an activity for which you will officiate as the main official. Prepare for this by making sure you know the qualities you must have as well as making sure you know the rules!

Most physical activities have rules which say exactly how the activity should be played. Often the rules of an activity are called laws or regulations. Some of the organizations that make the rules for certain activities are:

Activity	Ruling body
Cricket	Marylebone Cricket Club
Netball	All England Netball Association
Gymnastics	British Amateur Gymnastics Association
Tennis	Lawn Tennis Association
Hockey	Hockey Association

TASK 1

*Find out who sets the rules for **at least three** other physical activities.*

The need for rules

The purpose of rules is as follows:

- to aid basic organization
- to ease administration
- to ensure safety
- to promote enjoyment.

Most of the rules for the activities which are enjoyed today have developed over a long period of time. Some very old activities did not have any set rules but it soon became necessary to set out basic guidelines for all the popular activities, for the reasons listed above. One of the most important of these is safety. Many of our present-day activities would be very dangerous if there were not very strict rules about **foul play** and the equipment to be used.

The playing area or surface to be used has to be defined and clearly stated and so must such things as the length of time of the activity, the clothing to be worn and the number of people who can take part.

Disobeying the rules can be very costly

International rules

The ruling bodies listed on this page set the rules for activities in England or Great Britain but there are other organizations which set the rules throughout the world. In tennis for example, The International Tennis Federation (ITF) has responsibility for the rules which apply throughout the world and they can overrule any decisions made by the Lawn Tennis Association.

TASK 2

*Find out the **international** ruling body for **two** of the activities listed in the table.*

Many activities also have players' organizations which work closely with the ruling bodies, setting rules and often, more importantly, enforcing the rules! These players' organizations are more common in professional physical activities than they are in amateur sports.

Etiquette

This is a **conventional** rule or form of behaviour as opposed to an enforceable or **decreed** rule, law or regulation. This often takes the form of fair play, good manners or good sporting attitude.

In all activities there is acceptable etiquette but it is not written down in any rule book and it is up to the participants to behave in the correct way. Because it is not written down there is no real way to make sure that it happens, but players are very unpopular if they do not conform. This is another reason why there are players' organizations in many activities because they will often take action against someone who is in breach of etiquette. Here are some examples of etiquette.

- *Soccer* – if an opponent is injured a player will kick the ball out of play to stop the game to allow treatment. On the restart the team with the throw-in will throw the ball back to their opponents who originally kicked the ball out of play.

- *Tennis* – at the end of a match opponents shake hands and also thank and shake hands with the umpire.

- *Squash* – players will call their own foul shots such as 'double hit' and 'ball not up'.

Rule changes

There are often changes made to rules. These come about for a number of reasons, including:

- to make the activity safer
- to make the activity more exciting to attract more players or spectators
- to keep up with changes or developments in equipment or materials used.

TASK 3

*Name **one** rule change which has been introduced for **each** of the reasons above.*

Often changes are made for particular tournaments or events. Sometimes these are experiments to see what effect the changes will have, so that they can be introduced if they are successful. Many changes were introduced for the soccer World Cup in America in 1994 and have remained ever since.

Rule enforcement

Rules have to be obeyed and there is a system in every activity to make sure that this happens. If a player, participant, club or organization does not abide by (i.e. follow) the rules, action has to be taken against them. This can include:

- suspension
- a ban
- a fine
- expulsion.

All activities have penalties which can apply when the game is in progress, such as the yellow and red card system in soccer, the 'sin bin' in ice hockey and rugby league, and the 'fouled out' system in basketball. For more serious offences action will be taken after the event has ended; this can be for drug taking, extreme foul play, illegal payments or 'bringing the game into disrepute'.

Good etiquette at the end of a tennis match

When you are looking at a performance, it is important to know what you are looking for and what makes a performance good. The following factors of form, style and technique are all aspects of a performance which you should be looking at closely.

Form

In relation to physical activities, we talk about performance form and stylized form.

Performance form

This is the level of performance which a player is able to produce when taking part in an activity. It is linked to the likelihood of success in taking part because a player who is 'on form' is more likely to perform well. There does not seem to be any way either to predict or to control whether a performer will be on form as it seems to vary. No matter how a person prepares in terms of practice and training their performance form can change from day to day and from game to game.

Players or performers are often selected or dropped from games as a result of their being on or off form.

The following factors seem to have an influence on form.

- *Confidence* – if a performer is well prepared mentally and has a positive belief that they will do well, good form may be maintained. Many successful teams and individuals are referred to as having a 'run of good form'.

- *Match fitness* – regular performance seems to keep people 'sharper' and their form is more consistent if they can react well to the pressure of competing regularly.

- *Practice* – nearly all performers will lose form if they are not practising regularly.

A common saying in physical activities is 'class is for ever and form is variable'. This may be true – it does happen that a top performer is

TASK 1

*Describe a sporting situation where the 'form' of **one** of the players has affected the result.*

beaten by someone who is thought of as a lesser player due to the different levels of form they are able to produce 'on the day'.

Stylized form

This means the performer has to produce a good shape, position, appearance or manner of presentation. Often the activity itself requires them to perform in a particular way and there may even be marks awarded for the form they show. Trampoline is a good example of this because a judge will deduct points from a competitor if there is a loss of form in the movements which are performed. All the movements in a trampoline routine have a set way or shape in which they must be performed and it is fairly easy to see if they are not done correctly.

This kind of form is also very important because someone who uses the correct formis more likely to be performing effectively and safely.

Good form is essential for a good score in a diving competition

Style

Style is slightly different from form as it is the way in which an individual actually performs a set movement. The movement itself can be a standard one but two people with contrasting styles can present it quite differently.

Gymnastics is an activity where style is very important as it is something which is judged. The style in which a movement is performed is just as important as how difficult the movement is.

Style can be important in team games, too. Some teams may have a particular style of play which needs to be noted by opponents (cricket is a good example) and tactics may be needed to combat it. Also, style can be very important to spectators who can appreciate a stylish performance as it is pleasing to watch.

TASK 2

*Describe the contrasting styles of **two** different performers in one activity.*

Technique

Technique is the manner in which someone performs, or the way in which it is done. It is very closely linked to skill. Any newcomer to an activity should be taught the correct technique for the skills they must learn.

The importance of correct technique

- *Effectiveness* – if a skill or a movement is performed correctly it will be done more successfully. There will be little wasted or inefficient effort. For example, in swimming a poor technique can result in a lot of splashing and little progress whereas good technique results in a smooth, fast, efficient stroke.

- *Injury prevention* – a poor or incorrect technique can often result in injury. A rugby player using the wrong tackling technique can be at risk, as can a trampolinist or a gymnast if they do not use the correct technique in their activity.

The 'Fosbury Flop' is a relatively new technique

- *Marks* are often awarded for good technique, so in these events this is essential in order to be successful.

Within one activity there can be basic techniques, advanced techniques and there may even be totally new techniques. Taking the high jump as an example:

- *basic technique* – a simple scissors jump over the bar following a diagonal run

- *advanced technique* – a western roll, rotating over the bar

- *new technique* – the 'Fosbury Flop', devised by Dick Fosbury and used by him in the 1968 Olympics, at which time it was a completely revolutionary new technique. It became so successful that it is now the only advanced technique used by top-class high jumpers.

TASK 3

*Name both basic and advanced techniques which must be learnt for **two** physical activities.*

In all physical activities, performers are always trying to improve their own technique or even to find a new, better way in order to give themselves an advantage in competition.

Teacher

A teacher is usually the person who first introduces people to physical activities, starting from the basics. The basic skills, basic rules and basic techniques are taught at this stage.

The teacher also has a responsibility to *develop* all of these skills. This may be a role you are called upon to adopt instead of that of performer.

Most children start school between the ages of four and five and experience up to six areas of activity. They start with very basic introductory work, to prepare them for more complex work later. The following are the basic contents for the six areas of activity.

1 Dance

- *The body*, control of various body parts such as hands, feet and head.

- *Actions*, moving and stopping, holding still, travelling, jumping, spinning, twirling, spiralling, twisting and transferring weight.

- *Space*, moving in space, using pathways.

- *Dynamics*, moving to a rhythm, repeating patterns of movement and making simple dances.

- *Relationships*, with the teacher, the music and other pupils as individuals or groups.

2 Games

- *Footwork*, running, hopping, skipping.

- *Awareness of space and other people*, chasing, dodging, avoiding.

- *Jumping and landing.*

- *Ball skills*, sending using hands and feet, hitting, receiving, travelling with a ball.

- *Games*, make up and play games with simple rules and objectives with one person and a partner.

3 Gymnastics

- *Travelling* with use of space, using feet, hands and feet and large parts of the body.

- *Body shapes*, curling, stretching, twisting and turning plus changes of direction.

- *Supporting body weight*, when still and using different parts of the body as bases.

- *Transference of weight*, developing travelling, moving weight from feet to hands, jumping from two feet to two feet, hopping, sliding, rocking.

- *Levels*, low, medium or high levels of space.

- *Pathways*, transference of weight with straight and curved pathways.

- *Linking movements*, sequences on and off apparatus.

- *Directions*, forwards, backwards, sideways, up and down.

4 Swimming

- *Beginners and non-swimmers*, getting in and out of the pool, submerging, breathing in water, floating and supporting positions.

- *Stroke development*, gliding, strokes on front and back.

- *Elementary survival skills.*

- *Water safety*, dangers in and around water, actions in an emergency, helping others, activities near water.

- *Simple games*, walking races, treading water contests, picking up objects from the bottom, relays, ball games using targets and small-sided water polo.

5 Athletic activities

- *Running*, including speed work and non-competitive longer runs.

- *Jumping*, for accuracy, height and distance.

- *Throwing*, accurately, high, low and for distance.

6 Outdoor education

- *Exploring environments*, in and around the school grounds, looking at best and worst features, rope trails, short walks, places to climb, scavenger hunts.

Up until the age of seven only areas 1–4 are taught, the other two areas may be added.

> ## TASK 1
> *Choose **one** of the activity areas. In a paragraph, describe how you have progressed from the basic activities through to your present stage.*

Teachers do not just deal with the best performers but with groups of mixed ability. They aim to ensure that all of the members of the group can plan, perform and evaluate a physical activity at a basic level. Therefore a teacher does not concentrate on just one activity but teaches a variety – often at different levels.

Teachers often supervise inter-school fixtures out of normal school hours

Teachers work with pupils during core time (normal timetabled lessons) and also as an **extra-curricular activity** (usually after school or in lunchtimes) when most of the work is done with team practices and inter-school fixtures.

Although teaching PE is a specialist job, teachers don't just teach one activity. They need to be able to cover many. They must also try to **differentiate**, that is to make some tasks more difficult or even easier so that all ability levels are catered for and can be assessed.

> ## TASK 2
> *Choose **one** task that is important in **one** physical activity. How could that task be made easier? How could it be made more difficult?*

Trainer

A trainer's role is different from that of a teacher. The trainer is usually the person who is responsible for the physical condition of performers. Trainers deal with performers who have specialized and reached a high level in one particular activity or event.

It is not always easy for performers to push themselves hard enough. Sometimes they do not have enough knowledge about their event to know exactly what, or how much, they should do. A trainer therefore:

- *Sets training schedules* – this can be over a long period of time and will probably be based on ensuring fitness levels. The trainer will make sure the performer **peaks** at the right time, especially for a competition.

- *Takes training sessions* – this is to ensure that all the right things are included in each session, such as the warm-up, and once again the main aim is to achieve the correct physical fitness level.

Many trainers also have a responsibility for dealing with injury prevention, treatment and cure. They often have to double up as a **physiotherapist** (identifying and treating injuries) in order to make sure the performers are fit.

A coach is usually a specialist in one activity and is responsible for preparing a performer in:

- skill acquisition
- correct technique
- correct physical state
- correct mental state.

Coaches usually only work with performers at a higher level as it is a very demanding task. Many work full time and are paid. In individual activities, such as international athletics, many of the top performers employ a personal coach who works with them all the time. If you are adopting the role of coach you can assist a performer or a team in the following ways:

- *Prepare performances* – this includes choosing tactics, formations, strategies, game plans and fitness levels.

- *Analyse performances* – performers need as much feedback as possible both during and after a performance in order to find ways to improve. So one of the most important jobs of the coach is to analyse performances. This analysis can include the performers' actions or even those of the opponents.

- *Motivate and encourage* – this can occur before or during a performance and can often make the difference between a performer losing or winning.

- *Review performances* – the coach examines the last performance in great detail to look for ways in which improvements can be made or for any changes which are needed.

Coaching aids

Each activity has its own equipment which can make coaching easier. For example, cricketers use cricket nets, trampolinists may use harnesses, rugby players use scrummaging machines and tennis players can use automatic ball feeders.

A coach can make use of a variety of coaching aids to analyse performance

TASK 1

*List the coaching aids for **two** more activities.*

There are some common aids which can be used by coaches in all activities.

Video

Television or video film is now one of a coach's most important aids. They can film other people's performances to show how something should be done and they can also film their own performers to let them watch their own performance. Videos can be replayed in slow motion, which shows every little movement, and movements can be filmed and analysed from all angles and directions. For example, a trampolinist who is **travelling** (moving forwards in the air when rotating) can benefit a great deal from watching it on video, because they can actually see how far they are moving.

Demonstrations

Many coaches are ex-players or performers and they are therefore often able to demonstrate the right way to do something. If they cannot do this themselves, they can usually find someone else who can and they can then highlight the good points.

Often they will take their team or players to watch a higher standard team for the same reasons.

Books and coaching manuals

Coaches can recommend suitable books for performers to study. It is also important for them to keep up to date themselves. They may have to read a lot of articles in journals, and keep up with any rule changes.

Other specialists

To prepare their performer fully coaches may enlist the help of people such as **dieticians** (they will work out the correct diet for the particular event), sports **psychiatrists** (this is becoming a more important area as many coaches think that the only barriers left for performers at the top level are mental ones), qualified physiotherapists (to deal with any minor injuries, strains or pulls) and team doctors to deal with emergencies.

Coaches' chalkboards

These are small boards marked out with the playing area or pitch. The coach uses them during a game to point out positional changes or **tactics**.

TASK 2

Design and draw out a coach's chalkboard which could be used for a physical activity you take part in.

Modern technological advances

Many advances have been made in recent years which can help to monitor, assist and even predict performances. Computer developments are among the most significant because many programs are now available as CD-ROMs.

Some computer programs can select the most suitable training schedules for individual performers, who can then be linked directly into computers while they are training to see what the effects are. All this information can later be used by the coach who will make appropriate adjustments to the training.

Situations can be simulated by the computer so that the performer can almost experience a game or competition and work out ways to play.

More advanced equipment and training aids are being designed. This includes the materials that are used, such as lightweight clothing and lighter safety equipment.

One of the most important aids for a coach is a very accurate timing device. These are now very advanced and specific to many activities. Being able to record split times or lap times with a countdown facility is vital and many conveniently-sized watches are now available, designed for particular events.

Analysing performance

Analysing a performance is quite a difficult task. To analyse a performance means to divide it up into all of its separate parts, or units, and examine it in detail. You also need to study the separate parts of the performance and make a detailed description of it, including any criticisms.'

The main purpose of this analysis is to come up with ideas of how to improve performance.

You may analyse another person's performance or you may be able to analyse your own performance – especially if you have access to a video camera.

Like any other aspect of physical education, you may need to learn some new techniques yourself in order to be able to analyse this well.

To analyse someone's performance, you need to get yourself thoroughly prepared and be sure that you know exactly what it is you are looking for and expecting to see.

The following checklist may help you with your analysis.

A = *Arrange* what you are looking for into its separate parts.

N = *Note* down what you see and observe.

A = *Apportion* the different elements of the performance into their different categories.

L = *Look* for any specific details.

Y = *You* should then start to distinguish the separate parts of the performance.

S = *See* if you can find any solutions to problems which might have occurred.

E = *Evaluate* the whole process with an overview about how successful the whole performance was.

TASK 1

Produce your own recording sheet for an activity, or session, you are going to analyse. Then use it in an analysis session.

It is also useful to keep in mind what you will be looking to achieve in particular during an analysis session, especially when you are trying to come up with suggestions for ways a performance could be improved.

Some of the factors you could identify are:

- *accuracy* – is this required for the activity and is it being consistently achieved?

- *timing* – is there a need for this (any striking/hitting game will certainly need it), and is it being consistently achieved?

- *control* – this may include both control of the body as well as control of any equipment used, such as bats and balls

- *efficiency* – is the performance being carried out efficiently? Sometimes a good performer seems to use the minimum of effort but still achieves a good result

- *balance* – many activities require this. In gymnastics good balance might be obvious, but other activities also require it for a top quality performance

- *spatial awareness* – this means being aware of the people and situation around you. It can be a vital part of many game activities

- *hand–eye co-ordination* – this is important in any activity that requires control of equipment such as a bat or stick

- *form or tension* – this may be important in activities such as dance, gymnastics or trampolining, where it can be a factor in the judging of a performance.

The final stage will then be for the analyst to suggest ways in which the performance could be improved, modified, refined, adapted or developed to bring about an improvement. For the assessment of this particular part of your course you will be specifically required to recognize strengths and weaknesses within a performance, using the proper technical terms in your analysis.

You will be expected to do the following:

- identify a particular strength in a performance (2 marks)

- identify another strength or develop further your explanation of the first strength you identified (2 marks)

- identify a particular weakness in a performance (2 marks)

- identify another weakness or develop your explanation of the first weakness you identified (2 marks)

- use relevant technical terms in your explanations of the strengths and weaknesses of the performance. (2 marks)

This is the focus that you must concentrate on in your analysis component.

Improving performance

You should use the information you have gathered from analysing someone's performance. Then specifically look closely at the strengths and weaknesses you have already identified, to suggest ways in which the person's performance might be improved.

You will be expected to do the following:

- use your knowledge and understanding of the activity and principles of practice/ training/techniques (see unit 28 for details) to decide on and prioritise the area for improvement (2 marks)

- demonstrate your understanding of the nature, cause and reason for the strength or weakness (2 marks)

- set realistic and attainable targets for improvement (2 marks)

- measure/monitor progress – show you know how to check for and recognize progress towards the target (2 marks)

- corrective measure – describe a practice/ activity/exercise to improve technical/ tactical/ fitness/skill/techniques/outcome. (2 marks)

Not all factors in the bullet list will be relevant to each activity, so some have a choice, for example, practice/activity/exercise. You have to select the appropriate ones.

TASK 2

Using the analysis sheet you developed in Task 1, go on to suggest ways for improving a performance as outlined above.

Concentration is important when observing a performance

25

This unit covers Section 1 of your practical coursework and you should look carefully at units 28 – 31 as they contain a lot of useful information regarding the type of exercise programmes you might choose to follow. Many of the technical details you will need to know when planning and implementing your programme are included in these units. You will need to consider all of the following when dealing with this part of the course.

Planning your programme

These are some general points you should consider:

- *Set realistic goals* – do not make your programme too difficult
- *Predict some likely outcomes* – what is likely to result?
- *Explore and select the options* which might be available to you – do not make too hasty a decision.

These are the headings you will be assessed against for this part of the course. It is important to think about each of them carefully and make sure that your planning includes them all:

- The purpose or aim of the programme in relation to prior levels of fitness, performance levels as well as considering any possible injuries or health problems (see units 9, 10, 32 and 33)   (5 marks)
- Awareness of safety aspects including equipment, apparatus, physical and psychological factors (see units 9, 22 and 23)   (5 marks)
- The appropriateness or purpose of the exercises or techniques you have chosen to improve fitness or skill levels (see units 13 and 14)   (5 marks)

- The appropriate application of the activities within the programme in relation to other theoretical areas and principals of training (to include the factors of progression, overload, frequency, duration, time and tedium (see unit 28).   (5 marks)

Performing your programme

You have to perform your chosen programme over a period of time in order to make it effective. The minimum time you would be expected to do this is for a five-week period (remembering that you have to leave some recovery time between each session you perform). You must therefore plan accordingly.

The following factors are the ones you will be assessed on:

- the implementation of your planned programme – whether you performed the exercises or activity with control, consistency and ease   (5 marks)

Pupils performing their programme

- whether or not you managed to complete the exercises or techniques in a safe and/or efficient manner (5 marks)

- your attitude and motivation levels towards improving your personal targets you set and whether you were able to sustain activity over the set period (5 marks)

- how effective and appropriate your warm-up and warm-down were. (5 marks)

Another important requirement is that you keep evidence to support the information you will be providing regarding your programme.

Monitoring your progress

Throughout your programme you must monitor your progress – or lack of it if that is the case! These are the ways you should do this:

- using tables for recording results (2 marks)

- making brief notes or comments after each session (2 marks)

- recording heart rates (2 marks)

- recording recovery rates (2 marks)

- writing a concluding statement or summary of results. (2 marks)

It is important that you record your results regularly and accurately.

Evaluation of your programme

In terms of total marks available for this section, this is the area which is worth the most, so you must make sure that you consider the evaluation of your programme very carefully and thoroughly.
The marks you can be awarded are broken down quite clearly in different headings and it is important that you cover each of these.

1. Evaluation of planning the programme

- Reference to pre-test scores (2 marks)

- Assessment of the appropriateness of the level at which the programme was pitched (2 marks)

- The appropriateness of the order of exercises or activities within the programme (2 marks)

- The application of the principles of training, progression and overload (2 marks)

- An assessment or explanation of the exercises or activities in terms of whether they were the right choice – specificity. (2 marks)

2. Evaluation of performing the programme

- The application of the principles of training such as specificity, progression and overload (2 marks)

- The assessment or explanation of the exercises being the correct choice – specificity (2 marks)

- The manageability of the programme (2 marks)

- The appropriateness of the order of the exercises or activities within the programme (2 marks)

- The enjoyment, interest and motivation experienced within the programme (2 marks)

3. Evaluation of monitoring the programme

- The assessment or explanation of the exercises or activities being the correct choice – specificity (2 marks)

- The appropriateness of the order of exercises or activities within the programme (2 marks)

- The identification and explanation of any modifications which were made during the implementation stage of the programme (2 marks)

- Reference, with explanations, to the effects on you as a performer at any stage through the programme (2 marks)

- Reference, with explanation, to the results recorded by you at any stage through the programme. (2 marks)

4. Final evaluation/appraisal of the programme

■ Reference to post-test scores   (2 marks)

■ The manageability of the programme   (2 marks)

■ Reference, with explanations, to the effects on yourself on completion of the programme – considering any progress or development   (2 marks)

■ The enjoyment, interest, motivation experienced during the programme   (2 marks)

■ Reference to what might happen next, such as any adaptations to any future programmes or any future planning.   (2 marks)

Leading a warm-up/warm-down

The final part of this section requires you to adopt a leadership role, specifically during the warm-up/warm-down section of a training session or even a full practical session.

You should familiarize yourself with what these sessions should consist of (see pages 90 and 91).

There will be specific aspects of how you can carry out this role which will be assessed. These are the factors on which you will be assessed:

■ The suitability of the exercises or activities included in the warm-up/warm-down session to increase/decrease the intensity of movement as appropriate   (2 marks)

■ The utilization of exercises/skills/ equipment/stretches appropriate to the sport activity/muscle group   (2 marks)

■ The ability to organize and lead the group   (2 marks)

■ The use of verbal communication skills such as voice projection, volume, intonation, and clarity   (2 marks)

■ The use of non-verbal communication skills such as demonstration of the exercises or activities.   (2 marks)

Once again, there will be a requirement for you provide some evidence to justify being awarded marks in all of the above categories. This means that the session you lead will have to be observed by one of your assessing teachers. It would also be useful if you wrote out a plan, with details, about what your session is to be.

TASK

Plan out, in detail, a full warm-up and warm-down for a physical activity session. Make sure that it is appropriate for the activity being undertaken.

Pupils warm-up/ warm-down session in progress

SECTION 2

Health, fitness and factors affecting performance
and
Principles of training

This section looks at the **physiological** factors that affect performance, as well as health and safety and training methods.

It is very important for a performer to know how their body works, how it can be kept in good working order and how it can be maintained and even improved.

This section sets out the necessary information in a practical way, so that you build up a good knowledge of your own body, what it is capable of and ways you can improve it. Many of the tasks set targets to improve something. They are closely linked to the requirements you will have in your practical sessions in relation to organizing and running exercise/training programmes.

Remember that all units in this section are interrelated and should not just be considered as separate and unconnected topics. Much of the information on how the human body works may already be familiar to you from Key Stage 3 Science. What you will be expected to do for your GCSE PE course is apply your knowledge, not just identify various muscles or bones. You may be asked to consider how the various body systems work together for specific movements to take place and also to consider other effects which might be relevant, such as the effects of ageing on performance, the importance of flexibility, or how and why training influences performance.

The whole of this section covers all of the theory information you will required to have a knowledge of in order to answer sections A(9.1) and B(9.2) of the examination paper.

The World Health Organization defines health as:

a state of complete physical, mental and social well being and not merely the absence of disease or infirmity. Health is one of the fundamental rights of every human being without distinction of race, religion, political belief, economics or social conditions.

It is important that everyone should develop the knowledge and skills which will enable them to understand their own bodies and how to keep them healthy, and to have a regard for the health of the community.

The following nine components can influence your health.

1 Use and misuse of substances such as alcohol, tobacco, medicines and other drugs.

2 Sex education – the physical, emotional and social aspects of an individual's development as a male or female; personal relationships; responsible attitudes and appropriate behaviour.

3 Family life education – the value and importance of the family as a social institution; its contribution to the development of attachment, love and concern in caring for others.

4 Safety – the safety of the individual in different environments, e.g. at home, on the road, at school, at work, during leisure activities.

5 Health-related exercise – the importance of exercise in promoting good health.

6 Nutrition – the association between diet and health; the nutritional value of various foods; the quality of food preparation and handling.

7 Personal hygiene – personal cleanliness; avoidance of disease; social considerations.

Good health enables you to enjoy your life more

8 Environmental aspects of health education – the effects of various environments on health: social, physical and economic factors which contribute to health and illness.

9 Psychological aspects of health education – mental health, emotional well being, stress.

Health is very important and good health is something that everyone wants. There are ways to help maintain your health and there are also many things that can damage your health. Some of these are dealt with here and in the next unit. You will find others in units 11–13 and 32.

Alcohol

A survey by the Health Education Authority found that 90 per cent of people in the UK drink alcohol. Like many other things, moderate amounts of alcohol do not necessarily do any harm. However, if someone drinks too much then the immediate effect is that they become drunk. This can often lead to violent behaviour. It also causes a lack of co-ordination and usually vomiting too.

If excessive drinking continues over a period of time there can be more serious effects such as:

- damage to the liver, muscles and heart

- damage to the digestive system

- mental illness such as hallucinations, memory loss, depression, brain damage and extreme confusion

- damage to the immune system, leaving the body less able to fight diseases.

Alcohol is a mood-altering drug. Technically, it is a depressant drug as it slows down the action of the brain. Some people think that it is a stimulant but this is not the case. It only takes a small quantity for some effect to be felt. Any performer in a physical activity would be affected by alcohol and it is for this reason that performers should never drink alcohol before taking part in sport.

TASK 1

Describe some sporting situations where a performer could be put at risk because of the effects of alcohol.

Alcohol, in moderation, may not necessarily be a hazard to health – smoking always is!

Smoking

In the UK every packet of cigarettes carries a health warning which must be printed by law. These include, 'Smoking causes cancer' and 'Tobacco seriously damages health'.

There is no dispute about the fact that smoking is harmful, which is why these warnings have to be printed. The dangers caused by smoking are:

- greater risk of serious diseases such as heart disease, lung cancer and chronic bronchitis

- developing a 'smoker's cough'

- frequent sore throats

- shortness of breath

- nose, throat and chest irritation and breathing difficulties

- headaches

- dizziness

- nausea and lack of concentration.

The most dangerous thing about smoking is that it kills. Over 100,000 people a year die as a result of smoking and it kills more people by causing heart attacks than any other disease.

No one who smokes can expect to be healthy or maintain a good level of **fitness**. Even non-smokers can be affected by **passive smoking** by breathing in other people's tobacco smoke which can be equally harmful.

The only good news about smoking is that something can be done about the harmful effects. A reduction in the number of cigarettes smoked can help. Stopping altogether can enable the body systems to recover, although this may take several years.

The most simple solution seems to be not to start in the first place!

TASK 2

Describe ways in which a sportsperson's performance could be affected if they were a regular smoker.

31

Medicines

Medicines are drugs which are intended to help to keep people healthy, to cure illnesses or to aid recovery. Something as simple as cough medicine can be used easily and safely and many everyday medicines can be bought from chemists' shops. Other medicines are controlled more carefully and can only be acquired on a **prescription** authorized by a doctor. Again, many of these medicines aid good health as people with more serious illnesses, such as asthma, need them to control their condition.

A drug is a chemical substance. If it is taken into the body it affects the chemical balance within the body. Because of this serious effect, most drugs are controlled and should only be used on medical advice and with medical supervision, as they can be harmful when not used properly. For many people drugs are essential; they not only keep them healthy but may even keep them alive. However, drug abuse can be extremely harmful if the drugs are taken for the wrong reasons or in the wrong dosages.

Some drugs are known as **performance enhancing** (see unit 32). Their use in physical activity is often illegal (according to the rules of the particular activity) because it can give the people who take them an unfair advantage.

TASK 3

*Name **three** medicines which can be used to make people more healthy.*

The important thing to remember with all substances is that they can be both used and abused and any performer taking part in physical activity should be aware of this.

Safety and risk assessment

Safety is particularly important for anyone taking part in physical activity. All activities have some element of risk which can be reduced by taking the necessary precautions.

Many activities, especially games activities, have their own particular safety rules or precautions

TASK 4

*Think of **three** physical activities. For each one think of **three** different safety precautions which should apply.*

which players and performers should be aware of and stick to (see unit 3).

Some activities, especially outdoor and adventurous ones, can actually take place in a potentially dangerous environment. There is therefore extra need to make sure that all the necessary safety actions are taken. The challenge element of these activities is what attracts many people, but the safety aspect must not be ignored.

Some basic safety factors which apply to most activities include:

- lift correctly – when lifting heavy or awkward loads or weights always keep your back straight and bend your legs

- wear the correct clothing/footwear for the activity

A challenging activity might be dangerous if safety precautions are not taken

A careful and correct warm-up is an important safety factor

- do not wear jewellery
- abide by the rules of the activity
- check any of the equipment which is necessary and use it properly
- wear protective items where it is appropriate
- make sure the activity is properly supervised
- warm up before taking part and cool down when you have finished.

No activities are guaranteed safe but all of them should be carried out in as safe a manner as possible. In team activities each performer has a responsibility not just for themselves but for all the other performers as well.

Many safety regulations have been tightened up in recent years as a result of accidents. Most schools have very detailed guidelines for trips and physical activities.

Environmental factors

Environmental factors such as where you live can be related to health. In some areas pollution can be a very real problem as it can affect the air or even the water supply. People who live in large cities may have problems caused by car exhaust fumes or factory emissions, both of which can drastically reduce the air quality.

Many people – for example, those who suffer from asthma or hay fever – can be affected by such simple things as high pollen levels during the summer months.

Air quality can also be affected by pressure changes brought about by weather systems. This can result in smog (a mixture of smoke and fog) which can be dangerous for people who have respiratory problems.

Social and economic factors can be just as important and just as damaging. Poor housing, lack of main services such as a clean water supply, heat and light and lack of support services such as medical help (vaccinations, doctors, nurses and medical centres) can cause health risks. Poverty is also a problem as this can often result in lack of suitable clothing and food.

TASK 5

List some ways that environmental, social and economic factors could affect someone taking part in physical activities.

If you want to remain healthy it is very important that you follow the basic rules of **hygiene**. This is also linked with risk assessment because following good hygiene guidelines greatly reduces the risk of illness and injury.

Personal hygiene includes:

- washing
- cleaning
- prevention of disease
- prevention of infection
- food preparation practices
- dental care
- clothing
- **self-esteem** and confidence
- social considerations.

Most of these should be quite obvious but some need to be considered in more detail.

One of the things you must maintain very carefully is your skin. This is the largest organ of your body and on an adult male it can be about three square metres in area. It can be quite a job to look after it all carefully and well.

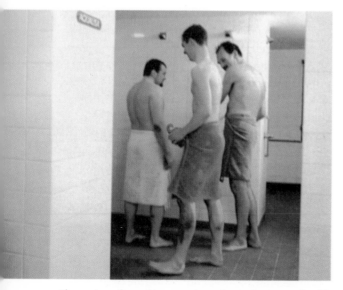
Showering after taking part in a physical activity should be encouraged

Washing

You should do this regularly. It should be fairly obvious that if your hands are dirty then you wash them, and this might be necessary several times a day. However, it applies equally to all parts of your body.

If you do not wash at all your skin will soon become dirty and an unpleasant body odour (commonly known as BO) will be produced. Many deodorants and anti-perspirants are available to buy but these do not cure the problem, they only cover it up.

The only solution is to wash regularly. Ideally this should include a bath or a shower where the whole body is thoroughly washed, preferably using soap. It is especially important to bath or shower after physical activity to remove the traces of sweat on the skin. It is just as important to make sure that you dry yourself thoroughly afterwards, especially between your toes, to help prevent **athlete's foot.**

It is also very important to wash your hair as it can quickly become oily or greasy, or you may develop an itchy scalp.

TASK 1

Design a poster which points out the importance of washing and which is designed to encourage people to keep themselves clean.

Cleaning

It is important that anything you come in contact with is as clean as possible. This is obvious for things such as knives and forks but it should apply to any equipment you might be using or wearing, and it is very important if it is clothing.

Clothes should be washed and changed regularly, especially your underwear. You should always change all of your clothes after

Prevention of disease can be achieved largely by washing and cleaning. Cleanliness can prevent an environment developing where germs can survive and multiply.

Any cuts or wounds should be carefully cleaned and antiseptic should be applied. This can help with the prevention of infection. Another great help is the **immunization** programme in which young people are **vaccinated** (usually by injections) to prevent them suffering from diseases such as:

- HIB (a type of meningitis)
- whooping cough
- diphtheria
- tetanus
- polio
- measles
- mumps
- rubella (German measles).

Other vaccinations are made available if there is an epidemic of a particular disease.

TASK 2

*Find out the symptoms and effects of **at least two** of the diseases listed above.*

You will probably need to clean yourself and your kit after physical activity

physical activity, particularly if it has been strenuous. Your clothes could be dirty and will almost certainly be sweaty. They should be washed before being worn again. This is why it is a good idea to have a sports kit which is just worn for a particular physical activity and to change into a clean set of clothes after you have had a shower or bath. If you have a PE kit, make sure that it is washed regularly, preferably after every time you use it.

Nails should be kept clean and toe nails, in particular, should be cut regularly as this can help to prevent **ingrown toe nails.** These can be most uncomfortable and painful and can stop participation in physical activity.

Ears should be kept clean and if earrings are worn in pierced ears these too must be carefully cleaned and maintained. Remember that earrings should be removed when taking part in physical activity.

Dental care is also very important. This doesn't only mean regular and correct brushing of teeth but also requires regular visits to the dentist for check-ups and any treatment which might be necessary. Tooth decay and gum disease are common and the condition of teeth declines with age, so regular check-ups are essential.

Food preparation must be carried out very carefully on clean surfaces, and with clean hands and equipment; and the necessary precautions must be taken both before and during the cooking. These include making sure that foods are stored correctly (fridges or freezers may be necessary), that sell-by dates are checked and that cooking instructions are followed carefully. People who are careful about hygiene may have higher self-esteem and are more likely to be accepted by other people socially than those who are unhygienic.

Everyone needs food to survive. Food provides the body with energy and nutrients. The nutrients in food are:

- carbohydrates
- fats
- proteins
- vitamins
- minerals.

Although not a nutrient, water is essential for life. Dietary fibre is also needed to keep the digestive system in good working order.

No single food provides all the nutrients the body needs, so it is important to eat a variety of foods. Most foods can be divided into four main groups and a smaller fifth (or 'extras') group, based on the nutrients provided.

1 bread, other cereals and potatoes

2 fruit and vegetables

3 milk and dairy foods

4 meat, fish and alternatives

+ fatty and sugary foods

It is important to achieve a balanced diet as all the nutrients needed by the body can be obtained by eating a wide range of foods from each of the four main groups shown above.

Energy

Even when a person is resting, energy is needed to keep the body ticking over. The amount of energy needed for important processes such as breathing and keeping the heart beating, is called the **basal metabolic rate** (BMR).

Activity levels also affect a person's energy requirements. A person who has an active job involving lots of walking is likely to need more energy than someone who sits at a desk each day. Physical activities such as football, cycling, swimming, tennis and hockey also increase the need for energy.

To keep body weight constant, the amount of energy provided by food needs to match the amount of energy used by the body. If the diet provides more energy than is needed, the extra is stored as adipose tissue (or fat) and weight gain occurs. In the long term, a person may become overweight or **obese**. In contrast, if the diet supplies less energy than is required, stores of adipose tissue are used to provide the extra energy needed and weight loss occurs.

The best way to lose excess body fat is to reduce the amount of energy provided by food whilst increasing the amount of energy used by the body.

The components of the diet which provide energy are: fats, carbohydrates and proteins. Most foods contain a mixture of these nutrients. The amount of energy provided by a particular food (sometimes called the energy value) depends upon the combined amount of energy provided by each of the nutrients. The energy value of a food is usually expressed in kilojoules (kJ) or kilocalories (kcal). In everyday language, most people refer to kilocalories as **calories**.

TASK 1

Collect the labels from a variety of different packaged foods. Compare the energy values of these foods. Which five foods contain the most energy and which five contain the least? Explain the differences.

Carbohydrates

Carbohydrates can be divided into two groups based on the number of sugar units:

- *Simple carbohydrates (sugars)* consist of one or two sugar units. Types of simple carbohydrate include **glucose**, **sucrose**, fructose (fruit sugar) and lactose (milk sugar).

Simple carbohydrates are found in sugar, sweets, chocolates, jam, honey, sweet drinks, cakes, biscuits, milk and fruit. With the exception of milk and fruit, most of these foods are not very nourishing and should not be eaten too often.

- *Complex carbohydrates (starches)* consist of hundreds of sugar units. Starchy foods such as bread, pasta, rice, potatoes and pulses are all rich sources of complex carbohydrates. These foods contain a wide range of other nutrients and should form the main part of most meals and snacks.

Carbohydrates provide the body with energy and so are an important part of the diet, particularly for people who are very active. During digestion, carbohydrates are broken down into single sugar units, such as glucose. Once absorbed, glucose can be used to provide energy. If it is not needed immediately, it is converted into **glycogen** which is stored in the liver and muscles. During exercise, the body can use stores of muscle glycogen to provide energy. But if glycogen stores are full, glucose can be used to make fat and is stored as adipose tissue.

Top sports performers have to work out their energy needs very carefully and will sometimes **carbohydrate load** (eating lots of starchy foods) in the week before an important competition or event, such as a marathon. Carbohydrate loading increases the amount of glycogen in the muscles which helps to delay tiredness and may improve performance in the end stages of a competition.

TASK 2

Suggest ways in which you could cut down on the amount of sugary carbohydrates you eat. How would you change your diet to include more starchy carbohydrates?

Fats

Fats contain substances called fatty acids. There are three main types:

- saturated fatty acids (*saturates*)
- monounsaturated fatty acids (*monounsaturates*)
- polyunsaturated fatty acids (*polyunsaturates*).

Most fats contain a mixture of different fatty acids. Foods which contain a high proportion of saturates are usually of animal origin such as meat, meat fats such as lard, and dairy products. Some margarines and oils also contain saturates. Monounsaturates are found in many foods – olive oil is a particularly rich source. Foods which contain a high proportion of polyunsaturates include margarines and oils made from seeds and nuts such as sunflower, soya and corn oils. Oily fish such as sardines are also a rich source of polyunsaturates.

Fats are important because:

- they provide a concentrated source of energy
- fat stored under the skin helps the body keep warm
- fat stored around major organs has a protective effect
- foods with a high fat content contain fat-soluble vitamins
- two fatty acids (called essential fatty acids) cannot be made in the body and must be provided by the food.

Although fats are an important part of the diet, most people should aim to cut down on the total amount of fat they eat. In particular, they should try to reduce their intake of saturates.

TASK 3

Suggest ways in which you could cut down on the amount of fat your diet provides.

Fats can provide the body with energy during exercise, but this depends on the intensity and duration of the exercise, and also on the fitness level of the person taking part. Fat tends to be used to provide energy during light activity and during prolonged periods of exercise. As a person becomes fitter, fat tends to be used to provide energy instead of glycogen.

Proteins

Proteins are made from building blocks called **amino acids**. The body needs twenty different amino acids to make all the proteins needed for good health. Nine of these (called essential amino acids) cannot be made in the body and must be supplied by food. The remaining amino acids (called non-essential amino acids) can be made in the body.

Proteins from animal sources such as meat, fish, eggs, milk and cheese contain all the essential amino acids in adequate amounts. With the exception of soya beans (which also contain all the essential amino acids), proteins from plant foods – such as beans, lentils, breakfast cereals, bread, pasta, rice, nuts and seeds – lack one or more of the essential amino acids.

Proteins are needed:

- for the formation, growth and repair of tissues such as muscle, hair and skin

- to make enzymes and hormones.

In general, proteins only provide the body with energy if the diet contains inadequate amounts of carbohydrates and fats. But during very strenuous activities or prolonged periods of exercise, proteins in muscles may start to be broken down to provide extra energy.

A person who is physically active needs a good supply of proteins to ensure that muscles grow and keep in good working order. Most people need slightly more protein when they train hard or for long periods. Someone with a lack of proteins could suffer from malnutrition.

Vitamins

Vitamins are only needed in small amounts, but they are still essential for good health. Vitamins can be divided into two groups.

- *Fat-soluble vitamins* (A, D, E and K) can be stored in the body

- *Water-soluble vitamins* (B group and C) cannot be stored, so the body needs a constant daily supply.

Vitamins are important:

- to protect the body and maintain the body's chemistry

- to enable growth and maintenance of bones, teeth, skin and glands (this is especially important in young children because of the growth process)

- to help with digestion, the stability of the nervous system and tissue growth, and resistance to bacteria and disease.

Although **vitamin supplements** are widely available, it is far more important to meet requirements for vitamins by eating a balanced diet. If a wide variety of foods are eaten every day, vitamin supplements are not necessary.

Compared with inactive people, individuals who exercise regularly or spend a lot of time training may have slightly greater needs for certain vitamins. For example, some of the B group vitamins convert nutrients in food into energy.

During exercise, the body uses more energy and so the need for some of the B group vitamins increases slightly, but vitamin supplements, taken in excess of a person's need, are unlikely to improve performance.

TASK 4

Find out the names of three diseases that are caused by vitamin deficiencies. What are the symptoms of each disease and how can the deficiencies be prevented?

Minerals

As with vitamins, minerals are necessary for the efficient working of the body. Some minerals are needed in smaller amounts than others. These are called trace elements.

The human body takes in minerals from a variety of vegetables and meats. For example, calcium is obtained from milk, cheese, yoghurt and boney fish (e.g. mackerel); iron is found in red meat, liver, eggs and dark green vegetables (e.g. spinach).

Runners may need to replace fluids lost when taking part in a race

Minerals:

- help to build tissues (zinc)
- are constituents of bones and teeth (calcium and fluorine)
- help to release and use energy in the body (potassium helps with heart and muscle contraction)
- provide soluble salts in the body fluids and cells (sodium) to maintain the fluid balance in the body and encourage the correct functioning of cells and muscles.

Requirements for minerals can be met with a varied diet, but as with vitamins, the need for some minerals may increase if a person exercises or trains regularly. Similarly, mineral supplements taken in excess of need are unlikely to improve performance. A mineral deficiency can result in stunted growth, damaged eyesight or weak, malformed bones.

TASK 5

Compare the different vitamin and mineral supplements available at a large supermarket. Consider the nutrient content and cost of each type.

Fibre

Fibre is needed to keep the digestive system healthy. A good intake of fibre or roughage helps to prevent constipation and may reduce the risk of developing conditions such as bowel cancer. Most people should eat plenty of fibre-rich foods. Good sources are wholemeal bread and pasta, wholegrain cereals, brown rice, pulses, fruits and vegetables (especially where skins can be eaten), nuts and seeds.

TASK 6

Suggest ways in which you could increase the fibre content of your diet.

Water

Water makes up about two-thirds of body weight and is essential for good health. Water is lost from the body in urine, sweat, expired air and faeces. An average-sized man loses about 2.5 litres of water from his body every day. If this is not replaced, **dehydration** occurs.

During exercise, more water is lost from the body than at rest. Some of this extra water is lost in sweat, and some is lost as water vapour when a person breathes out. The amount of water lost depends upon:

- the intensity of the exercise
- the duration of the exercise
- the temperature and humidity of the surroundings.

In general, more fluid is lost when a person exercises vigorously, for a long time, or in a hot environment.

Everyone needs to follow a balanced diet, to make sure that they stay in good health. It is very important that people who take part in regular physical activity consider their diet carefully.

Different activities may require different diets but individual needs also vary greatly. Dietary needs can be affected by the following.

Age

Younger people have various periods of rapid growth when they need a greater amount of food to enable their bodies to cope with the demands put upon them. As they get older, the demand for food decreases and tends to level out.

The trend seems to be that as we get older we need to regulate our food intake and our weight more. This is almost certainly linked with the fact that we tend to take less exercise as we get older.

The amount and type of activity undertaken

People taking part in different physical activities may need different diets depending on the activities they choose to do.

- *Gymnasts* need to remain fairly small and light and so need to avoid very fatty foods which could lead to an increase in body weight. They need strength and energy to keep going so they need a good balance of carbohydrates, proteins and fats. They need to monitor their body weight regularly.

- *Hockey players* don't need to be particularly light or heavy to take part in their activity but they do need energy to keep going in matches and training. Body weight is not a major concern but players would have to

monitor it if excess weight caused them to slow down during games. They need a fairly normal diet with sufficient carbohydrates, proteins and fats to supply their energy needs.

- *Weightlifters* need to have a great deal of body weight and may even need to increase it if they wish to get into a certain body weight category (there are ten of these ranging from 52 kg to 110+ kg). Because of this, weight lifters may eat to increase **bulk** so the quantities consumed would be large, with carbohydrates and fats as a priority. They also need to increase strength, so proteins are needed to help with muscle development.

As shown in the examples above, quantities eaten can be just as important as the types of food.

TASK 1

*Think of **two** other types of performer. What sort of diet will they need for their sport?*

Dietary needs

Performers also need to pay particular attention to their dietary needs at particular times, such as:

- before activity
- during activity
- after activity.

Before activity

This is always a period of preparation for performers and they must make sure that they are as ready as they can be to take part. If their activity requires them to be particularly light, or even large, this has to be planned out and

This weightlifter will require a specialized diet

maintained over quite a long period of time. Their diet would become a routine with some adjustments from time to time.

A top performer might adjust their diet for up to a week before an important event. Many long distance runners decrease the amount of carbohydrates at the start of this period and then increase it substantially towards the end, especially the night before (carbohydrate loading). The timing of this is important. It can be dangerous to eat within two hours of an event because the body finds it very difficult to cope with digesting food *and* meeting the demands that the increased amount of exercise makes. Fats and meat are particularly difficult to digest so they should not be eaten for several hours before an event. Liquids can be taken just before an event without causing the same problems.

During activity

No food should be eaten during activity because the digestive system would not be able to cope and it could cause extreme discomfort or even illness. What is important is that the performer replaces lost fluids and drinks enough to prevent dehydration.

Failing to take in enough liquid can lead to collapse and, in extreme cases, hospital treatment may be required to replace the liquid.

After activity

When an activity is over, the performer must replace all the energy that has been used up. This should not be done immediately – it is unlikely that the desire to eat will be felt anyway (remember that exercise can suppress the appetite). It is possible to take liquids almost straight away and many track athletes can be seen doing this immediately after a race.

At least two hours should be left before any substantial amounts of food are eaten and then the cycle of eating, following the correct diet, can start again, ready for the next performance or event.

Possible dietary problems

Being underweight can be just as unhealthy as being overweight. In some cases a person may be **anorexic**. Anorexia is a mental illness which results in someone refusing to eat. The person may suffer a loss of appetite, or may appear to follow a normal diet but then force themselves to vomit later. This results in them being extremely thin and **undernourished**. It is a very serious condition and can lead to death.

Obesity is the opposite condition. Being extremely fat and greatly overweight can also be very dangerous as it puts a great strain on the heart, joints and muscles.

TASK 2

Using the information in this unit and in unit 11, choose a physical activity and consider the dietary needs for a performer before, during and after the activity.

The most basic way to be physically active is to exercise or to experience 'healthy physical exertion'. Exercise is something in which everyone should take part. It does not have to be particularly strenuous and the amounts of exercise will vary from person to person. Some people exercise to maintain their general good health and well-being. Others exercise to achieve a very high level of **fitness** (see unit 14).

We have seen that exercise plus a balanced diet can help to keep body weight down (see page 36) but exercise has other benefits, such as:

- improving your body shape

- helping with the relief of tension and stress

- helping you to sleep better

- reducing the chances of getting illnesses and disease

- giving you a physical challenge to aim for

- toning up the body and the muscles, which leads to an improvement in **posture**

- increasing your basic levels of strength, stamina and flexibility.

Exercise can take many forms and it can be fun!

Exercise can also be a very social thing as it can involve joining clubs and associations and starting up new friendships.

Physical activity is important for everyone because it improves our general health. many jobs require a good level of strength and stamina in order to manage tasks like stacking shelves or standing on one's feet all day. Other jobs, called **sedentary** jobs, involve sitting down for long periods with little regular body movement, so it is very important for these people to exercise.

How much exercise is necessary?

This very much depends on two things:

- the physical condition of the person

- the long-term aims of the person.

Physical condition

If someone is not very healthy or has not been exercising regularly they may need to see their doctor before they decide how much to

exercise. This would also be a good idea if the person was middle aged or older because the advice would be to start off with fairly mild exercise and then to increase it gradually.

Many doctors are now prescribing exercise to their patients instead of drugs and many have arrangements with local leisure centres so that people can go there to exercise.

Long-term aims

Exercise has to be done regularly to enjoy the benefits, and the amount of exercise can be increased gently. A long-term aim can be to move on from the mild levels of exercise which are appropriate when you start off, to much higher levels. After a while you could reach the level that a person who takes part in regular, quite strenuous physical activity would need.

Many activities have playing seasons and 'closed seasons' when the sport is not played competitively. Performers in these activities would therefore need to plan their exercise around this and carry out exercise training during the closed season. Some performers even travel abroad to do this where the climate is better – if they can afford it!

Good exercise habits

Here are some simple and easy ways of increasing the amount of exercise you can take.

- Don't drive, or be driven, short distances but walk instead.
- Try to walk at least part of a journey. This is easy to do if you travel by bus.
- Use a bicycle.
- Walk up stairs rather than using an escalator or a lift.
- Do some simple stretching or **flexibility** (see unit 16) exercises at various times daily.

TASK 1

List some other simple exercise habits you can start.

Exercise guidelines

The following are some general guides to the type and quantity of exercise advisable.

- Being slightly breathless is not a bad sign but if you are unable even to talk when exercising you have probably overdone it.
- Try to exercise for periods of 15–20 minutes about four or five times a week.
- Exercise until you are pleasantly tired; do not overdo it. 'No pain no gain' is not necessarily a good slogan.
- Go for good all-round exercise. Swimming is particularly good because it includes some stretching movements, allowing the muscles to move freely, without straining the body.
- Establish an exercise routine which becomes a regular part of life. Joining a club is a good idea as it can help organize your exercise routine.

Effects of exercise

The long-term effect of exercise is the enjoyment of all the benefits that have been listed. There are also some short-term effects which occur as exercise takes place.

- The rate at which the heart beats (the pulse rate) will increase .
- The rate of breathing will increase.
- The body temperature increases and sweat appears on the surface of the skin.
- Skin will appear to redden, especially on the face.
- There may be a feeling of tiredness or 'heaviness' in some muscles which are being used.

TASK 2

Observe someone who is exercising. As the exercise continues, note down the differences in: pulse rate, skin colour, amount of sweat and breathing rate. What changes have you

It is important to keep a level of both physical and mental fitness which is relative to your needs and requirements.

A basic level is always necessary, but you may have to work very hard to achieve high levels. Fitness can only be achieved through hard work and it is relative to the standard at which you perform.

Some of the factors of fitness are:

- age
- sex
- somatotype
- strength
- power
- flexibility (also known as suppleness or mobility)
- endurance (also known as stamina)
- speed.

The first three are different because an individual does not have any real control over them. They will be dealt with later (see units 19, 20 and 21). The other factors can be changed. The ways in which they are important will be dealt with in this unit.

Some activities only require a level of general fitness

So what is fitness? Basically it is having a highly efficient body which can cope with a high level of physical demand. We have seen the importance of being healthy (unit 9) and the way in which physical activity can help (unit 13). Both of these are vital if a high level of fitness is to be achieved. It is possible to be healthy without being fit, but it is not possible to be fit without being healthy.

There are two different levels of fitness depending on the type of physical activity being undertaken. They are general fitness and specific fitness.

General fitness

For general fitness, an individual needs to be in good health and be able to carry out everyday tasks comfortably. She or he should also take part in a number of physical activities at a low level of performance. Some individuals may be able to compete at a relatively high level in a particular activity due to natural ability or because they have acquired a high skill level in that activity.

TASK 1

*Make a list of **five** activities which only require a general fitness level.*

Specific fitness

This is necessary if the activity in which the individual takes part is particularly demanding or if they are competing at a high level.

It is therefore an extension of general fitness because the physical demands require that the individual must prepare very carefully for the specific needs of that activity.

Natural ability and skill alone will not be enough to compete at the highest level, where specific fitness is essential.

Achieving specific fitness

Clearly, the first thing needed is a good level of general fitness. This can be achieved by following the exercise guidelines in unit 13. It would be very dangerous to do too much too soon because you could make demands on your body which it might not be able to cope with.

The activity for which a person is trying to get specifically fit will dictate the amount and type of **training** (see unit 29) needed. This training will, in some way, aim to improve:

- strength

- flexibility (suppleness, mobility)

- endurance (stamina)

- speed

- agility.

This does not mean that you will only need to consider one aspect, as all of them need to be considered to some degree. What is important is that certain activities need greater concentration in one area than in others, and it is important to be able to identify these and work on them specifically.

All of the factors can be identified and all of them can be improved so it is important to recognize them and look at ways of improving them.

It is also important to remember there are factors which, if not considered carefully, can have a damaging effect on fitness. Not all of them can be controlled but they must be noted.

- Physical handicap can limit fitness in certain areas, depending on the severity of the disability, but many physically handicapped people concentrate on particular aspects of fitness for their chosen activity and reach high levels, often using adapted training equipment. They may have to accept a limitation on the activities which are

High level activities require a high level of specific fitness

available, considering their particular handicap, but the variety and standard of physically handicapped sport shows that these barriers can be overcome.

- Illness, injuries and medical conditions – little can be done about these. Short-term illnesses or injuries such as broken bones may mean only a temporary reduction in fitness levels. If the illness or medical condition is fairly serious, it could greatly restrict the level of fitness which can be achieved.

- Diet (see units 11 and 12).

- Drugs, alcohol and smoking (see unit 9).

- Weight, height and somatotype (see units 20 and 21).

- The stress and pressures of competition. Many performers will be trying to become fit in order to compete. The pressures they experience both before and during competition are very high and can be damaging. These psychological factors (see pages 64–5) can prevent fitness being achieved or maintained.

Muscular strength

There are different types of strength, each one having a different effect on the efficiency of the body. Muscular strength consists of:

- static strength
- explosive strength
- dynamic strength.

A performer can use different methods to improve his or her strength. The method they choose may depend on which particular type of strength they want to develop.

Static strength

This is the greatest amount of force which can be applied to an immovable object. It is very important in any activity where you have to brace yourself against another performer, or some object or weight.

Arm wrestling requires static strength. A member of the pack in a rugby scrummage needs it to be able to push against the opponents. Sometimes it will be used just to stay still and sometimes to push the other pack backwards.

Static strength being demonstrated in a rugby scrum

TASK 1

Think of some other sporting situations that require a great deal of static strength.

Explosive strength

This is muscular strength used in one short, sharp movement. A sprinter leaving the starting blocks uses a great deal of explosive strength to push forwards and upwards as quickly as possible. A great deal of explosive strength is needed in the leg muscles for this.

TASK 2

Think of some other sporting situations that require a great deal of explosive strength.

Dynamic strength

This is the muscular strength a sportsperson needs to support their own body weight over a prolonged period of time, or to be able to apply force against some type of object.

This type of strength is very closely linked with **endurance** (see unit 17) because the muscles need to work continuously, moving and supporting the body. Compare this with explosive strength which only occurs for a short space of time, and you can see the difference. A gymnast performing on the rings or the pommel horse needs a lot of dynamic strength to be able to complete a routine.

TASK 3

Write down some other sporting situations that require a great deal of dynamic strength.

A sportsperson, or performer, will always require some degree of static strength, explosive

This speed skater has clearly developed leg strength

strength and dynamic strength to be able to take part in their chosen physical activity. They must be able to identify which are the most important and which they need to work on most as part of their training programme.

Sometimes it is easy to see the types of strength which top sportspeople have developed. Speed skaters have very well developed muscles at the tops of their legs as they need explosive power to accelerate, and they will work on these muscles specifically.

Many male gymnasts need considerable arm strength, especially for the rings exercise, and they have very clearly defined arm muscles.

TASK 4

Think about a physical activity that you do. Try to work out when you are using static, explosive or dynamic strength. Which type of strength do you use most? Which muscles do

How can strength be increased?

Developing and increasing strength is relatively easy as long as you follow the right training programme and understand the principles of training (see unit 28).

In recent years there has been an increase in the number of gyms where strength can be improved. This has been helped by the improvements in the equipment and facilities available. Previously, the only way to 'weight train' was to use weights on bars. These would have to be frequently changed, and it was necessary to work with others who could help to load and unload and supervise lifting.

The new, purpose-built equipment means that people can train on their own with equipment which is safe and easily and quickly adjusted. The new equipment can also be much more specific to certain muscles, or muscle groups, so it is easier to work on the areas you want to.

Although free weights (bars with weights which can be added or subtracted) are still used, by far the most popular method of training is to use multi-gyms or gyms fitted with weight training stations.

TASK 5

What advantages do multi-gyms have over free weights as a method of improving

This gymnast requires upper body strength

Flexibility is the range of movement around a joint. Sometimes it is called suppleness or mobility but all these terms mean the same thing.

Advantages of flexibility

The amount you can bend or stretch your joints is very important for just about all the movements you do in everyday life. It is particularly important when you are taking part in physical activities. Every sportsperson should work to try to improve flexibility. Flexibility is often ignored by performers who may not realize all the advantages which increased flexibility can bring.

Less chance of injury

Most physical activities require performers to reach or stretch. Quite serious injuries can occur if you stretch too far. A hooker in rugby needs flexibility in the shoulders to bind on to the lock forwards, a tennis player needs it to be able to stretch and reach for shots and a cricket or rounders player needs it to be able to bend and stretch when fielding.

TASK 1

List some more activities where flexibility is important in reducing the chance of injury.

Preparing the body for performance

If flexibility exercises are done immediately before taking part in a physical activity, as part of the warm-up, it not only reduces the chances of an immediate pull or strain but also means that the performer is properly prepared for taking part.

Improving body posture

Good posture means that the muscles are holding the body in position correctly and that there are no over-tight muscles which can cause aches and pains.

A hurdler needs flexibility to hurdle efficiently

Better, more efficient performance

With a full range of movement at the joints all performances will be improved. In many activities you cannot perform some of the movements without flexibility. Gymnastics is a good example of this. In others, you become more efficient – a swimmer performing butterfly stroke is a good example of this.

Dancers will be able to provide a more pleasing performance because increased flexibility will enable them to be more expressive.

Some events have scores awarded for how well certain movements are performed and for an event such as hurdling, a flexible athlete is able to clear the hurdles far more efficiently.

TASK 2

Name some activities in which marks would be awarded for performing movements that require a lot of flexibility.

Flexibility occurs around joints. The main joints involved in movement are as follows.

- *Shoulders and arms* – where the flexibility occurs at the shoulder joint and also at the elbow and the wrist. Most people have quite a good range of movement in all these areas as they are used all of the time in many everyday activities. Just putting on clothes requires quite a lot of flexibility in these joints.

  Shoulder and arm flexibility is used in any activity requiring lots of arm movements, such as throwing or swimming.

- *Back* – the majority of movements require some flexibility in the back and it is an area which is often ignored in flexibility exercises. Very few people have much range of movement here which is why it is an area prone to injury (bowlers in cricket are a good example).

- *Hips* – lot of movements involve bending at the hip joints, where it is possible to have a very large range of movement in various directions. Any form of leg raising or lowering requires flexibility here. Any movement from the waist involves a combination of hip and back flexibility. This is an area where many people do not have a particularly good range of movement and it is a good area to test for flexibility (see unit 31).

- *Legs* – movement is mainly in the knee and ankle joints. Many people have a fairly good range of movement here because they are areas which are used often. Any walking or running movement, and certainly any kicking movement, require full flexibility.

If joints are not regularly used and exercised, flexibility decreases quite rapidly so it is very important to do flexibility exercises regularly for all areas and concentrate particularly on those areas which you use in your chosen activity.

Ways of improving flexibility

All flexibility exercises need the joints to be moved as far as possible but this can only happen if the muscles surrounding it contract (see unit 25) and if they are able to work against some kind of resistance (some force which is pushing back against the muscles). Here are some examples.

- *Passive or isometric contraction* is where you bend or stretch as far as possible pushing against something. Then you try gradually to push farther and farther to increase the range. Sometimes a coach can help you to push but this must be done very carefully.

- *Active or dynamic contraction* is where you get into a stretched position, as far as possible, and then bounce or bob further. This must also be done very carefully. Some coaches even advise against it as it can cause a sudden strain which can damage muscles.

Stretching in a warm-up helps to improve flexibility

TASK 3

Name an activity you take part in and describe how improved flexibility could improve your performance.

Endurance is probably the most important aspect of fitness and most training usually concentrates on improving it. It is important for all performers to be able to keep going with a movement or activity for as long as possible, or at least as long as is necessary. Endurance is also sometimes called stamina and there are very few physical activities for which it is not a priority.

Muscular endurance

Muscular endurance is the ability of the muscles, or a group of muscles, to keep working against a resistance. The amount of dynamic strength you have (see unit 15) relates to the amount of muscular endurance you have. When a muscle is no longer able to continue working properly, **muscular fatigue** takes place and the muscle will literally not be able to work against, or hold, a load any longer.

Signs of lack of muscular endurance can soon set in. Muscles begin to ache and feel tired, limbs feel heavy and even the most determined performer has to stop.

The only way to improve muscular endurance is to increase dynamic strength. This can be done by using weight training methods (see unit 30).

You can use press-ups to test your muscular endurance

Your ability to improve muscular endurance can be affected by the different muscle fibre types which you have in your body. There are two types.

- *Slow twitch fibres* contract slowly. They can keep doing so for quite long periods of time and they are essential for endurance.

- *Fast twitch fibres* contract quickly so they also tire quickly. They are therefore more suited to speed and power.

Different individuals have different quantities of these fibres. Performers are more likely to be able to improve their muscular endurance if they have a greater proportion of slow twitch fibres in their muscles.

Cardiovascular endurance

Cardiovascular endurance is the ability of the heart and lungs to keep supplying oxygen in the bloodstream to the body to provide the energy to sustain physical movement. In any activity that requires you to keep moving for quite long periods of time you will be far more effective if you have a high level of cardiovascular endurance.

Anyone who has felt out of breath when performing an activity has felt the effect the activity has had upon their heart and lungs. When at rest (this can mean just sitting or standing but not doing anything strenuous) the average person has a heartbeat of about 72 beats per minute and a breathing rate of about 14–16 breaths per minute. That is enough to keep your body working efficiently as enough oxygen will be available to satisfy your needs.

As soon as your body starts to exercise there is a greater demand for oxygen as your body is working harder. The heart rate goes up and so does the breathing rate and if you are performing strenuous activity for long periods it goes up quite considerably. Your ability to keep

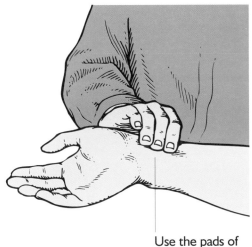

Use the pads of
your fingers.
Don't use your
thumb, as it has a
pulse of its own

Locating a pulse at the wrist

going at this high level of demand is a measure of your level of cardiovascular endurance.

It is important to be able to monitor the heart rate as this is one of the basic ways of measuring and testing endurance. You can check your heart rate (commonly called **pulse rate**) by placing your fingers on the inside of your wrist or on your neck. Use your fingers and not your thumb because there is a pulse in your thumb which can give you a false reading. Simply count the number of beats you can feel in one minute and this will give you your pulse rate.

TASK I

Count your own resting pulse rate for one minute and write it down. Practise to make sure that you can locate your pulse quickly and easily.

Unit 13 describes the effects of exercise. It is very easy to experience the effect exercise can have upon the pulse rate. Once you have learnt how to find your pulse you can check it after several minutes' exercise and you can see for

yourself how much higher it is. There are now watches available which have sensors that can give a very accurate pulse reading and many sportspeople use them.

These watches are also used to help you to improve your level of endurance. Unlike muscular endurance, you cannot exercise your heart and lungs on weight training machines to make them more efficient. To improve them you have to make them work harder by working your body hard. This increases pulse and breathing rates. It is most important to keep them at a high level for some time. The graph gives you an indication of the levels the pulse should be relative to age.

On the graph:

■ *Maximum pulse* is worked out by taking your current age away from 220 (for example, if you are 15 your maximum pulse would be 205). This is the absolute highest level that you should achieve.

■ *Training zone* is the level to which your pulse should be raised and maintained for maximum benefit (see page 52).

■ *Aerobic zone* is from 60 to 80 per cent of your maximum pulse and also benefits increased endurance levels but is not as intensive, or beneficial, as the training zone.

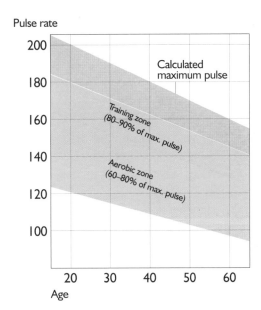

Pulse rate graph

Improving levels of endurance

To be able to benefit fully from exercise in terms of improving endurance it is necessary to work at a high level (aerobic zone and training zone) for at least fifteen minutes. This is a long time to work at such a high level so it is very important that you build up gradually to this standard.

No one should attempt to exercise at high levels or in a strenuous way unless they have carefully built up to it. If you are in any doubt you must seek medical advice. Excessive exercise can be just as harmful as a lack of exercise.

TASK 2

Work out your training zone and see if you can exercise at that level comfortably for a period of time. Only build up to longer periods if you are able to. Try to do this regularly and keep a record of your progress.

Unit 30 looks at ways of training and unit 31 looks at ways of testing. These are very closely linked to improving endurance. If you want a simple way of exercising in your training zone then jogging, cycling, swimming or running on an exercise treadmill (if you have access to one) are good ways to do it.

Pulse recovery rate

This is another way to check endurance levels. It involves taking your resting pulse before you begin to exercise, raising it to a high level and then recording how long it takes to return to normal. The quicker it returns to normal, the higher your level of cardiovascular endurance and the fitter you are considered to be.

There are specific tests (see unit 31) which are used to check recovery rates but it is easy to check your own recovery rate after any period of strenuous exercise.

TASK 3

Before exercising, or taking part in a physical activity, check your resting pulse rate. Afterwards, record how long it takes your pulse rate to return to normal after you have finished. Try to do this regularly and keep a record of the results.

If you regularly exercise using the guidelines set out you will be able to reduce your resting heart/pulse rate and you will have made your heart more efficient. Reducing your resting pulse rate by ten beats a minute (and this is quite possible) means that your heart beats five and a quarter million times less in a year.

Top sportspeople who have a great deal of cardiovascular endurance have a very low resting pulse. The lowest recorded is 16 for a cross-country skier.

Oxygen uptake

As the cardiovascular system is concerned with the heart and the lungs it is important to consider the amounts of oxygen your body needs when exercising, as well as the heart rate.

Oxygen uptake is the total amount of oxygen that the body needs and takes in at any time. It is also referred to as VO_2. Obviously this increases when you exercise, as the body needs to take in more oxygen to produce energy. This cannot go on indefinitely so the maximum amount that a person can take in is known as VO_2 **maximum.**

It is possible to test a person's VO_2 maximum (see unit 27). The higher it is, the greater their level of endurance.

Just as there is a level of heart rate to aim for during exercise in order to improve your level of endurance there is also a level to which your VO_2 should be raised. This should be between 55 and 75 per cent of your VO_2 maximum. One simple way of recognizing when you are working at this level is that you will not be able to carry out a conversation with anyone, as you will not have enough breath to do so.

Cross-country skiers often have a very low resting pulse rate

The oxygen system is sometimes referred to as the aerobic system. (Do not confuse this with 'aerobics' which simply refers to a method of exercising that affects the aerobic system.) There are two terms which relate to it.

- **Anaerobic energy** is used when physical activity is carried out without the use of oxygen. In this case oxygen is not used to generate the energy, it is in fact ATP (to be precise: adenosine triphosphate). This can only be used in short bursts and for short periods.

- **Aerobic energy** is used when the body is continuing with activity for a long period of time and the energy to do so is produced with oxygen.

Unit 27 looks at the respiratory system in more detail and the way in which oxygen is converted to energy.

If you work very hard during a physical activity you may find that you are out of breath for quite a time after you have finished. This is because your body has needed more oxygen than you were able to supply and you have experienced **oxygen debt**. Your body has managed to keep working by using the **lactic acid system** where glucose is broken down in the muscle system. Too much lactic acid can lead to fatigue and tiredness and even stiffness in the muscles after exercise.

The feeling of being short of breath after exercising is not unusual, but you need to repay the oxygen debt and you also need to be able to disperse the lactic acid that has built up. One of the best ways to do this is to exercise lightly after you have finished. This is called the cool-down (or sometimes the warm-down) because this helps its removal.

One important thing to remember about endurance is that most physical activities require a high level of both muscular endurance and cardiovascular endurance. It is only very specialist activities that require just one.

In any activity there are often times when muscular endurance is needed and then cardiovascular endurance takes over. This often works in cycles.

TASK 4

Choose a physical activity (preferably one you take part in) and analyse a performance to see how and when it requires each type of endurance.

Speed

Two factors contribute to this.

- *Reaction time* is how quickly a performer can respond to something. It could be a sprinter reacting to the gun or a tennis player reacting to a tennis ball coming towards them.

- *Movement time* is how quickly a performer can carry out the actual movement. For example, it could be how long it takes the sprinter to run 100 metres or the tennis player to play and follow through their stroke.

The total speed of a performer is the combination of reaction time and movement time, so clearly reaction time is very important. It can certainly mean the difference between a winning or a losing performance, especially in events which last a short time.

A 100 metre sprint race takes less than ten seconds at the top level so if someone reacts to the gun and is out of their blocks quickly they will have a considerable advantage.

Reaction time is very important at the start of a sprint race

Because of the importance of this and the advantage it can give, there are sensors in the starting blocks, linked electronically to the starting gun, to check how quickly the sprinter has reacted to the gun. If it is too quick it will register as a false start and the race is restarted. Top performers react so quickly that electronic checking is the only way of knowing for sure.

Although it is possible to train to improve speed there may be restrictions on how effective this may be.

- *Inherited factors.* In unit 17 we saw that a high proportion of fast twitch fibres can help improve speed. If you have inherited a lower quantity your chances of substantially improving your speed are reduced.

- *Body shape and size.* Because of body weight, muscle size and bone structure you may not be able to increase speed.

- *Duration and distance of the event.* It is not possible to maintain speed indefinitely. A sprinter will slow down progressively, the farther they go. Distances up to 400 metres are considered sprint events and even then sprinters cannot maintain the speed at which they can run 100 metres.

However, speed can be improved by:

- increasing strength, particularly in the main muscles required

- developing action and style for your activity or event

- making speed-work part of your training programme. This involves ways of training the muscles to contract quickly.

Another factor often thought to be a part of fitness is **agility**. This is a combination of flexibility and speed as it is the ability to move quickly, changing direction and speed whenever necessary.

Being agile can be a great advantage in a great many physical activities. The way to improve it is quite straightforward – you should practise the particular aspect of the sport which requires agility. For example, soccer goalkeepers will regularly practise saving footballs fed to them from different angles and heights and at different speeds.

TASK 1

*Name parts of **three** physical activities needing agility and describe a practice for each that could improve it.*

Power

Power is the combination of the maximum amount of speed with the maximum amount of strength.

There is a very strong link between power and explosive strength (see unit 15) and there are a great many physical activities which require power, although not necessarily all the time, as the table below shows.

Activity	Power required for
Tennis	Serving and smashing
High jump	Take-off phase
Rugby	Scrummaging
Golf	Driving
Soccer	Shooting
Cricket	Fast bowling and batting
Athletics	Throwing events, sprints
Hockey	Hitting/shooting
Table tennis	Smashing

Power is not something which can be maintained for long periods. The table includes sports which would not normally be considered 'power events'. This is because power is only used in short bursts. It is impossible to sustain it for long.

Events such as weightlifting and power lifting only require the performer to use power for a very short time. In weightlifting it is actually to lift the weight above the head and then it is only necessary to control it for a few seconds.

This weightlifter needs a great deal of power to lift these weights

TASK 2

Make a list of other events, or stages in a physical activity, where it is important to have power.

It is clear that to have effective power you do not have to be particularly strong. The table includes several examples of activities where strength is not a priority. What is important is the combination of strength and speed, but there are other factors which also help.

- *Co-ordination* You must be able to link all the parts of a movement into one efficient, smooth movement.

- *Balance* Being in control of your movement is vital, without it power will be reduced.

Age constantly affects a person's level of fitness in varying ways. It is a factor to be considered for young people as well as older people. For all forms of competitive sport there are age divisions, usually junior, youth and then senior. These exist because of the great effect age can have.

Within these age divisions there are usually subdivisions. For example, typical age divisions which a tennis club might use for its annual championships would be:

- under 10
- under 12
- under 14
- under 16
- under 18
- seniors
- veterans (40+)
- super veterans (50+).

Some activities would have even more categories.

TASK 1

*Choose **one** physical activity and find out the different age groups which exist for competitions.*

Gymnasts are at their most flexible in their early teens

Why are age divisions necessary?

- *Practising and learning*
  Very young people are not able to cope with too much information, especially if it is quite complicated. They may simply not understand how to do things, so tasks must be kept simple.

- *Flexibility*
  This decreases with age. People are usually at their most flexible in their teens. This is one of the reasons why gymnasts, especially girls, tend to be at their best in their early teens when they are able to perform really well. The decline in flexibility tends to be more noticeable after the age of 30, although it can start in the 20s.

- *Strength*
  A young person will not achieve their maximum strength until they are fully grown. Muscle mass starts to increase in the mid teens. Up to the age of 20 the body is still growing and developing in terms of bone size and muscle. Therefore young people should not start weight training until their mid to late teens. Doing so before this could cause problems.

  During a person's 20s and 30s, there is ample growth hormone so strength tends to peak at this age. There is a loss of protein over the next 40 years and there can be a decline in strength of up to 40 per cent.

- *Diet*
  The body's metabolism slows down as people get older so weight is likely to be gained. This tends to occur in the 40s when the body also loses lean muscle mass, so fewer calories are needed than before and the extra may turn to fat. As you get older you preserve less fluid so there is a tendency to dehydrate quicker.

- *Oxygen capacity*
  This reduces with age; a 50 year old has a reduced capacity compared to a 20 year old.

- *Injury and disease*
  The older people get, the more likely they are to suffer injuries (and the longer it takes to recover from them) and there is an increased chance of disease. For instance, there is a far greater chance of heart disease among older people.

- *Reaction time*
  This decreases with age; the very young have been tested as having very good reaction times.

- *Skill*
  This can improve due to growth (high jumpers may appear more skilful as they get taller, so might basketball players). However, experience is an invaluable asset and it can only be gained over a period of time.

Some of the ways in which age affects our bodies are more important than others because there is little which can be done about them. For example, it is not possible to prevent protein loss as this is just a part of the ageing process, but it is possible to improve or maintain flexibility by regularly performing flexibility exercises. It is also possible to regulate the diet to take account of the changes in the metabolism. If you are aware of the effects of ageing, there are steps you can take to lessen them.

Age and physical activity

Some activities are regarded as young people's sports and some are regarded as old people's sports. Sometimes there are good reasons for this and sometimes there is no real need for it to be true.

If an activity requires a great deal of physical exertion, it is going to be more difficult to compete at a high level as you get older, for all the reasons already mentioned. For any other activity which is less strenuous there does not need to be any bias concerned with age.

In many professional sports there are few performers under sixteen years old or who have not at least left school or college. Tennis has been an exception to this several times in the past, when female players appeared to mature earlier than males. In most activities top performers do not seem to be able to master the range of skills necessary until their late teens or early 20s. Their 'playing career' can quite often last only between ten and fifteen years, due to the very demanding nature of playing full-time sport at the top level. Veteran players in these sports are the exception rather than the rule.

TASK 2

In which sports would you expect players to be in their:
a *teens*
b *20s*
c *30s?*

Many female tennis players play at the highest level while still in their teens

The drawings below show three different **somatotypes** (or body types). These were first identified by an American called W H Sheldon.

Your body type is something you are born with because it is determined genetically. Body shape can be improved but you cannot make drastic changes such as increasing your height or your basic bone structure.

The three classified groups are **endomorph** (fat), **mesomorph** (muscular) and **ectomorph** (thin). The drawings show the extremes of these three body types.

Endomorph

People with this basic shape are short and rounded with a tendency to gain fat. They have short legs in relation to their trunks.

Extreme examples of the three basic body types

Mesomorph

This body is a basic Y-shape, well muscled with wide flexible shoulders, long arms and hands, a narrow waist and lightweight legs.

Ectomorph

These people are relatively short with thin arms and shoulders. They often have a small head with a long neck, a short waist and long legs.

Not many people fall clearly into one of these categories, as most people are a mixture of all three. To classify body type Sheldon used a scale of one to seven for each somatotype, giving seven points for an extreme somatype. To work out *your* body type give yourself a mark somewhere between one and seven for each of the three types, depending on how close you are to the extreme of the type.

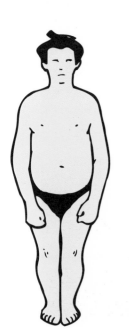

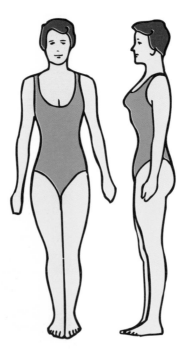
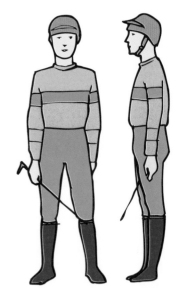

Endomorph   *Mesomorph*   *Ectomorph*

TASK 1

Attempt to give a somatotype rating either for yourself or a sports player of your choice. How does this body shape make the person you have rated especially suited to a particular sport or activity?

Somatotype and sport

Somatotype is a very important factor in physical activities because it may mean that you are particularly well suited to one sport or that you are particularly unsuited to another.

It makes a lot of sense to identify the activities you are suited to, with your natural advantages, rather than trying to overcome the limitations that your body type might impose.

In Australia in the 1990s, there was a national programme called Sport Search. Schoolchildren were measured in an attempt to match them to particular sports. Somatotype characteristics were not the only things tested; other factors of fitness were also taken into account.

In the past, many Eastern European countries used similar programmes to try to identify potential sportspeople. Female gymnasts are at an advantage if they are extreme ectomorphs, so it was not uncommon for very young children to be selected and sent to specialist training schools. There, full advantage could be made of the potential advantages of their body type. At the other end of the scale, an extreme endomorph would be very well suited to become a weighlifter. The large body weight, short legs and low centre of gravity are all useful to them and they can add to this advantage by a suitable training programme which would enable them to increase muscle size and strength.

An extreme mesomorph is very well suited to swimming or perhaps basketball or high-jumping. Their height is a tremendous advantage and it is true that all top performers in swimming and high jump are well over six feet tall.

The former communist countries of Eastern Europe used body typing to identify potential medal winners

There are still many sports for the 'normal' shaped person, who is not of an extreme body type, and there are many activities where it is possible to succeed at the highest level whatever your type. It is also worth remembering that some aspects of your body type, such as your height and weight, may change quite a lot as you grow and develop. Your true somatotype will not be established until you are fully grown.

Rugby is a good example of a sport where all different body types can play and each can use their somatotype to advantage. An endomorph could be in the pack, possibly as the hooker, where their bulk and shortness could be an advantage. A mesomorph could be one of the forwards, as one of the main line-out jumpers where their height would be a great advantage and an ectomorph would be well suited to the scrum-half position where being small, quick and agile would be an advantage.

TASK 2

*Choose an invasion game and identify **at least one** somatotype. Explain the advantages that type would have in a particular position.*

All people are different. These differences can be a very important factor when taking part in physical activity. They can affect the amount of success you are likely to have. All of the following will vary in individuals:

- strength
- flexibility
- endurance levels
- speed and power
- age
- somatotype
- the senses (sight, hearing, touch)
- physical ability
- mental ability
- experience
- motivation
- environment and culture
- gender or sex (male or female).

Some of these factors have been dealt with earlier as factors of fitness but the others may be equally important.

The senses

One of the most important factors related to the senses is the quality of your eyesight. Having poor vision can affect your performance quite dramatically. For most activities, being able to see clearly is an advantage and even a slight sight problem can lead to mistiming shots or strokes, not being able to see targets properly or not picking up the flight of a ball or shuttlecock. Wearing glasses may not be the solution as even these could leave you with 'blind spots'. There may even be activities where it is impossible to wear glasses due to the degree of physical contact involved and the safety factor.

People taking part in physical activities do not always fully appreciate the importance of hearing. A good rackets sports player can tell by the sound of the impact just how well a shot has been struck. Being able to hear other people in a team game is very important. Calls by team-mates must be clearly heard and understood.

Touch can also be important. Many sports involve holding a ball, bat, racket or even a piece of specialist equipment. Holding them correctly can be dependent upon the sense of touch.

Physical ability

This can vary greatly and it is not always possible to say why one person is 'better' than another. It is often explained as one person just having a 'greater amount of natural ability'. No matter how much research is done there does not seem to be any scientific answer to this but, clearly, some people do find some activities easier than others.

Mental ability

There are factors which can affect your level of mental ability such as your intelligence, your levels of concentration, your perception (your awareness of things around you) and your use of reasoning and logic to solve problems which might arise.

Experience

This is something which can only be gained over time. A young or new player will often be called 'inexperienced' and may be the loser because of it.

Not all people benefit from experience. It is how you learn from experience that is important. Some people make the same mistakes time after time whereas others seem to benefit and improve.

Motivation

This is how determined you are to do well and how much effort you are prepared to put in. Some people seem able to motivate themselves very well, but some need the help of others such as team-mates, managers or coaches (see unit 23).

Environment and culture

People living in different parts of the world obviously live in different cultures, but it is possible to live in a different environment even within the same town or street.

The availability of money and facilities – or lack of them – or even the type of climate you live in can all have a big effect.

Gender

Whether you are male or female is probably one of the most influential factors there is. There are real differences between men and women, and this is not an unfair comment but a fact!

There are very few activities where women compete against men on equal terms. Horse riding is the main one. Other physical activities are strictly organized separately for men and women, for the following reasons.

Strength

On average, women have only two-thirds the strength of men, as men have a greater muscle mass. Because men have higher **testosterone** levels they have greater muscle growth.

Rate of maturity

Girls mature earlier than boys so competition between them when young can be fair. From the age of about eleven, though, boys start to overtake girls in terms of height, weight and strength. Because of this, many sports become single sex from eleven years upwards.

Body type

Women have a flatter, broader pelvis (designed for childbearing) and have a higher percentage of fat. Women also have smaller lungs and a smaller heart, which affects cardiovascular endurance levels. **Menstruation** (periods) can also affect performance.

Flexibility

Women tend to be more flexible than men since they have less muscle mass.

TASK 1

In what activities would greater flexibility give women an advantage over men?

Discrimination

There is little doubt that women are discriminated against in terms of prize money and finance for their sport. They are also prevented from taking part against men by many of the rules and regulations of activities. Pregnancy and the birth of a child may cause a woman to miss up to a year of competing, for each child.

TASK 2

a Why do you think that horse riding is an activity totally open to both sexes?

b Are there other activities which should be open to both sexes? Give reasons for your answer.

Physiological factors are things which can affect you physically and will in some way have an effect upon your body. Like the individual differences covered in the last unit, these factors also vary between people, and they can have important effects upon performance. Some factors affecting performance were explained in unit 9 but there are others which can also have an influence:

Illness or medical condition

An illness is often something which is only temporary but a medical condition could be something which a performer has to cope with permanently. If they are taking some sort of medicine or receiving some form of treatment it will affect how well they perform, even if it does not stop them taking part altogether. The following are some of the most common conditions.

- *Asthma* – a disease which causes difficulty in breathing. Unfortunately it is becoming more and more common. It can be brought about by allergies, infections or even emotional situations and it causes an involuntary contraction around the **bronchioles** (see unit 27) which makes the sufferer wheeze and struggle for breath.

  It can be controlled by drugs and medicines, the most common of which is an inhalant spray. However, a person suffering from asthma is likely to be less successful at endurance events because of their condition.

  The effects of asthma do tend to decrease with age so there is a chance of the condition improving.

- *Hay fever* – this also affects the breathing system but more directly affects the nose. It is caused by an allergy, often to the pollens of grasses. It causes an inflammation of the membranes in the nose which makes the sufferer sneeze and their eyes water. It only affects people during the time that the pollens are produced, which is in the spring and summer months, but it can be extremely uncomfortable and can actually stop them from performing.

  There are medications available which ease the condition but they will not stop it completely and some of the drugs may cause drowsiness.

- *Colds and flu* – these are infectious diseases because they can be passed from one person to another. The common cold affects the nose and throat and causes sneezing, sore throats, running eyes, coughs and even headaches. It usually lasts only for a matter of days but some of the symptoms can last longer. Flu (or influenza) mainly affects the respiratory system but it can affect the whole of the body causing fever, headaches and general weakness.

TASK I

*Choose **one** physical activity and describe the ways that a bad cold or flu could affect a player's performance.*

- *Blood disorders* – many of these are very serious (especially leukaemia which is cancer of the blood cells) but there are other less serious ones which can also have an effect.

- *Anaemia* occurs when there is a shortage of oxygen being transported through the blood. This can be put right by taking iron tablets. **Fainting** is sudden unconsciousness which happens when a lowering of blood pressure causes lack of supplies of blood to the brain. It is only temporary but can be quite dangerous if a player is performing at the time of the faint.

- *Menstruation* – the menstrual cycle affects some women quite badly, causing vomiting, headaches and feelings of extreme tension. The extreme hormonal changes may affect performance and the fact that it happens on a 28-day cycle can certainly affect training.

Lack of sleep

Tiredness can have a very bad effect on performance as it reduces levels of concentration and co-ordination. Movements become sluggish and thoughts can often be confused, speech can even be slurred.

Depriving people of sleep has been used as a form of torture due to the confused mental state it can bring on, so it is no surprise that it can seriously affect a physical performance.

There can be a vicious circle if someone is nervous or worried before an important event, as this may lead to sleepless nights and the tiredness then affects the performance.

Staleness

This can occur if a performer overdoes physical activity. It can lead to patches of bad form, caused by the over exertion of either too much play or too much training.

In many physical activities now, there are opportunities to play all the year round instead of just throughout the traditional season, so it is very easy to overdo it. The pressure is on continually to improve so performers are stopped from having breaks or rests from their sport. They just have to hope that a stale patch will not occur.

Fatigue

This is one of the most serious and damaging factors which can affect a performance. It occurs when the body, or parts of the body, get so tired, through the amount of work they have been called on to do, that they stop working properly.

We have already seen in unit 17 that fatigue can occur in the muscles so that they will not

Substitution can prevent a fatigued player from being injured

be able to carry on whatever work they are doing. As fatigue starts to set in it will lead to a decrease in skill levels, the performer will not be able to move the extra yard to intercept a pass or play a shot. More mistakes will be made as the tiredness sets in and the effects get worse, not better. If the performer tries to keep going without a rest the chances are they will have to stop completely. There are cases where this has happened even at the top levels of sport.

This can be a dangerous condition. Injuries are more likely to occur because of the performer's inability to carry out movements properly. Techniques can also start to suffer.

The only solution if fatigue has really set in is for the performer to stop before they do themselves harm. It is important that coaches and managers of teams can recognize the signs of fatigue and substitute a player if possible.

TASK 2

*List, in order, the signs of fatigue. Choose **one** physical activity and describe how fatigue could affect a performer.*

Many trainers and coaches feel that the physical boundaries of performance are stretched nearly to their limits and that the main boundaries that need to be broken through are psychological barriers, taking account of:

- personality type
- tension
- anxiety
- boredom
- stress
- pressure
- motivation
- psyching up.

There is often a great link between these factors, and they can have an enormous effect on performance and skill levels. All of these factors can affect the actual aquisition of skills as well

Personality type

People can be divided into two identified types:

- *introverts* – these are people who are quiet and self-centred, not high in confidence, not looking to lead

- *extroverts* – confident and outgoing people with high opinions of themselves, they tend to be leaders.

An extreme introvert would be unlikely to be able to fit in well in a team game and would probably be far more suited to an individual sport or activity.

Tension

A performer can experience tension personally, in anticipation of an event. It is also an atmosphere which can be generated by spectators.

Tension is related to excitement or suspense and it is easy to see how these feelings can be transferred from performers to spectators and back again. Tension can also exist just between two players or teams.

Tension does not always have a bad effect on performance. Some competitors find that they cannot compete properly unless there is some

tension, and they respond to it positively. Others find that tension makes them nervous and uncertain and this results in a poor performance.

Anxiety

A person who is anxious is uneasy or troubled and clearly this is not a good state for a performer to be in. All performers experience some level of anxiety before or during a performance and, to some extent, this is not only normal but it can actually help. However, when a player becomes over anxious, or nervous, their performance can get worse, especially if they are already in a tense situation.

The main reason why someone feels anxious is that they are worried about losing or performing badly and this is made even worse if people they know are watching.

TASK I

Describe a sporting situation where you have felt anxious. Explain how you felt and what caused you to feel this way.

Boredom

When you are bored you are totally uninterested in what you are doing, your concentration lapses and the chances are that you will try very little, if at all.

It is unusual to choose to be in a sporting position that is boring, but boredom can set in if you are being unsuccessful and it will lead to a decrease in the standard of performance.

Stress

In a stressful situation, you feel extreme tension or pressure. A certain amount of stress can be a good thing as it can make you more alert and ready to perform your best. However, if your stress level rises too high it can cause you

The atmosphere generated by a big crowd can enhance performance

problems. Different people react in different ways to high levels of stress. Some seem to cope very well, even to the point of enjoying it, while others find that their performance can be ruined.

Stress will almost certainly increase if there is an audience or a crowd watching. Top performers usually respond very well to this situation and actually look forward to it, being disappointed if there are not many people watching. It is very unlikely that anyone would reach the top level of their sport if thuld not cope with this situation.

TASK 2

Describe the ways a crowd can influence a player or team. Explain the differences between how a 'home' team and an 'away' team might

Pressure

This is something which others, usually opponents, bring to a physical activity. If a player is unable to cope with it ('cracking under pressure' is the popular term), it will certainly have a bad effect on the way they perform.

Players, or competitors, are always trying to put their opponents under pressure by the way they play the game. If they find a weakness they make the most of it.

Being able to keep going when under pressure is vital for a player to be successful. This is what is meant by the expression 'soaking up the pressure'.

Motivation

This is the amount of determination a player has to do well. Highly motivated players are more likely to cope with anxiety, tension, boredom, stress and pressure because they are positive about what they are doing and they want to succeed.

Some people can be motivated just by the desire to win. For others it is the rewards that go with winning, such as money and fame, which are most important.

It is probably more difficult to motivate people who are used to winning because of this. They have become used to being the best and it can then be difficult for them to motivate themselves sufficiently to stay at the top in their sport. This is why top sportspeople often employ a personal coach or trainer to help, not only with their physical preparation but also with their mental preparation and motivation.

Psyching up

This is how players are prepared to perform well. Different approaches are used, from calmly talking them through the game or match, to arousing them to an emotional state of excitement and commitment to winning.

Functions of the skeleton

The human skeleton has five functions:

- support
- protection
- movement
- shape
- blood cell production and storage of mineral salts.

These functions all contribute to the skeletal system helping with a performance, most notably in allowing movement.

Support

The skeleton provides support for muscles and many delicate vital organs. It is the framework around which the body is constructed. Without it our bodies would collapse.

Protection

The skeleton provides a protective cover. The skull protects the brain and the ribs protect the heart and lungs. Without this protection injuries would be far more common and serious.

TASK I

Name some other vital organs which are protected by parts of the skeleton. Name the bones which protect them.

Movement

Where two or more bones meet there is a joint and it is here that movement occurs, with the help of muscles (see unit 25). The amount of movement differs between different joints (see page 71).

Shape

As the basic framework of our bodies, the skeleton gives us our shape. Muscle size and the amount of body fat also contribute to this.

Blood cell production and storage of mineral salts

These are lesser known functions of the skeleton. Red and white blood cells are produced in the bone marrow and mineral salts, such as calcium, are stored in the bones.

Classification of bones

The diagram opposite shows and names the bones which make up the skeletal system. The four types of bone are:

- long bones
- short bones
- flat (or plate) bones
- irregular bones.

Long bones

These are coloured blue in the diagram. They include the femur, humerus, tibia, fibula, radius and ulna. These bones are used in most of our movements, including any type of running or throwing. The greatest ranges of movement occur at the joints of these bones. These are the main points of flexibility (see unit 16).

TASK 2

Identify and find the length of the longest bone in your body.

Short bones

These are coloured green in the diagram. They include the wrist and ankle bones (carpals and tarsals). They are used to help you to grip things and to enable you to balance and perform fine movements.

Flat (or plate) bones

These are coloured brown in the diagram.
They include the skull, ribs, pelvis and scapula
and they are very important for protection.
They are also the bones to which the larger
muscles in the body are attached.

Irregular bones

These are coloured in yellow in the diagram.
Most of these are in the face and the vertebrae
in the spine (also known as the **vertebral
column**). There are a total of fourteen bones
in the face. There are 33 bones in the
vertebral column.

The main bones in the skeletal system

Key

Long bones

Short bones

Flat bones

Irregular bones

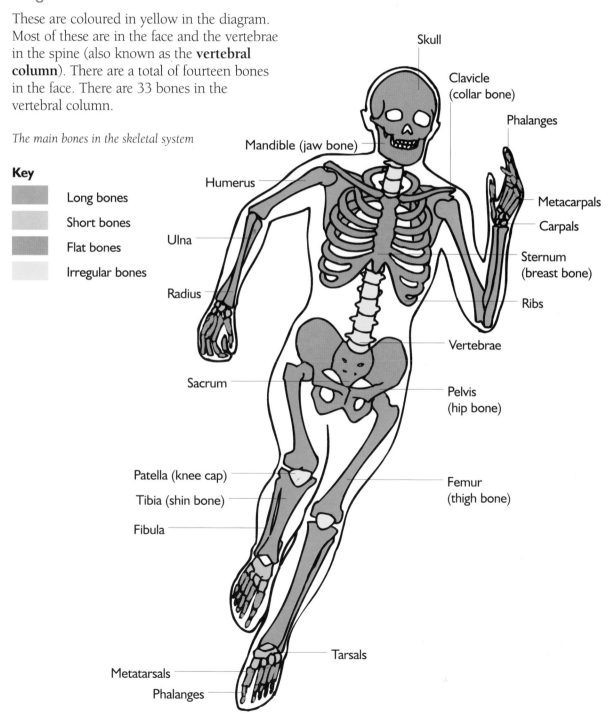

Joints and movement

All bones are solid and rigid and do not bend, so movement has to occur in areas where the bones are connected by joints. Examples of these joints are shown in the diagrams opposite. The types of joints (or areas of articulation) are:

■ immovable (**fibrous** or fixed) – e.g. the skull bones and the pelvic bones

■ slightly movable (**cartilaginous**) – e.g. the vertebrae of the spine and the pubic bones

■ freely movable (**synovial**) – these are the majority of joints which allow the greatest amount of movement. There are different types of freely movable (synovial) joints.

TASK 3

Identify which of your joints has the greatest range of movement.

Freely movable (synovial) joints

The six types of joints are shown in the diagrams on this and the opposite page. These joints all have some things in common although the type and range of movement they allow is quite different. Common characteristics are as follows.

■ *Hyaline cartilage* – this is a shiny, smooth and white covering on the surface and end of the bone. It serves two purposes as it protects and reduces friction (rubbing) between the bones at joints.

■ *Ligaments* – these are bands of fibre attached to each of the bones and linking the joints. They keep the joints stable and control the amount of movement.

■ *Synovial membrane* – this is a thin layer of tissue which is on the inside of the articular capsule (tissue which surrounds the joint). It produces synovial fluid which is like a type of oil as it lubricates the joint and allows smooth movement.

■ *Articular discs or menisci* – these act like shock absorbers and are attached to the capsule on the outside edges of the joints.

Connective tissue

We have already seen that bones need to be connected up in order to allow movement. The various forms of tissue which allow this to happen are as follows.

■ *Cartilage* – like the hyaline cartilage in the synovial joints, this is tough but flexible tissue which acts as a buffer between the bones at joints. There is quite a complicated arrangement of cartilage in the knee joint (as can be seen in the diagram) and many injuries result in damaged cartilage. Your ear flaps and nose are almost all cartilage.

■ *Tendons* – these are very strong, non-elastic cords that join muscles to bones. Some are flat and broad. There can be one or more tendons, depending on the size of the muscle.

■ *Ligaments* – as above.

The six freely movable types of joints

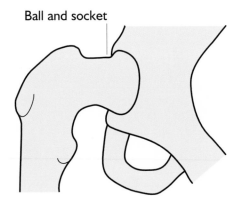

Ball and socket

*The hip and shoulder are examples of **ball and socket** joints*

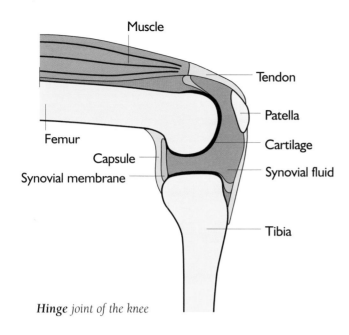

Hinge joint of the knee

Muscle
Tendon
Patella
Cartilage
Synovial fluid
Tibia
Femur
Capsule
Synovial membrane

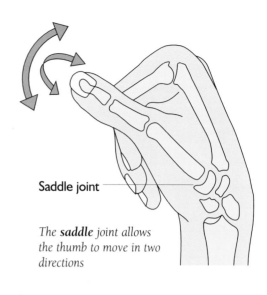

Saddle joint

*The **saddle** joint allows the thumb to move in two directions*

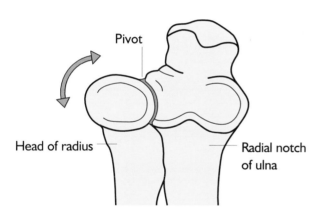

Pivot
Head of radius
Radial notch of ulna

*A **pivot** joint such as the one which allows us to turn our hands over and back*

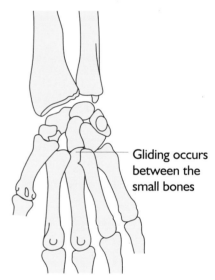

Gliding occurs between the small bones

*The **gliding** joint*

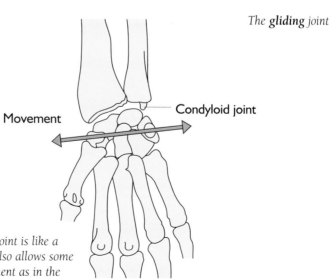

Movement
Condyloid joint

*The **condyloid** joint is like a hinge joint but also allows some sideways movement as in the wrist*

69

The vertebral column

The general functions of the spine are:

- to keep the body upright
- to help posture and movement
- to act as a shock absorber
- to protect the spinal cord.

The vertebral column can be broken down into five separate regions, each with its own specific functions.

The five regions of the spinal column and their functions are as follows.

- *Cervical vertebrae* (or neck) – seven vertebrae make up this region, the top two are known as the atlas and axis. This region allows head movement, such as nodding and shaking, and also bending and twisting of the neck. The neck muscles are attached here.

- *Thoracic vertebrae* (or chest) – twelve vertebrae make up this region. These vertebrae are attached to the ribs and support the rib cage. There is some movement here allowing some bending and turning of the trunk.

- *Lumbar vertebrae* (or lower back) – there are five vertebrae in this region and they are the largest of all the vertebrae. The back muscles are attached here. This is where there is the greatest amount of movement for bending forwards, backwards and from side to side. This is the most common area for back injuries due to the amount of movement and it is an area which should be especially worked upon for flexibility exercises.

- *Sacral vertebrae* – there are five vertebrae in this region which are fused together to become one. This is where the spine is joined to the pelvis and where body weight is transmitted to the hips and legs.

- *Coccyx* (or tail) – this is the very base of the spine and is made up of four vertebrae fused together. It is all that remains of what was a tail before humans evolved.

During any physical activities, it is very important to protect the back. Any injuries to the back should be treated as serious and with caution as it possible that the spinal cord could be damaged. In extreme cases, back injury could lead to paralysis.

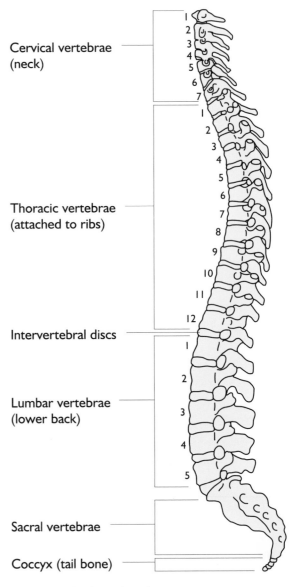

Cervical vertebrae (neck)

Thoracic vertebrae (attached to ribs)

Intervertebral discs

Lumbar vertebrae (lower back)

Sacral vertebrae

Coccyx (tail bone)

The vertebral column (spine)

Types of movements at joints

Joints allow us to move in different ways. These different movements have technical names to describe them.

- *Flexion* – this is the decreasing of an angle between two bones, such as bending the leg at the knee or bending the arm up at the elbow towards the shoulder. This is the movement needed for a bicep curl, for example.

- *Extension* – this is when the angle is increased between two bones (the opposite of flexion), such as straightening the leg at the knee or lowering the arm from the shoulder. Kicking a ball requires extension of the leg.

- *Rotation* – this is when a bone may move round freely in a curve, such as the movement of the arm at the shoulder. Bowling a delivery at cricket is an example of this.

- *Abduction* – this is the movement of a bone or limb away from the body. Lifting your leg up and outwards sideways from the hip is an example of this.

- *Adduction* – this is the movement of a bone or limb towards the body (the opposite of abduction), so returning the leg back down to its straight position after lifting it up would be an example of this.

TASK 5

Work in pairs. Take turns to ask your partner to perform a movement, describing it by its technical term only. See how many you each get right.

All movement involves one or more of the types mentioned above. It is no coincidence that most of the movements have *opposite* movements to counteract them. We shall see in unit 25 that muscles are always arranged in pairs so that movement can take place in both directions.

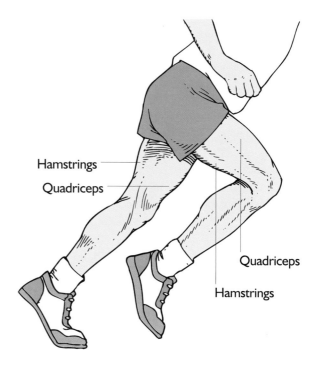

The upper leg showing quads and hamstrings relaxing and contracting during movement

Movement and levers

A lever is something solid or rigid which can be used to apply force. In human movement this is brought about by the action of the muscles moving the bones. The central point of this movement is always the joint around which the movement is taking place.

If you do a chin-up on a chin bar the muscles and bones of your arms are acting as levers and the central point (known as the fulcrum) is your elbow joint. When performing chin-ups it is an advantage to have short levers (a short overall arm length) as this makes it easier to do chin-ups.

If you want to add more strength to a movement you can make your levers shorter by bending. For example, pushing in a rugby scrum with bent legs is more efficient than trying to push with straight legs. You can get more power into a tennis volley with a bent arm than you can with a straight one.

Muscles

There are more than 600 muscles in your body and they make up half of your total body weight. The muscles and muscle groups (when specific groups of muscles work together) combine with the skeletal system (see unit 24) to allow movement.

Just how effective this movement is able to be through the combined actions of the body systems will have a great effect on the levels of performance you are able to achieve.

There are three particular types of muscle: voluntary (or skeletal) muscle, involuntary (or smooth) muscle and cardiac muscle.

Voluntary or skeletal muscle

These are sometimes called striped or **striated muscle** and they make up the majority of the muscles in the human body (see the diagram opposite). They also help to give the body its shape. They are called voluntary because they are under your control (through the nervous system) and only move when you want them to.

Involuntary or smooth muscle

These are muscles which you cannot control. They are found in the walls of the intestine and in the blood vessels. Even though you cannot control these muscles at all, they work automatically all the time that you are alive.

Cardiac muscles

These are also involuntary muscles as they work constantly and automatically. They are a special type of muscle only found in the wall of the heart. The beating of your heart is a muscular action which goes on all of the time. As we have seen (page 50) your heart beats approximately 72 times a minute, so cardiac muscles work very hard.

Muscles and movement

Muscles can only pull, they cannot push so they have to work in pairs in order for any movement to take place.

As one of the muscles contracts (becomes shorter) the other one of the pair has to relax (it lengthens). This causes movement at the joint around which the two muscles are attached. An example of this is shown in the diagram on this page where you can see how the arm can be moved around the elbow joint. If the biceps contracts, the triceps relaxes and the arm bends at the elbow. If the triceps then contracts and the biceps relaxes, the arm straightens back up.

The muscles invoved in these movements are called:

- *prime mover* (*agonist*) – this is the muscle which contracts to cause the movement. In our example of bending at the elbow the prime mover is the biceps.

- *antagonist* – this is the muscle which relaxes and lengthens to allow the movement to take place. In the example of bending at the elbow it is the triceps.

The action of the muscles working together to enable movement is often referred to just as antagonistic movement.

The way in which the muscle is actually

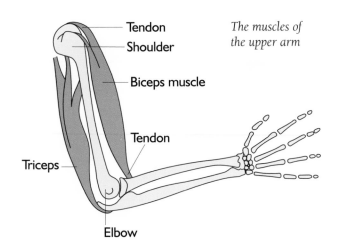

Tendon
Shoulder
Biceps muscle
Tendon
Triceps
Elbow

The muscles of the upper arm

attached to the bone is also very important and there are terms used to describe this.

- *Origin* – this is the end of the muscle which is actually fixed to the bone by **tendons** (see page 68).

- *Insertion* – this is the part of the muscle which actually moves the most and it is at the opposite end of the muscle to the origin.

In our example of the bending of the arm at the elbow, the origin of the triceps and biceps is at the shoulder and the insertion of both of them is at the elbow.

TASK 1

Bend and straighten your arm. As you do so, use the fingers of the other hand to press gently on the triceps and biceps muscles. See if you can feel the movement which is taking place. Try to feel the location of the origin and insertion of each of the muscles at the elbow and shoulder.

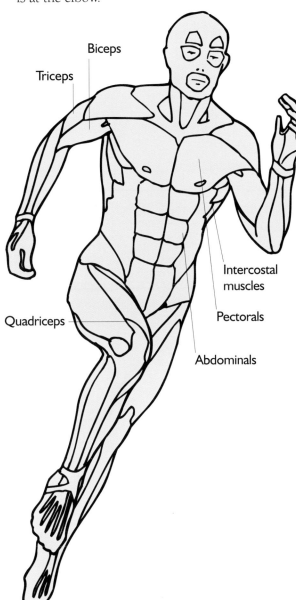

Major skeletal muscles – front view

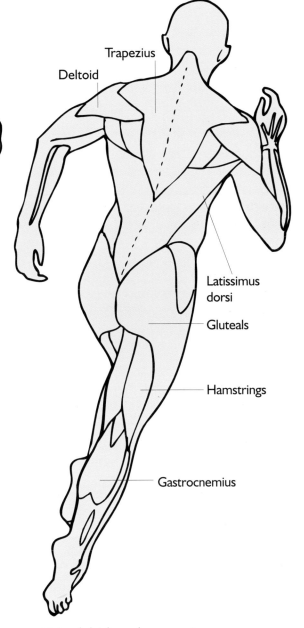

Major skeletal muscles – rear view

Types of muscle contraction

We have seen that muscles need to contract so that movement can take place. There are different types of muscle contraction, called:

- isotonic
- isometric.

Isotonic contractions

There are two types of isotonic contractions.

- **Concentric contractions** – when the muscle shortens. In the elbow bending example (see page 72) the biceps muscle undergoes a concentric contraction because it shortens as the arm bends. This is also sometimes known as a dynamic contraction.

- **Eccentric contraction** – when the muscle gradually lengthens and returns to its normal length and shape. The biceps muscle undergoes an eccentric contraction when the arm straightens back up after it has been bent. This is sometimes also known as a static contraction.

Isometric contractions

In these contractions, there is no actual movement of a limb or a joint so the length of the muscle is not affected. The muscles are working although they are actually stationary – for example, when a gymnast performing a handstand holds themself in position by isometric contraction of the muscles in the arms. Once again, the triceps and biceps would be working but this time they would be undergoing an isometric contraction.

TASK 2

Put your hands flat against a wall and push hard with both arms straight. Feel the muscles contracting in your arms. Now work with a partner and feel how their biceps and triceps are both contracting.

Categories of muscles

While all the different muscles in the body have different names they can also be put into categories depending upon the type of job that they do.

When the muscles are working as pairs to allow a movement at a joint, the muscles involved are known as:

- *prime movers* – the main muscles which contract to produce the movement

- *antagonists* – the muscles which work against the prime movers and relax to allow the movement to take place

- *flexors* – the muscles which bend a limb at a joint by contracting

- *extensors* – the muscles which work against the flexors and straighten a limb at a joint by contracting

- *adductors* – the muscles which move a limb towards the body

- *abductors* – muscles which move a limb away from the body.

The photos on the opposite page show a dual-use specialist weight-training machine which works on the adductors and the abductors of the legs.

Muscle tone

Muscles are not usually completely relaxed, but keep some tension in them. It is very difficult to relax any of your voluntary muscles completely, no matter how hard you try.

TASK 3

*Work with a partner. Try to relax your arm or leg completely so that your partner can raise it easily and let it fall freely. Is it **completely** relaxed and moving freely?*

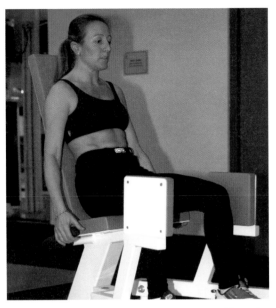 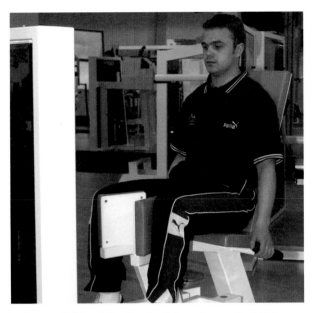

These machines can be used to develop either the adductor leg muscles (as in the left-hand photo) or the abductor leg muscles (right)

The tension that remains in the muscle is known as muscle tone. It is important because it makes contracting your muscles, for a movement to take place, easier. It means that the body is in a state of readiness as the muscles are prepared to do their job.

When you are asleep you lose body tone, whereas if you are particularly agitated or anxious your body tone will increase.

This is often called 'tightening up' or 'stiffening up', which is exactly what your body is doing!

Body tone affects your whole appearance as it helps you to maintain posture.

Posture

This is the way you hold your body and it is very important, not just so that you can look good (this could be especially important in some physical activities such as dance or gymnastics, where body shape and position is important), but also so that you can maintain good health. Poor posture can put a strain on certain parts of your body and cause muscular and skeletal damage. It can also cause damage to some of your internal organs so they become unable to operate properly.

The two types of posture are:

■ *static posture* – when you are sitting, standing or even lying down

■ *dynamic posture* – when you are walking, running or moving more actively.

In both cases it is important that your posture is correct and that you are carrying or supporting your body correctly.

TASK 4

Either check yourself or observe a partner sitting, standing and walking. Is the posture good or bad? What makes it good or bad?

There is obviously an important link between the muscular system and good posture. There are some important rules to remember.

■ Sit, stand and walk correctly.

■ Exercise your muscles regularly.

■ Wear sensible clothing and footwear.

■ Lift and carry correctly; always lift with a straight back and bent legs.

Muscle fatigue

This occurs when the muscle – or a group of muscles – is unable to carry on contracting and the movement you would like to make will simply not happen.

If you want to experience, or see the effect of muscle fatigue just do the following task.

TASK 5

Hold a 1 kg bag of sugar (or any other object of similar weight) at arm's length with both arms straight out in front of you. See how long you can hold it, keeping your arms straight. You will eventually reach the point where the contraction of the muscles (the biceps and triceps) cannot be sustained any longer and you will have to lower your arms.

Muscle cramp

This occurs when the muscle is locked in a contraction and the muscle is in **spasm**. It is really an involuntary contraction of the muscle and it often follows a period of intensive exercise where the muscles have been overworked.

The way to relieve the cramp is to massage or rub the muscle and straighten the limb or affected area. Cramp can be extremely painful and the effects can last for some time, leaving a dull pain in the affected muscle. It can quite easily stop a performer from continuing or taking part in a physical activity.

Muscle fatigue will set in eventually if any load is applied to the muscles

Muscle atrophy

This is a wasting, or a decrease in size, of a muscle and it can occur through a reduction of blood supply to the muscle over a long period of time. It may be due to inactivity or lack of use.

If someone has a broken leg which has to be placed in a plaster cast to immobilize it, the muscles of the leg can't be used to their full extent to contract and relax. There will therefore be a reduced amount of blood flow to them due to their inactivity and this will result in a certain amount of muscle wastage.

This can be put right by a programme of exercises to increase the activity of the muscles and build them up to their previous state.

Muscle structure

Muscles are made up of a mass of fibres which are wrapped in bundles. The middle, or belly, of the muscle usually bulges out (the biceps is a good example of this) and the muscle narrows at the ends where the tendons (see page 68) attach it to the bones.

Major muscles – location and their function

The major skeletal muscles are listed below, with a description of where they are found on the body and the movements they help with. On some occasions their common names have been added in brackets.

- *Triceps* – located at the back of the upper part of the arm, between the elbow and the shoulder, they allow the arm to straighten.

- *Biceps* – located at the front of the upper arm, between the elbow and the shoulder, they allow the arm to bend and also to rotate slightly.

- *Deltoids* – located on the back of the shoulder joint, they allow the shoulder to move in all directions, up, down, backwards, forwards and to rotate.

- *Pectorals* (pecs) – located on the front of the upper chest, they help movement of the shoulders.

- *Trapezius* – located by the neck on the upper back, they help with shoulder movement as well as keeping the shoulder in position.

- *Abdominals* (stomach) – located at the front on the side of the stomach (external oblique abdominals) and across the front (rectus abdominus) of the stomach, they allow bending and turning of the trunk and also assist with breathing (see unit 27).

- *Latissimus dorsi* (lats) – located on the back from the armpit to the lower back, they allow movement at the shoulder backwards, forwards, up and down.

- *Gluteals* – located at the lower back around the bottom region at the back of the hips. The medius assists with walking and the maximus with climbing and standing up, as well as some rotation at the hips.

- *Quadriceps* (quads) – located at the upper front of the leg in the thigh region between the knee and the pelvis, they allow the leg to straighten.

- *Hamstrings* – located at the upper back of the leg between the knee and the pelvis, they allow movement of the hips and the knee, mainly the bending of the knee.

- *Gastrocnemius* (calf) – located at the back, bottom rear of the leg between the knee and the foot, they assist in walking, running and jumping movements and the pointing of the toes.

The muscles listed above do not perform all of the movements on their own. Instead, they work together with other muscles to allow all of the complicated movements your body is capable of, especially when you are performing physical activities.

TASK 6

Either on your own, or with a partner, perform a movement from a physical activity and try to identify which major muscles you have used. Try to use the correct terms for movement from unit 24 (page 71) to describe what the types of movement were.

The blood carries the body's 'fuel supply' and the circulatory system makes sure that it gets to all parts of our body, not only to keep us alive but also to ensure we function properly.

The circulatory system must be considered very closely with the other body systems because its efficiency can be greatly affected by the type and amount of training you do. Just as training affects it, the efficiency of this body system also affects how much training you are able to do!

The main functions of the circulatory system are:

- *transport* – carrying blood, water, oxygen and nutrients throughout the body, and transport and removal of waste

- *body temperature control* – the blood absorbs the body heat and then carries it to the lungs and to the skin, where it is then released

- *protection* – it helps to fight disease, e.g. antibodies which fight infection are carried in the blood and the clotting of blood seals cuts and wounds.

The circulatory system has four main parts:

- the heart
- the blood vessels
- the blood
- the pulmonary and systemic circuits.

The heart

The diagram opposite shows the heart with the various parts labelled.

The heart is a muscle and, like any other muscle, it contracts and relaxes. Each time it does this it performs a **heartbeat**. We have seen before that your heart beats about 72 times a minute and this is increased a great deal when you exercise or take part in physical activity.

TASK I

What is the name of the device that a doctor uses to listen to a person's heartbeat?

A typical human body has about five litres of blood (about ten pints) and this amount of blood is pumped by the heart in less than a minute.

The heart is composed of four parts: two chambers at the top of the heart, called the **atria**, and two chambers at the bottom called the **ventricles**. The ventricles have thicker walls than the atria.

The main function of the heart is to act as a pump, so that it can move the blood around the body. This is how the pumping action works.

- The blood enters the right-hand atrium. At this time the blood is dark red because it does not contain much oxygen, but it does have some waste products, including carbon dioxide. (In the top diagram opposite, blue has been used to represent deoxygenated blood.)

- The right atrium pumps this blood into the right ventricle, through the valve (see lower diagram opposite).

- The right ventricle pumps the blood through the **pulmonary artery** to the lungs where oxygen is picked up and carbon dioxide is deposited. The blood is now bright red due to the extra oxygen.

- From the lungs the blood returns to the left atrium through the **pulmonary vein**.

- The left atrium pumps the blood into the left ventricle and the blood leaves here through the aorta to be distributed to the rest of the body.

As the blood moves through the body, it loses its oxygen which is used by muscles and for other body functions. Then it returns to the right atrium and the cycle takes place all over again.

This means that your heart works very hard. Unit 17 showed just how important monitoring your heart rate is for assessing levels of fitness and particularly endurance.

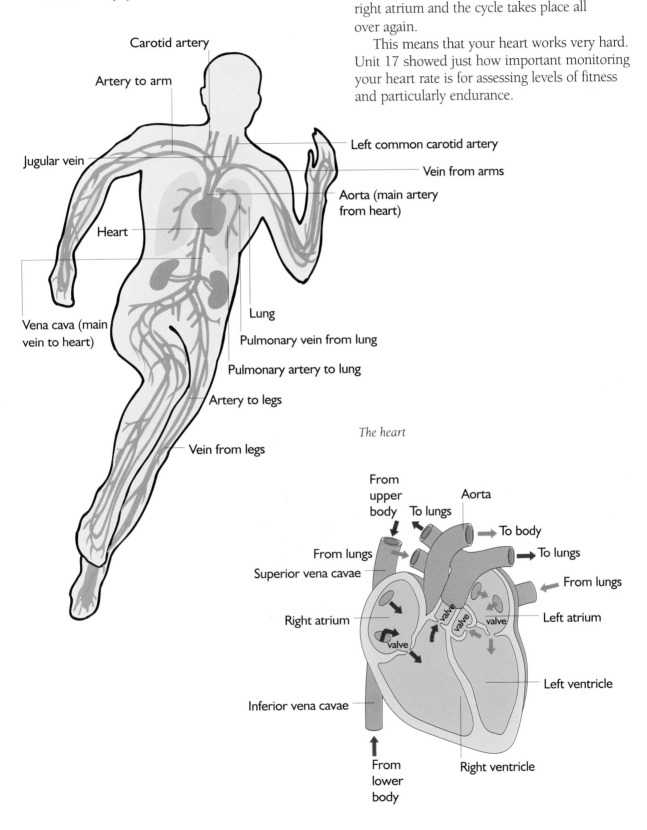

The circulatory system

Carotid artery

Artery to arm

Jugular vein

Heart

Vena cava (main vein to heart)

Left common carotid artery

Vein from arms

Aorta (main artery from heart)

Lung

Pulmonary vein from lung

Pulmonary artery to lung

Artery to legs

Vein from legs

The heart

From upper body

Aorta

To lungs

To body

From lungs

Superior vena cavae

To lungs

From lungs

Right atrium

valve

valve

valve

Left atrium

Left ventricle

Inferior vena cavae

From lower body

Right ventricle

Blood vessels

The three types of blood vessel are:

- arteries
- capillaries
- veins.

Arteries

These carry blood, at high pressure, away from the heart and they are the thickest of the blood vessels.

As the diagram below shows, the artery has an inner lining called the endothelium, then a layer of involuntary muscle and elastic fibres which control the diameter of the artery (so that it can expand and contract depending on the amount of blood flowing through), then an outer layer of tough fibrous tissue.

The aorta is the largest artery in the body and the arteries divide into smaller arteries known as **arterioles** and then into even smaller vessels known as capillaries.

TASK 2

Explain why arteries are the thickest of the blood vessels.

Capillaries

These are subdivisions of the arteries and are fed by the arterioles. They are so small that they are only one cell thick. Because they are so thin they are **semi-permeable**, which means that they allow carbon dioxide, oxygen, nutrients and waste products to pass through their walls.

Capillaries are found in clusters where they feed the muscles, organs and body tissue and at the end of the capillaries the blood flows into the veins.

Veins

These are thinner than arteries although their structure is the same. The two outer layers of involuntary muscle and tough fibrous tissue are much thinner but the central layer (endothelium) is much the same (see diagram). The veins transport the blood back to the heart. One important feature that the veins have is a system of **valves** (also known as pocket valves) which stop the blood from flowing backwards.

The veins also receive some help pumping the blood. Muscles near to the veins help by their muscular contractions (this is known as the **skeletal pump**). These press on the veins and have a squeezing pumping action. Arteries nearby push against the veins when there is a

Cross-section of an artery

Cross-section of a vein

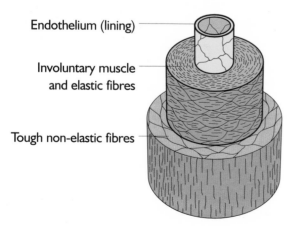

Endothelium (lining)

Involuntary muscle and elastic fibres

Tough non-elastic fibres

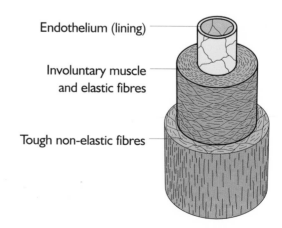

Endothelium (lining)

Involuntary muscle and elastic fibres

Tough non-elastic fibres

surge of blood through them and this has a pumping effect. Gravity assists blood flow in the veins above the heart, although it cannot help below. The action of breathing causes pressure changes which have a sucking effect on the blood.

As the heart pumps blood out it also causes a sucking action which affects the veins close to the heart.

The blood

Cells

Cells make up 45 per cent of the blood and are its 'solid section'. There are three types.

- *Red blood cells* (erythrocytes)
  These are extremely small but there are so many of them that they give the blood its red colour. They are produced in the bone marrow and contain **haemoglobin**. It is this that transports the oxygen and carbon dioxide. Production of these cells is very high. Up to two million are produced and destroyed every second.

- *White blood cells* (leukocytes)
  There are not so many of these as red cells but they are also produced in the bone marrow and in the lymph tissue. Their main function is to fight against infection. They engulf foreign bodies or bacteria. The pus in wounds is formed from dead leukocytes.

- *Platelets*
  These help to clot the blood and are small fragments or particles of larger cells. They help to clot and seal the skin but also do the same job on small blood vessels that are damaged.

Plasma

This forms the remaining 55 per cent of the blood. It is the 'liquid section' and is mainly composed of water. It also contains fibrinogen protein (which helps in clotting), nutrients such as glucose and amino acid, waste products such as urea and some carbon dioxide and oxygen.

The pulmonary and systemic circuits

The pulmonary circuit

This carries the deoxygenated blood (via the pulmonary artery) from the right-hand ventricle of the heart to the lungs where it exchanges the carbon dioxide for oxygen, to become reoxygenated. Then the pulmonary vein transports the oxygenated blood to the left atrium of the heart.

The systemic circuit

Through this, the aorta carries the oxygenated blood from the left ventricle of the heart to all of the various body tissues, through the capillaries. The blood then flows back through the veins, having deposited the majority of the oxygen, and into the right atrium through the vena cava.

The main areas that the blood visits on this circuit are the cardiac muscle of the heart, the stomach, intestines and liver, the muscles and the skin.

The oxygen transported through this system is vital for physical activity. Because the muscles demand more oxygen when they are being used, the supply of oxygen has to be increased, through a greater flow of blood.

During physical activity the muscles require an increased supply of oxygen

Pulse

The pulse is caused by the action of the heart as it pumps blood around the body. Every time the heart beats (this is the heart, or cardiac muscle contracting) it registers as a pulse. The amount of blood being pumped through the arteries makes the artery wall expand and contract and the blood rushing through the arteries causes the pressure wave that you feel as your pulse.

You can check your pulse in any of the following places.

■ *Radial pulse* – at the base of the thumb on the inside of the wrist.

■ *Carotid pulse* – on either side of the neck.

■ *Temporal pulse* – just over the temple at the side of the forehead.

■ *Femoral pulse* – in the groin.

TASK 3

Use the diagram to help you locate your pulse in each of the different areas. Make a note of the area in which you can locate it most easily, as this is useful for certain types of fitness testing.

Blood pressure

The blood in the circulatory system is always under pressure. This is how it is pumped around the body. The pressure has to be higher in the arteries than in the veins because this is where the blood starts its journey.

Blood pressure is a measurement of how much pressure the blood flowing through the artery puts on the artery wall. It can be measured very accurately using a **sphygmomanometer** which puts pressure on the artery wall by squashing it and then gives readings of the pressure exerted.

Two readings are always taken:

■ *systolic pressure* – the pressure of the blood in the arteries when the left ventricle contracts

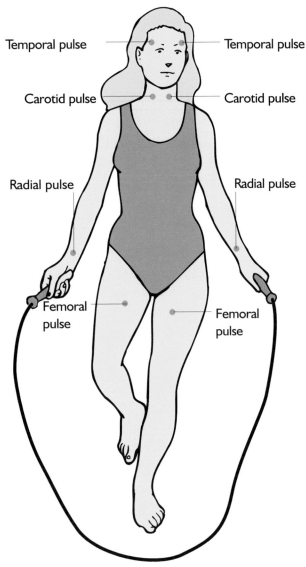

The four pulse points of the body

■ *diastolic pressure* – the pressure of the blood in the arteries when the left ventricle relaxes.

The final reading is like a fraction, with the systolic pressure at the top and the diastolic underneath.

Blood pressure readings should be taken when you are resting, not exercising, and should range from 100 over 60 (that is 100 systolic pressure over 60 diastolic pressure) to 140 over 90. The average for a young person is about 120 over 80.

Your blood pressure reading is taken in any medical test you might have as it is a very good indicator of ill health and a measure of how efficient you heart is. Blood pressure can be affected by:

- *age* – blood pressure is usually lower in young people than in adults

- *sex* – blood pressure readings vary between males and females

- *exercise* – exercising increases the blood pressure

- *stress and tension* – both can increase blood pressure

- *circulatory system condition* – if the heart or blood vessels are not in good condition, blood pressure will increase.

Blood pressure does vary but there is only cause for concern if it is consistently high.

High blood pressure may indicate that the heart is finding it more difficult to pump blood around the body. This could be caused by narrowing or blocked arteries, and would mean that the heart has to work harder to maintain circulation.

This may lead to a state where the heart muscle temporarily gets starved of oxygen. This can result in a sharp pain in the chest which is known as angina. The situation may become even more serious and can result in a **heart attack** (where the heart stops because it is starved of oxygen) or a **stroke** (where the brain is starved of oxygen). Both are very serious, life-threatening conditions.

Blood pressure can be reduced by:

- increasing regular exercise

- following a sensible diet to reduce or control weight

- stopping smoking

- taking medications

- avoiding stress (or 'managing' stress).

Diseases associated with the heart are the most common cause of death in the Western world. Keeping your blood pressure under control and within the acceptable limits is one of the most effective ways of avoiding these diseases.

Exercise and the circulatory system

Exercise affects the body in several ways.

Heart rate (pulse rate)

This increases greatly during exercise and can easily double. The reason for this is the increased demand for oxygen as the muscles, in particular, need more oxygen to be able to work at the increased rate. There are certain areas or zones which you should be aware of and work to when exercising (see page 51).

Heat production

Exercise causes an increase in body temperature and heat is produced. Extra water and salts in the capillaries need to be removed as waste products. This is achieved through sweating. Waste is dispersed through the skin via the blood capillaries and pores in the skin surface.

Blood pressure

This increases with exercise as more blood is circulated. This is not a bad thing as the increase is only temporary, while the exercise is going on. It should return to normal afterwards.

Skin colour

The blood vessels at the surface of the skin have to open up or dilate to allow the heat to escape. This causes the 'flushed' or reddening effect. It is usually most clearly seen on the face.

There is clearly a strong link between the circulatory system and the respiratory system, which is responsible for initially drawing oxygen into the body (see the following unit).

TASK 4

Design a promotional poster entitled 'Exercise can seriously improve your health', based on the information above.

The respiratory system consists of:

- the air passages
- the lungs
- the diaphragm.

Together, these are responsible for bringing air into the body, circulating it and then expelling it (see diagram opposite).

The air passages

These are made up of the following parts.

Nasal cavity

Air enters through the nostrils and in each of these two cavities there are three ridges which are covered in a thick, mucous membrane which filters the air and warms and moistens it. The filtering is done by the cilia, which are small hairs that trap dust, pollen and any other airborne impurities.

Mouth

Air also enters here. The mouth is separated from the nasal cavity by the palate which allows you to chew food at the same time as you breathe.

TASK 1

Pinch your nose tightly and breathe only through your mouth. What difference does it make to your breathing?

Pharynx

This allows both food and air to enter; the food goes into the **oesophagus** and the air travels through the larynx.

Epiglottis

This is a flap at the back of the throat which prevents food from going down the trachea or windpipe.

Larynx (or voice box)

The epiglottis is at the upper opening of the larynx and the air passes through here to the trachea. It is in the larynx that the voice is produced, as air moves over the vocal chords.

Trachea (or windpipe)

This is a large tube consisting of rings of cartilage. It is flexible but the cartilage rings are rigid and keep it open.

Bronchus

These are at the base of the trachea where it branches out into two smaller tubes known as the left and right bronchus or bronchi.

Bronchioles

The bronchi in turn branch out into smaller tubes known as **bronchioles** and these subdivide into smaller air sacs which are called **alveoli**. There are literally millions of these and they make up the majority of the lung tissue. It is here that the exchange of oxygen and carbon dioxide takes place. This will be dealt with in more detail later (page 87).

The lungs

These are the main organs of the respiratory system. They are inside the chest cavity protected by the ribs at the back, sides, front and the diaphragm at the bottom.

The lungs are like two balloons. There is a slight difference between the two as the right lung is slightly larger, with three sections (or lobes), while the left has only two sections.

The lungs are surrounded by a layer of membrane, called the **pleura**. This acts like a lubricant, as it is smooth and moist, and protects the lungs from any friction as they get bigger and smaller during breathing.

The diaphragm

This is a large muscle sheet which seals off the chest cavity from the abdominal cavity. Also, by contracting and relaxing, it is responsible for the action of breathing.

Training

The respiratory system is also greatly affected by the amounts and levels of training you do. Endurance training (see unit 17) is specifically linked to the respiratory system, which is why knowledge of how the system works and functions is important.

The respiratory system showing the air passages and lungs

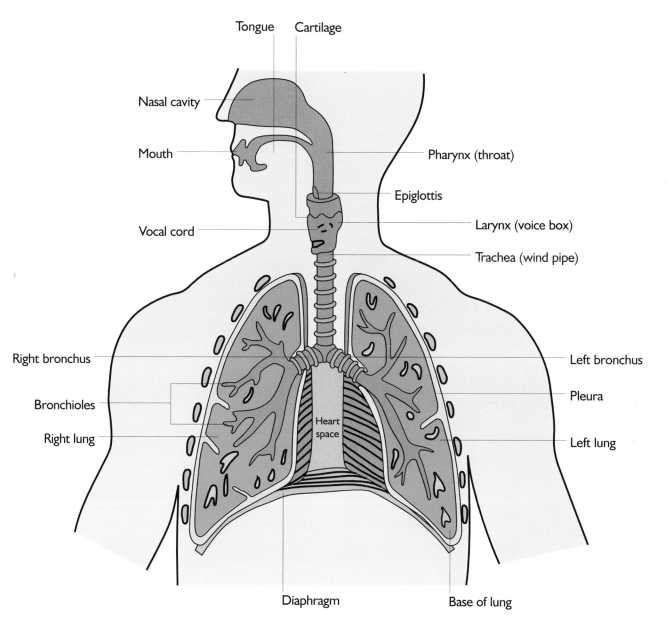

The action of breathing

Breathing involves two types of movement:

- *inspiration* – breathing in
- *expiration* – breathing out.

Inspiration

When we breathe in, the chest cavity changes shape and size. The diaphragm changes from a dome shape, flattens and moves downwards. At the same time the **intercostal muscles** raise the ribs and push out the sternum which makes the cavity larger. This reduces the pressure inside the chest cavity and causes air to be sucked into the lungs.

Expiration

When we breathe out, the reverse procedure takes place. The diaphragm relaxes and so do the intercostal muscles. Because of this the chest cavity returns to its normal size and the pressure on the lungs is increased, which forces the air out.

When our bodies are at rest we breathe between fourteen and sixteen times a minute. If we increase our activity or movement by taking part in physical activity this rate increases greatly. This type of breathing is called **forced breathing** and the rate can increase to anything up to 50 a minute!

In unit 26 we saw that the body needs more oxygen to be supplied via the blood so the breathing rate has to increase as well.

TASK 2

Check your resting breathing rate by counting how many breaths you take in one minute.
Try to check your breathing rate when you are taking part in strenuous exercise.

Types of lung volume or capacity

- *Tidal volume* – the amount of air which you breathe in and out, normally. It increases with exercise.

- *Inspiratory capacity* – the amount of air taken in after a normal expiration when forced breathing is taking place. It increases with exercise.

- *Expiratory reserve volume* – the amount of air which can be forced out after a normal expiration. There is a slight decrease in this during exercise.

- *Vital capacity* – the largest volume of air which can be expired after the deepest possible inspiration. There is a slight decrease in this during exercise.

- *Residual volume* – the amount of air which remains in the lungs after the maximum expiration. There is a slight increase in this during exercise.

The total lung capacity is worked out by adding the vital capacity to the residual volume.

It is possible to measure the lung capacities but this is not always a good indicator of either fitness or levels of endurance, although the greater your capacity, the more likely you are to be successful at endurance events. It will show up any abnormalities which could be caused by asthma or excessive smoking but it is the efficiency of the respiratory system that is most important.

Inhaled air and **exhaled** air are completely different. Inhaled air is high in oxygen and nitrogen, low in carbon dioxide. Exhaled air is high in nitrogen and oxygen but has much higher levels of carbon dioxide.

It is a misconception that we simply breathe in oxygen and breathe out carbon dioxide, as neither of these makes up the highest proportion of the air we breathe. Nitrogen has the highest level, at approximately 79 per cent for both inspiration and expiration. The oxygen levels are 21 per cent for inspiration and 16 per cent for expiration. The levels for carbon dioxide are 0.004 per cent during inspiration and 4 per cent during expiration.

The exchange of these two gases occurs in the lungs.

Gaseous exchange

This is the process which allows oxygen to be taken in from the air and for it to be 'exchanged' for carbon dioxide. This is how it happens.

- Oxygen, which has been breathed in, passes through the minute alveoli air sacs and into the red blood cells.

- The oxygen combines with the haemoglobin to form **oxyhaemoglobin**.

- An enzyme in the red cells breaks down the carbon dioxide, which is being transported in the blood (in the form of sodium bicarbonate), and turns it into a gas.

- The carbon dioxide gas then passes back through the alveoli and is breathed out through the lungs.

This process is vital for our bodies because it is the combination of food and oxygen acting together which produces the body's energy. The carbon dioxide and water are the waste products which must be removed.

Runners at the end of a race are often left gasping for air

Exercise and the respiratory system

An increase in the activity of the body, such as vigorous exercise, will have the following effects.

Breathing rate

This will increase greatly, up to three times the resting rate. The breathing becomes noisier and more obvious, especially to someone watching. The rate can increase so much that you can literally be left gasping for air.

VO_2 (or oxygen uptake)

This will increase greatly (see unit 17 for details). The body will need more oxygen as energy so the uptake will have to increase to cater for this. Quite simply, the more activity you do the more oxygen you need, but this can only go up to certain levels, so when you are at your limit you have achieved your VO_2 maximum.

Oxygen debt

You will develop oxygen debt after about five minutes or more of constant exercise. This is the point when the exercise becomes **anaerobic** (without the use of oxygen, which has to be paid back later – hence oxygen debt). If the exercise is just aerobic (with oxygen) then there will be no oxygen debt (see unit 17 for details).

TASK 3

*List **three** activities which would be anaerobic and three which would be aerobic.*

Vital capacity

This will increase, as the volume of air required has increased.

Residual volume

This only increases slightly, and so does the **tidal volume**.

The reason for training is to improve your ability to take part in physical activity. This improvement can only come about through a change and you may be trying to make a physical change. You must, therefore, have a thorough knowledge of the various body systems and all the other factors which can affect a performance. You will need to know *how* and *why* training is able to make these changes possible and the links that exist with health and fitness.

Training has certain principles which apply no matter what type you undertake. It is important to know what they are and the effects they will have. The main principles of training are:

- specificity
- overload
- progression
- reversibility.

As well as these, there are other terms which also apply to the general principles of training. These are:

- frequency
- intensity
- duration.

All training requires a combination of the above factors if it is to be successful and lead to improvement.

Specificity

Any type of training must be suitable, or specific, to the physical activity or sport you are training for. It would not be wise to choose a strength-training method if you were hoping to build up to running a marathon.

You may wish not only to choose one particular type of training but also to concentrate upon one particular area. It may

mean building up strength in the legs or the arms, or increasing flexibility in the shoulders, or improving reaction times.

Specific exercise will produce specific results and this must be considered with two other points.

- Individuals will respond differently to the same methods.
- Each activity will have different, and specific, demands.

One thing you must not forget is that most physical activities require a combination of exercises and perhaps even training methods. There are very few activities where it is easy to choose just one particular method and stick to that. That is why it is important to plan out and analyse exactly what is required and how those requirements can be met.

When you have done this, you will have a specific programme that will meet your needs. You may even find that there is specifically designed equipment to help you achieve this.

TASK 1

Name a physical activity and state what the specific training requirements are. What muscles – or muscle groups – would need most attention?

Overload

This is making the body work harder in order to improve it. You will have a 'capacity' to train which will be the normal level you work at. In order to improve you must extend that capacity by increasing your workload. It can be achieved in the following ways.

This 'pec deck' machine is designed specifically to exercise the pectoral muscles

- *Frequency* of training needs to be increased. To start with you may only train twice a week with a recovery period in between, but this could be increased to every other day and then up to five days a week. Top performers would probably train on some aspect of their activity every day.

  It does not necessarily help to have more than one session in a day. Just one is more advisable.

- *Intensity* must be increased. You can do this by simply working harder at the training method you are using. You may want to increase your heart rate to a higher level, to increase your endurance levels (see unit 17) or you might wish to add more weight if you are trying to increase your strength.

- *Duration* may refer to the length of each training session and this should be increased. It can also refer to the amount of time you wish to spend on a particular aspect of your training. If you are working in training blocks on certain areas you may want to do these over a longer period of time.

Your body responds to overload by adapting to it. Used sensibly, it will lead to an improvement.

Progression

The training you are doing, and particularly the amount of overload, must be increased progressively. In other words, as your body adjusts to the increased demands which you are putting upon it then that demand must be steadily increased.

If you stay at the same levels the improvement will not continue but you must be careful not to do too much too soon. If you do, it may lead to injury or muscle damage which will then set your training programme back.

Another factor to be aware of is plateauing. This happens when you get to a certain level and then seem unable to move on. This is common and it is likely that it will happen more than once, so it is best to be prepared. When it happens you have to be prepared to stay on that level for some time. Eventually you will improve or adjust enough to progress further. This is when you must be mentally strong and motivated to continue through a difficult period.

Reversibility

Just as progression can lead to an improvement, if you either stop or decrease the training you go into reverse and lose the effect. All the good you have done will be lost.

Sometimes you cannot avoid stopping if you have an injury or if you are ill. An example of the effect of reversibility can be seen if someone breaks a leg. Part of the treatment is to put the leg in a cast to immobilize it. This also prevents the muscles from being exercised properly. We have seen in unit 25 that muscles which are not used quickly **atrophy**, so strength is lost.

TASK 2

Work out a basic training programme for a specific activity, considering all the principles that have been outlined.

Once you are aware of the principles of training it is time to put them into practice with a training programme. This will consist of a number of training sessions. Each of these sessions should have four parts or phases, as follows:

- warm-up
- fitness or exercise phase
- skill or team play phase
- cool-down (also known as warm-down).

These sessions may be individual but they are often more effective, and more enjoyable, if they are done in a group or at least with a training partner.

Warm-up

This is absolutely essential in any training session because:

- it prepares the body for the activity to come. It increases the blood flow through the muscles, helping them to contract quickly. The nervous system is also stimulated which makes you more alert and aware, getting you psychologically prepared

- it reduces the possibility of injury, most notably muscle injury. The increased blood flow increases the temperature in the muscle and this makes it more responsive and able to contract and relax. Muscle fibres and tendons are more likely to be damaged if you fail to warm up properly.

If possible, the warm-up should be specific to the type of activity you are training for and you should aim to warm up the appropriate major muscle groups.

These are the types of things you should include in your warm-up.

- *A continuous movement activity* – something that is going to continue long enough to

increase the heart rate and body temperature so that the blood flow to the muscles will be increased. You must be careful not to overdo this stage. Many training sessions are ruined by an overly energetic warm-up phase!

- *Light exercises* that specifically work the major muscle groups to be used. Again, these must not be overdone. A couple of press-ups may be all that is required. Prolonged performance of the same exercise may lead to muscle fatigue.

- *Flexibility exercises* – these should really concentrate on all areas of the body and all major joints should be gently worked on to prepare them for a full range of mobility.

The time spent on the warm-up will vary, often with the type of activity. Many gymnasts, for example, will spend at least fifteen minutes warming up and most of this would be spent on the flexibility stage. For other performers a few minutes might be all that is required.

What is important is that if you do wish to emphasize one of the stages you do not ignore the others or give them too little time.

TASK 1

Choose an activity and write down an appropriate warm-up. Make sure that you consider all the stages of the warm-up and try to relate them to the activity you have chosen.

Fitness phase

During this phase you should work on the particular aspect of fitness which is most appropriate for the physical activity you are training for.

Most activities require cardiovascular fitness so some sort of endurance exercise should be included.

One of the benefits of training is that you can get your body used to coping with fatigue, so you should actually try to get yourself close to fatigue in the training session. The most useful training is that which most closely resembles a game or competition, as it should then make you more effective.

You must also apply the principle of overload during this part of the session if it is to have the full benefit.

> ## TASK 2
>
> *Choose an activity in which you take part. What kinds of exercises or fitness work would be suitable for this phase?*

Skill phase

If the activity you are taking part in is a team game, it would be essential for you to use this as a team session because it may be the only opportunity you get to practise together. The whole team, or units within the team, should practise group skills and there should also be the opportunity to practise individual skills as well.

If your activity is an individual activity, such as gymnastics, then you can practise the various skills you need. However, it is not wise to do this alone; you should always try to have a coach or training partner with you in case of accident or injury.

It may be that the activity you are training for does not require any particular skills – for example, a marathon run. In this case you would probably concentrate on the fitness phase and increase endurance training.

> ## TASK 3
>
> *Choose an activity. Write down some useful skills practices you could perform for this phase.*

Cool-down

This is also known as the 'warm-down'. It is often missed out in a training session.

Instead of just stopping completely after you have finished the other phases you should continue some part of the activity, but at a reduced rate. This can be as simple as just gently walking or performing some flexibility exercises.

The reason for this is that when you stop exercising, the heart is still beating at a fast rate. If you stop suddenly the muscles are not pumping the blood back at the previous rate, and this can cause the blood to 'pool' in the veins. This means that the waste materials such as lactic acid are not being removed. A build up of this can cause stiffness and soreness.

Just as your body is gently built up to strenuous exercise by the warm-up, so it must also be gently returned to its normal state by the cool-down.

Cricket nets provide a very specific type of skills practice

Weight training

Weight training is designed to increase muscle strength. Unit 15 covered the types of strength as well as their importance.

Many activities require some form of strength and weight training. Using the type of specialized equipment shown in the photo below is becoming increasingly popular. Linked with this is the fact that there have been many recent developments in the range of equipment and its availability.

Weight training can be used:

■ to increase muscle strength

■ to improve muscle tone.

To increase muscle strength means following a programme designed to increase the size of the muscles and therefore increase their strength. This uses the principle of overload (see unit 28) which will stress the muscles, gradually making them bigger.

To improve muscle tone, performers can use:

■ *repetitions* – the number of times you actually move the weights; one chest press, moving the weight up and down once, equals one repetition

■ *sets* – the number of times you do a particular weight activity; so, each time you complete your repetitions of the chest press you have done one set.

There is now a wide range of specialized weight training equipment available

You should always have an instructor or training partner to help you with free-standing weights

Different effects can be achieved by varying the repetitions and sets and the 'load', or weight, used each time. The weights are adjustable. To increase strength (to overload) you have heavy weights with small numbers of repetitions and you may do several sets of these.

To improve muscle tone you would use lighter weights and increase the repetitions, probably somewhere between ten and fifteen times. You would probably only do a maximum of three sets.

Additionally, there are more specific ways in which weight or strength training can be used. 'Free-standing weights' are weights which can be fixed on to long or short bars. These traditional weights are often preferred by people who want to increase strength because it is easier to add more weight. One of the drawbacks to the weight training machinery is that it does not always have enough weight, and it is not possible to add more.

If free-standing weights are used it is vital that you do not train alone. You should always have an instructor or training partner with you to help load and unload the weights and to help you to start and stop the weightlifting

movements. At times, it will be necessary to have two people to lift the weights up for you to start and to take the weights from you when you have finished. You should also ensure that you warm up thoroughly.

Other weight training methods are as follows.

- *Isotonic training* – where the amount of weight moved, or lifted, remains constant throughout the movement. This is important as it relates to the way the muscles contract when they are exercised. In a concentric contraction the muscle shortens (for example, a biceps curl, when the arm is bent and the wrist moved towards the shoulder) and an eccentric contraction when the muscle lengthens. For the biceps curl example, this would be the arm extending back to a straight position. (see page 74)

The principle of isotonic training is that the weight is kept constant on both the eccentric and concentric contraction. This would be the type of training preferred by those who wished to improve strength, power or endurance.

- *Isokinetic training* – where specialist equipment is necessary because you need the weights to vary the effort as you work at a constant speed. These 'variable resistance' machines are expensive because they adjust the load so that the muscles are worked evenly throughout the movement. The value of these machines is that they can duplicate movements such as throwing and kicking.

- *Isometric training* – where a contraction is held at a particular point. This can be useful for activities such as gymnastics where you are required to hold a position, so in training you would hold the muscle in the required position for about five seconds, and then repeat. In this case the length of the muscle stays the same while contracting.

TASK I

*Work out your own weight training programmes. Design **one** for a specific physical activity and **one** for improved general fitness. How would they differ?*

Circuit training allows a variety of exercises to be performed in different areas or 'stations'

Circuit training

The photo above shows a typical circuit training layout which would be useful for a general fitness circuit. One of the advantages of circuit training is that it is very adaptable. Another advantage is the variety of ways in which either an individual or group can use the circuit. The time taken, the amount of work done and the load for each area can all be varied and changed.

The various parts of the circuit are known as **stations**. It is very important that these stations work properly, following these rules.

■ The stations must be clearly marked with the movement or activity to be performed.

■ The activities must be demonstrated and/or practised to make sure that they are performed correctly. For example, you will not get the maximum benefit from a burpee (see opposite page) if you do not do it properly. Also you must check when the circuit is under way that all the activities are being performed properly.

■ Activities must be varied around the circuit. This means that there should not be a group of stomach muscle exercises all arranged together. They must be spread out at even intervals throughout the circuit, otherwise a performer may fatigue a muscle area by overworking it. Spreading the exercises evenly allows the muscles a little time to recover before they are exercised again, so overload can be more effective. It also makes the circuit less boring if there is a variety of exercises rather than repeating the same thing.

■ A recovery period should be allowed between each exercise so that performers recover sufficiently to do the next one. Some circuits can last up to 30 minutes and it is unrealistic to expect someone to work constantly at a high level for that long.

There are two main types of circuit, as described below.

Fitness circuit

Types of exercises which could be included on a fitness circuit include:

■ press-ups

■ squat thrusts

■ sprint starts (press-up position and with legs positioned as for a sprint start, quickly switch the right and left legs over to the front and back position)

■ burpees (a squat thrust followed by a star jump and then back into squat thrust position)

■ triceps dips

■ sit-ups

■ trunk curls

■ leg raising

■ squats

■ shuttle runs

■ hyperextensions (lying flat on the stomach, raise the head and feet, arching the back)

■ step-ups (on a bench or even a chair)

■ running on the spot (this can be with high knee raising or at sprint speed)

■ star jumps

■ skipping

■ alternate elbows to knees (arms clasped behind the head; turn the trunk and lift the knee at the same time twisting to lower the elbows)

All of these exercises can be performed with the minimum of equipment – just a bench and a rope are required. If you have more equipment you can have an even more varied circuit.

Skills circuit

This also includes various stations but the exercises are aimed at developing particular skills needed for an activity. An example could be a basketball circuit which might include:

■ chest passes against a wall

■ dribbling around cones

■ continuous free throw shooting

■ continuous lay up shots

■ bounce passes against a wall

■ continuous long throw passes.

Others could be added or the circuit could cater for a combination of skills with suitable fitness exercises as well.

Running the circuit

There are various ways to run a circuit.

■ *Timed circuits* – where performers work for so long at each station and then rest before moving on (for example, 30 seconds work, 30 seconds rest).

■ *Fixed load* – each station is labelled with the amount of work the performer must do (it could be fifteen press-ups each time).

Both of these methods can be varied. The number of laps can be adjusted, or the periods of work and recovery, or the load and skills could be changed.

TASK 2

Devise circuits for:
a general fitness
b a specific physical activity
(name the activity you have chosen).

Interval training

Interval training consists of periods of work followed by periods of rest. The principle is much the same as for circuit training (which allows a rest period between stations) and prevents the performer from becoming too fatigued to carry on.

There are several ways that interval training can be done but the following factors have to be considered.

■ *Duration of the work* – this could relate to how far a performer may need to run or for how long they may work.

■ *Intensity of the work* – this could be the speed at which the performer works or the load they have.

■ *Repetitions* – this could be the number of work repetitions or the number of rest ones.

■ *Duration of the recovery period* – this would usually refer to time but it may involve a recovery distance, such as a certain distance a performer is allowed to slow walk.

The two most important factors in interval training are the *work* related to the *rest*. When at work, the heart rate should go up to a high training zone level (see page 51) which could be somewhere in the region of 180. During the rest, or recovery, periods it should drop into the aerobic zone which is about 140.

The two general categories of interval training are long interval training and short interval training.

Long interval training

This is particularly good for players in team games and middle distance athletes, as it works in bursts of from fifteen seconds up to three minutes. Because the work periods are quite long, those taking part in it cannot be expected to work flat out so they would normally work at about 80–85 per cent maximum. The rest or recovery periods would also be quite long; after three minutes of work there should be three minutes of recovery time.

The majority of this work would consist of running, usually for a set time. It would not be possible to do this over a distance because of the times worked, as not everyone would be able to cover the same distance in three minutes. If shorter times were used it would be possible to use distances and ensure they were covered within a certain time, e.g. sets of 400 metre runs in less than 75 seconds.

Short interval training

This is designed more for short bursts of activity so it would suit sprint athletes or some sports, such as racket sports, where there is much stop and go action.

The work periods are much shorter, probably no more than fifteen seconds but performers would be expected to work flat out for that time at maximum work rate. Because of this the recovery rates would be longer; up to two minutes would be necessary to recover sufficiently.

Again, this would mainly involve running and, specifically, sprint running. In some cases the full speed running could only be for five seconds.

Continuous training

Unit 17 covered the need to keep the heart rate at a high level, to improve endurance. Continuous training is a method that can achieve this because performers take part in activities which keep the pulse and heart rate high.

Examples of these activities are:

■ running and jogging

■ cycling

■ swimming

■ exercise sessions (such as aerobic classes).

There are also many specialist machines which can be used for continuous training. Many of them, such as treadmills and exercise cycles, duplicate the activities mentioned above but allow them to be done indoors.

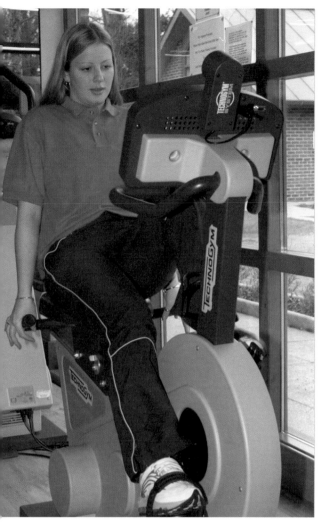

An exercise cycle allows you to exercise in warmth and comfort

This work must be carried out within the training zone (see page 51) if it is to be effective and the performer should aim to work for at least fifteen minutes at this level. This will then improve the cardiovascular and respiratory system. This type of training would therefore be suitable for anyone who wished to improve their general fitness levels.

Fartlek training

This is based on a Swedish method of training. It means 'speed training' and is a form of continuous training. It alternates walking, brisk walking, running, jogging and fast steady running. This can be performed as required in a session, so the individual decides when they are ready to build up to a fast run after progressing from a walk. However, it is probably more effective to set off on a planned programme based on times and distances which will be walked, jogged and run at speed.

TASK 3

Work out your own fartlek training programme, then try it out.

Altitude training

This involves performers (and these tend to be endurance athletes who take part in long-distance events) going to specific areas in the world where they can train at high altitude. The reason for this is that at high altitude the air becomes less dense and the pressure of oxygen decreases. This means that the performer is able to make some actual physiological changes occur which increase the oxygen-carrying capacity of the blood. This can make them more efficient runners by improving their endurance levels.

Continuous shuttle run

This is more correctly called the 'multi-stage fitness test', or commonly the 'bleep test'. It is covered in detail in the next unit but is included here because it is now often used as a method of training. Many international sports teams have adopted it as a training method and it has, as a result, been commonly accepted as such.

One important rule to remember with all training methods is that they should be carried out with care. They should be built up gradually and safely.

TASK 4

Draw up a chart and list the advantages and disadvantages of all the training methods described.

Just as specific training methods may be chosen to improve certain aspects of fitness it is also possible to test specific aspects of fitness. This is very important when planning a fitness training programme because the testing you do before, during and after the programme will give you an idea of just how successful the training programme you followed was.

The following testing methods are linked to the specific aspects of endurance, flexibility and strength.

Progressive shuttle run

This test of fitness is often called the multi-stage fitness test or the 'bleep test' (see page 97). It is also often used as a training method, although this is not what it was originally intended to be.

The test is designed to be a general test of endurance and with the use of various tables it can test a performer's VO2 maximum (see page 52).

The test is very easy and simple to set up and administer. All it needs is a tape cassette player and an area (preferably indoors) at least 20 metres long. The test consists of a tape recording which has a series of pre-recorded bleeps on it, at various intervals. The people who take part in the test line up at a start point and run to a distance 20 metres away, then run back again. However, this must be in time with the electronic bleeps on the pre-recorded tape, so they have to run at the pace the bleeps are dictating.

At the start this is quite easy because the bleeps are quite a long time apart, but every minute they change levels and the time between the bleeps decreases! This means that performers still have to run 20 metres but, as each level changes with each minute, they have to speed up. There are 25 levels in all but performers are at sprinting speed long before that!

The longer a performer is able to continue – and they must turn after each 20 metre run in time with the tape – the higher their score and the higher their level of endurance. If they turn after the bleep has gone on three consecutive occasions they must stop, so they are not allowed to run at a slower pace.

The progressive shuttle run, or 'bleep test', in operation

Flexibility testing

Testing flexibility is quite simple and doesn't require a lot of expensive equipment. Unit 16 dealt with flexibility and the ways it can be improved. It is quite easy to perform flexibility exercises and keep a record of the amount of movement achieved.

Even a simple exercise like bending with straight legs and trying to touch your toes with your outstretched fingers can be measured each time you do it. You just need a partner with a ruler to measure the gap between your finger tips and the ground. This would be a test that would measure your own flexibility and any progress you might be making, but there are also tests which can be used to measure you against other set scores.

The most commonly used one is the 'sit and reach test' which is shown in the photo.

The distance you can move the slide forwards is a measure of the amount of flexibility in your lower back and hamstrings.

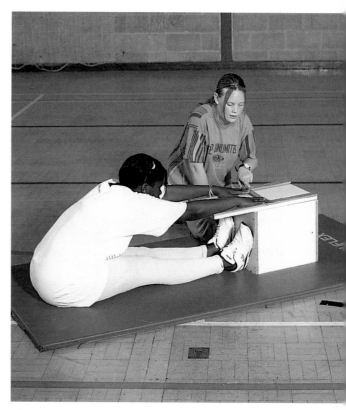

The 'sit and reach' flexibility test

TASK 1

Work out your own flexibility test for any part of your body and regularly perform flexibility exercises while recording any progress you may be making.

Strength testing

Strength can be a difficult thing to test because it is often related to body weight and shape. Unit 20 covered somatotypes. Body size can be a dominating factor when testing for strength.

It would be reasonable to expect a really strong person to be able to lift up, or move, a large amount of weight and to be quite big themselves with a large body weight. However, it is possible to test someone for strength by finding out how strong they are in relation to their body weight and this is often a fairer test.

For this reason, the chin-up test, or pull-up test is often used. For this you need a bar which is suspended in the air. It needs to be above your full stretch height as you have to hang from it. You hold the bar, with your fingers pointing away, and lift your body up so that your chin is level, or above, the bar. You then lower yourself until your arms are completely straight and then lift yourself back up again. You score one for every properly completed chin-up.

The important thing about this test is that it is measuring your strength in relation to your body weight. It does actually favour smaller people and being tall or heavy is a disadvantage. Unit 24 covered the reasons for this (see page 71).

Other strength movements such as press-ups, squat thrusts or dips (arm bends performed on parallel bars) can all be used as strength tests as they all test the performer's ability to move their own body weight.

Pure strength can be tested using weights or even specialized equipment such as a **dynamometer** which measures the strength of your grip.

Weightlifting is a test of pure strength; the more you lift, the stronger you are.

The Harvard step test being performed

The Harvard step test

This is a test of the pulse recovery rate which is explained in unit 17. It is very important when carrying out the test to be able to take an accurate pulse reading (see page 51).

The test is very easy to do and to administer. All that is needed is a bench (or step or block which is about 50 centimetres high), a stopwatch and some paper and a pencil to record the results. Before doing the test you should make a note of your resting pulse rate.

To take the test you do step-ups on the bench continuously for five minutes, at a rate of 30 per minute. You can use a metronome to help with this or find someone to count out every two seconds to keep the pace constant.

At the end of the five minute period you make a note of your pulse rate at particular intervals as you are recovering. This should be after one minute, two minutes and three minutes and you should record each of these numbers. There is a calculation you should do to give a score which you can then compare to the table on this page.

The calculation is 300 (this is the total number of seconds you worked) divided by twice the total number of pulses you recorded during the recovery period (i.e. add together your three pulse counts). Then the result is multiplied by 100. Scores can be matched to the following.

Below 55	=	Poor
55–64	=	Below average
65–79	=	Average
80–89	=	Good
90 and over	=	Excellent

This very common test is based on the fact that if you have a quick recovery rate after taking part in strenuous activity, you have a higher level of cardiovascular endurance.

TASK 2

Perform the Harvard step test and compare your rating score with the table above.

Cooper 12-minute run

This is another test of aerobic capacity, or VO_2 maximum, so it tests the same thing as the bleep test.

One of the main advantages of this test is that it is easy to set up and to do because it does not require any specialist equipment. All you need is a stop watch and a marked out running area.

The test involves running for twelve minutes around the marked out area and making a note of how far you get in that time. The results can be used in two ways.

■ You can chart you own progress by keeping a record of how far you get each time. An improvement in distance covered will show that you are improving your cardiovascular endurance.

■ You can compare your performance to the rating chart below. The distance covered is in metres so you must make sure that your course is measured out in metres.

Age	Excellent	Good	Fair	Poor
13–14				
Males	2700	2400	2200	2100
Females	2000	1900	1600	1500
15–16				
Males	2800	2500	2300	2200
Females	2100	1900	1700	1500
17–20				
Males	3000	2700	2500	2300
Females	2300	2100	1800	1500

If you don't have a running track or area which is easy to mark out, then it is best to use the first method. As long as you run in the same place or area each time you will be able to keep an accurate record of your improvement.

TASK 3

Perform the Cooper 12-minute run and compare your score with the table above.

Cardiovascular and endurance testing

Modern technology means that there are now many ways of testing these. There are watches which can monitor anything from pulse rate and blood pressure to calorie expenditure as you train.

Other tests involve the use of training machinery such as running treadmills. It is possible to connect a performer up to monitoring equipment which will measure very accurately the amount of oxygen they are taking in and the amount they are expiring. Using the treadmill, they can exercise hard with all the monitoring equipment attached, so very accurate readings can be obtained.

Much of the modern equipment has programmable tests built into the readout monitors so it is quite easy to test yourself regularly. What they do not do is compare those results against set standards, which some of the other tests described do.

Nearly all of these training machine tests work on the principle of monitoring the heart rate and comparing them to training zones (see unit 17).

A specially designed marathon runner's watch

Performing a correct sit-up with a partner

Muscular endurance

This is fairly easy to test because muscular endurance can be worked out by seeing how many times you can do an exercise – in other words, your maximum number of repetitions.

One of the easiest of these is the sit-up test. For this you just need to do correct sit-ups with your knees bent at right angles and your feet firmly on the floor. It is often easier to find a partner to hold your feet down and keep you in position.

You perform as many sit-ups as you can and record your score. This will indicate the muscular endurance level of your abdominal muscles. You can do a similar test for arm strength by doing press-ups, or even chin-ups. The maximum repetitions you can perform for any exercise will give a clear indication of your muscular endurance. Specialized weight training machinery can allow you to do even more specific tests on muscles, or muscle groups, so you can work out your own tests.

TASK 4

Either work out – and try out – your own muscular endurance test or test the abdominal muscular endurance in your group.

Warning: Be very careful not to overdo testing to the point where you are unnecessarily straining yourself. The idea is to see how many repetitions of a particular exercise you can do, not to lift one very heavy weight once – that would be a test of strength. You will find that you will not be able to continue once you have reached your maximum and it is not wise to try to carry on past this point as you could injure yourself.

Power

Power can be tested by using activities which require explosive strength. The **standing broad jump** and the sergeant jump can be used to measure power.

Standing broad jump

Stand, with feet together. Bend at the knee then jump forwards, landing on both feet. Measure the total distance travelled from the start point to the landing point. If you use gym mats it is quite easy to start from behind one of the mats and mark, with chalk, where you land on the other. This has the added advantage of allowing you a soft surface to land on.

Sergeant jump

This is a vertical jump (unlike the broad jump which is horizontal), and it can easily be performed just using a wall and some chalk.

Stand next to the wall and reach up with your arm nearest the wall. Make a mark at the highest point your fingers can touch, with both feet flat on the floor. Then heavily chalk your finger tips, bend, and jump upwards slapping your fingers against the wall at the highest point, leaving a mark. The measurement to take is the distance between the two marks, so you actually measure how high each person can jump in relation to their own height. This makes it a much fairer test than just measuring how high they can jump.

Both of these tests measure the explosive strength, and therefore the power, of the leg muscles.

Agility

This can be tested by setting up any kind of obstacle course which makes you change direction regularly. It can even involve getting over and under obstacles such as gymnastic boxes or beams.

A simple test can just be running around marker cones over a particular course or distance and timing the run. You must make sure that you always set the course out exactly the same if you devise your own test. There is a set test for this which is known as the Illinois Agility Run, based on a zig-zag pattern run, with cones for the performer to run around in the middle section.

Agility tests can be devised to match physical activities so, for example, they can include dribbling tests for basketball, hockey and soccer which are very easy to set up.

TASK 5

Work out your own agility test course. It can be just a general running course or related to a physical activity. Try out your test and keep a record of the results.

Combination tests

Often, tests will be done to test a combination of factors, not just one. This is often the case when organizations such as the Armed Forces want to test the fitness levels of new recruits. They test for strength (often using the chin-up test) and endurance (usually a timed run over a particular distance such as the 12-minute run) as this is an accepted combination test for general fitness.

Another test is the JCR test which includes a Jump (the sergeant jump), Chin-ups and a Run (usually a timed shuttle run over a set course).

There was also a test devised in Europe known as the Eurofit test, which was a combination of the various factors of fitness. This combined many of the tests already described.

Body measurements

These are often tested, or more accurately, measured. The measurements taken are:

- height
- weight
- body composition.

The first two are very easy to take but body composition requires a specialist piece of equipment known as skinfold callipers. This device can accurately measure the amount of fat tissue in the body. Readings are taken at five body points: at the back of the arm by the triceps, at the front of the arm by the biceps, just behind the shoulder blade (this is known as a 'subscapular reading'), just above the waistband on the side of the abdomen (known as the 'anterior supra-iliac reading') and at the back of the calf muscle.

With all these readings it is possible to calculate the levels of excess fat in the body.

Measuring body fat levels using skinfold callipers

A drug is a chemical substance which, when introduced to the body, can alter the biochemical system.

Most drugs are designed to improve an imbalance caused by a disease or illness. For example, a simple and common drug is paracetamol. If you have a headache and take paracetamol, the headache goes away due to the change the drug has caused in your body. However when drugs are used in a healthy body they do not always have the desired effect. It must always be remembered that all drugs have some side effects.

The law and drugs

In 1971 a law was introduced called the Misuse of Drugs Act. It identified a list of dangerous or harmful substances and called them 'controlled drugs'. These fall into three categories, or classes, and there are differing penalties for unauthorized possession or use of these substances. These classes are based on the potential harmfulness of each drug. The main ones listed are:

- *Class A* – opium, heroin, methadone morphine, hallucinogens (such as LSD), injectable amphetamines and 'designer drugs' such as 'Ecstasy'
- *Class B* – opiate drugs, certain barbiturates, cannabis, cannabis resin, and six stimulant drugs of the amphetamine group
- *Class C* – other amphetamine drugs, 36 benzodiazepine tranquillizers and several non-barbiturate sedatives.

These drugs are often called 'social drugs'. Penalties on conviction range from life imprisonment for a Class A drug to two years' imprisonment and/or an unlimited fine for a Class C drug.

There is evidence of sportspeople using these drugs, but there is little to indicate that their performance is improved. If they were found guilty of using any of the drugs listed they would probably face a police prosecution and the governing body of their sport would also deal with them (see pages 110–11)

Most sportspeople who are involved in drug taking do so in the hope that it will make them perform better. They take drugs which are known as 'performance-enhancing drugs'. These drugs are banned by the International Olympic Committee.

IOC classifications

In January 1999 the International Olympic Committee published the following list of prohibited classes of substances and prohibited methods, together with the following statement:

'Doping contravenes the ethics of both sport and medical science. Doping consists of:
1 *the administration of substances belonging to prohibited classes of pharmacological agents, and/or*
2 *the use of various prohibited methods.'*

I Prohibited classes of substances
A Stimulants
B Narcotics
C Anabolic agents
D Diuretics
E Peptide hormones, mimetics and analogues

II Prohibited methods
A Blood doping
B Pharmacological, chemical and physical manipulation

III Classes of drugs subject to certain restrictions
A Alcohol
B Cannabinoids
C Local anaesthetics
D Corticosteroids
E Beta-blockers

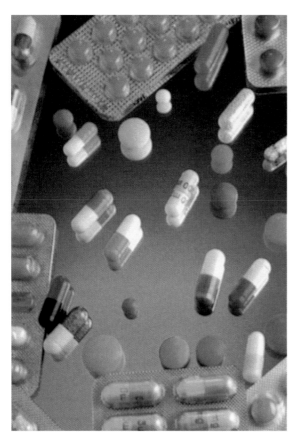

Not all drugs are harmful and banned – many have beneficial uses

- strokes and increased and irregular heartbeats
- anxiety and tremors
- insensitivity to serious injuries
- addiction.

There is an unusual group of stimulants known as the **beta₂agonists** and these are classified as being both stimulants and anabolic agents.

Many of the compounds found in stimulants are found in treatments for colds, hay fever and asthma, so it is very important to check with a pharmacist before you take any medications prior to an event.

Another recognized stimulant is caffeine (this is found in tea and coffee) and there is a maximum level, of 12 micrograms per millilitre, above which it would be considered performance enhancing. Cocaine is another stimulant and it is one of the controlled, and therefore illegal, drugs.

These drugs are not strictly illegal although it is illegal to deal in, sell and/or supply, and obtain anabolic steroids. The governing bodies of sport have banned their use and taken steps to stop performers using them.

The types and effects of each of the prohibited classes of substances are detailed below.

Stimulants

These substances increase alertness, reduce fatigue (see page 63) and may increase competitiveness and hostility. They can also produce a loss of judgement and this can lead to accidents in some sports.

An overdose of stimulants can cause death. This has occurred twice in cycling events: once in an Olympic event and once in the Tour de France. Other side effects can include:

- high blood pressure and headaches

TASK 1

Write down some activities where stimulants might help a performance. Explain why you think so.

Narcotics

These include morphine and heroin. The main reason that they are banned is because they hide the effects of illness and injury. They suppress the feeling of pain but their side effects are:

- respiratory depression
- physical and psychological dependence
- exhaustion or over training
- constipation
- extreme apathy.

Performers must be very careful to draw the line between treating an injury and actually concealing its full extent by taking narcotics. A far more serious injury could occur and an addiction to these drugs can lead to death.

Drug-taking can be tempting in sports where the margin between winning and losing is a fraction of a second

Anabolic agents

These are probably the best known and most commonly abused drugs in sport. The main type is known as **androgenic anabolic steroids**. These are a group of both natural and synthetic compounds which are very similar to the natural male hormone known as testosterone. Testosterone has two main effects:

- *androgenic* – promotes the development of male characteristics
- *anabolic* – stimulates the build up of muscle tissue.

There are more than a hundred types of anabolic steroids available. The most common ones are nandrolone, testosterone, stanozolol and boldenone. These are taken in tablet form, but some of the steroids are taken by injection directly into the muscles.

Steroids were developed originally because they helped to cure anaemic conditions, eased wasting conditions and bone diseases and were useful in the treatment of breast cancer.

The first records of performers taking steroids were noted in the 1950s when some body builders and weightlifters started to use them. This has now spread to other sports as performers feel that it can help their performance by:

- increasing muscle strength

- enabling them to train harder and for longer
- increasing their competitiveness.

There is no real evidence to back up claims that these drugs can have such a marked effect, but there is evidence to suggest that they can help with training. Taking steroids can enable a performer to have better and longer training sessions. Because of this they are often called 'training drugs'. They enable the performer to train very hard and then stop taking the drug in enough time before a competition to make sure that traces of it are not found during testing. This makes accurate testing for the use of this type of drug very difficult.

A sprinter who used steroids as a training aid would only need a 10 per cent improvement to change from being a borderline international athlete to a world record holder.

The risks involved in taking steroids are quite serious, and are listed below.

- *Liver disorders and heart disease* – there can be serious damage to the liver structure leading to jaundice, liver failure, liver tumours and bleeding of the liver. In one case a 26 year old body builder who had been taking steroids for several years died of cancer of the liver.

  The heart can be affected by changes in its fatty substances, which can lead to an increased liability to heart attacks and strokes, as well as increased blood pressure.

- *Sexual and physique problems* – in children, growth can be affected or even stunted. Men can suffer from reduced sperm production and sterility. There can be shrinking and hardening of the testicles, impotence and even the growth of breasts.

  Women can have a disruption of the menstrual cycle and ovulation, changes in the sex organs, balding, acne, growth of facial hair and deepening of the voice. Steroids can also cause miscarriage, still birth or damage to the foetus, especially during early pregnancy.

- *Behavioural effects* – there can be quite marked changes of behaviour in some individuals. This can be seen as increased moodiness and aggression. The changes can be so extreme that they would constitute a psychiatric disorder.

All of these disorders depend upon the amount of steroids being taken and the period of time over which they are taken. The effects can be reversed if their use is stopped quickly enough.

It must also be remembered that beta$_2$agonists have anabolic effects and can have similar side effects.

Corticosteroids also have quite serious side effects which include:

- high blood pressure
- salt and water retention
- potassium loss
- bone and muscle weakness
- mental disturbances such as euphoria, depression or paranoia
- diabetes
- suppression of growth in children.

TASK 2

Draw up a table listing the possible advantages and disadvantages of taking

Diuretics

These are used medically to reduce excess body fluids and for the management of high blood pressure. Sports performers could misuse them:

- to reduce weight quickly in sports where weight categories are important
- to reduce the concentration of substances by diluting the urine.

Because of this second effect, some authorities reserve the right to obtain urine samples from competitors at the weigh-in prior to a competition.

The following side effects can occur through injecting diuretics into the system:

- faintness and dizziness
- muscle cramps

- headaches and nausea
- dehydration.

The body needs a certain amount of fluids during exercise to perform properly and safely and diuretics can cause kidney and heart failure due to the excessive loss of water.

TASK 3

Name some activities where taking diuretics could assist a performer. Explain why.

Peptide hormones, mimetics and analogues

Peptide hormones 'carry messages' around the body to increase growth, influence sexual and general behaviour and to control pain.

Mimetics and analogues are synthetic drugs which have a similar effect to peptide hormones. Both the natural and synthetic versions are banned in sport.

This category include the following drugs:

1 Chorionic gonadotrophin (hCG)

2 Pituitary and synthetic gonadotrophins (LH)

3 Corticotrophin (ACTH testracosactide)

4 Growth hormone (hGH)

5 Insulin-like growth factor (IGF-1)

6 Erythropoietin (EPO)

7 Insulin – permitted only to treat insulin-dependent diabetes. Written notification of diabetes must be given by an endocrinologist or team physician.

Some of the above are already present in the human body but drug misuse increases the levels artificially. It is these higher levels or 'abnormal concentrations' that are tested for and banned.

The side effects of increasing the levels can include:

- muscle wastage through prolonged use
- enlarged internal organs
- unusual growth patterns such as enlarged hands and feet.

Blood doping

Some years ago, endurance athletes used this to make their blood more efficient in carrying and supplying oxygen. It involves having a transfusion of blood (this is when blood is actually added back into the bloodstream). It can involve an athlete having blood taken away, training with depleted blood levels, then having the blood replaced. It can even be replaced with someone else's blood, red blood cells or related products.

This used to be tolerated, but is now banned. Possible side effects are:

- development of allergic reactions such as a rash or fever

- acute kidney damage if the incorrect blood type is used

- delayed transfusion reaction which can result in a fever and jaundice

- transmission of infectious diseases such as, viruses, hepatitis and AIDS

- overload of the circulation and metabolic shock.

As well as banning the use of blood doping, the IOC has also banned any interference by what it calls pharmacological, chemical and physical manipulation. This covers such things as interfering with urine samples or using medical knowledge to assist performers.

Shooting is one of the activities that specifically bans the use of beta-blockers

TASK 4

In what sort of sports could performers obtain an advantage through blood doping?

Beta-blockers

These are prescribed to people who have a medical condition affecting their heart. They calm and control the heart rate. They would not be of any real benefit in some activities, but in others they have been identified as providing an advantage. Beta-blockers are therefore banned in:

- archery

- bobsleigh

- diving and synchronized swimming

- luge (a form of bob sledge)

- modern pentathlon

- shooting

- ski jumping

- free-style skiing.

TASK 5

Look through the list above and say how taking beta-blockers might help the performer.

Use of beta-blockers in events requiring endurance would actually decrease performance, but there are cases where they have been used in sports to calm nerves and keep the performer steady.

Creatine

Not all drugs that seem to have some properties of improving performance are banned and some performers take these 'supplements' to help with their training.

One of the most controversial of these is **creatine**, which is often referred to as a 'legal steroid'.

Mary Pierce caused controversy by using creatine as part of a training programme to increase her physical strength

It is a nutritional supplement which gives a massive dose of amino acids similar to those found naturally in meat, helping athletes to train harder to build muscle. Some take a daily dose of 30 grammes which produces creatine levels equivalent to eating between 25 and 30 steaks!

Some nutritionists warn against using the supplement, which is available as powder, tablets and even chewing gum, and warn against taking it for too long in order to avoid side effects. These can include:

- diarrhoea and nausea
- involuntary clenched teeth
- the sound of rushing to the ears
- muscle cramps in the legs.

The supplement is taken as a training aid in addition to extreme levels of training. The extreme exercise forces the body to produce protein for thicker muscle and the creatine aids this process.

Without adequate supplies of creatine, muscles tire quickly. The supplement can delay the onset of fatigue, allowing the athlete to train to the very limit of their capability and therefore aiding muscle growth.

TASK 6

Compare the 'advantages' which taking creatine might have for a performer to those which taking steroids have.

One performer who took creatine was tennis player Mary Pierce. The French tennis player caused quite a sensation in 1999 when her physique changed quite dramatically after she had greatly increased her physical training along with creatine as a nutritional supplement.

Doping control

The use of drugs to improve a performance is clearly cheating and it can also be very harmful, sometimes even fatal. Despite all of this, some performers still use them in an effort to gain an unfair advantage.

Their use is banned and there are procedures in force to try to catch those who use drugs, and to discourage others from doing so. The procedure is called doping control and it involves obtaining a urine sample, testing it for any banned substances and following that up with any disciplinary procedures which might be necessary.

Recommended sanctions

The following sanctions can be imposed following a positive drug test.

■ *Scale 1* – (all the main listed doping classes)

Two year ban for the first offence, life ban for the second offence.

■ *Scale 2* – (ephedrine, phenylpropanolamine etc.)

A maximum three month ban for the first offence, two years for the second offence and a life ban for the third offence.

Unfortunately, these sanctions do have to be used. There are many cases where performers have used drugs to improve their performance.

TASK 7

Find out the penalty imposed on anyone who recently tested positive for banned drugs.

Drug use in sport

The first recorded use of drugs in sport goes back as far as 1865. Here are some more recent cases.

1988 – In the Seoul Olympics there were ten positive doping results, five of these were in the weightlifting, two in the modern pentathlon, one each in wrestling and judo and one in athletics. The athlete found guilty was Ben Johnson. This was one of the most famous cases of drug abuse as he had just won the Olympic 100 metres championship.

Johnson was given a two year ban and returned to racing with little success. He then subsequently failed another test and was banned from the sport. There is little in sport more controversial than the drug situation, and several athletes have battled against the authorities after their bans.

1998 – In January 1998 it was revealed that there had been an organized system of drug use by athletes and performers in the now disbanded German Democratic Republic (East Germany). Files were discovered which revealed that the 'Stasi' (the secret police force) had been running and organizing a state-controlled drug/doping programme where sports performers were encouraged, and even forced, to take performance-enhancing drugs.

One of their Olympic swimmers, Petra Schneider, won a gold medal in the 1980 Olympics for the 400 metres individual relay. She was known on the Stasi files as 'sportsperson 137' and had been given drugs since the age of fourteen. In adult life she has suffered many of the side effects which the drugs can have.

Another East German performer, shot put champion Heidi Kruger, was so badly affected by the amounts of steroids she was given that she was forced to undergo a sex change operation.

East German swimmer Petra Schneider was given performance-enhancing drugs from the age of fourteen

In February 1998 there was controversy at the Winter Olympics when Canadian snowboarder Ross Rebagliati was allowed to keep his gold medal despite being tested positive for traces of cannabis. His excuse that he inhaled it when at a party mixing with cannabis smokers was accepted!

In July and August 1998 there was an ongoing scandal throughout the Tour de France cycle race when individuals and even whole teams were banned from the race following police investigations and several failed dope tests.

This controversy was quickly followed within days when Juan Antonio Samaranch, the President of the International Olympic Committee suggested that athletes should be allowed to use 'harmless performance-enhancing drugs'.

In September 1998, US sprinter Florence Griffith Joyner, who had won the Olympic gold medal in the 1988 Seoul Olympics, died of a heart attack. There were allegations that she had achieved her success with the help of performance-enhancing drugs – although she never failed a drug test. Doubts had been expressed when she was at her most successful, due to the deepening of her voice and her noticeably more muscled physique.

1999 – In June 1999, triple Olympic gold medallist Michelle de Bruin (formerly Michelle Smith) the Irish swimmer was found guilty of 'tampering with a drug sample' and banned following a seventeen-month case in which she had protested her innocence. There had been doubts expressed over her achievements in the Atlanta Olympics because of her swift and spectacular progress and improvement.

One of the most recent controversies has been that over the use of creatine, which is a legal food supplement. Creatine can give massive doses of amino acids, such as those found in meat, which can help athletes train harder to increase muscle bulk (see page 108).

TASK 8

Make up a scrapbook of any recent drug controversies reported in newspapers.

The Canadian sprinter Ben Johnson, who failed a drugs test after winning the Olympic 100 metres in 1988

Making sure that you are performing safely is one of the most important factors when taking part in any physical activity. The topics covered in this unit all need to be considered as being potential risks and may require you to take steps to deal with them.

Injury – prevention and causes

In most cases, if you are able to spot a possible cause of injury, you can take steps to prevent it, but you must always consider preparation, participation, equipment and environment.

Preparation

It is important to get yourself ready to take part in physical activity properly. Many people fail to do it thoroughly. You need to consider:

- *Training* – you should not take part in any activity if you have not undergone some form of training so that you are physically prepared. Each sport makes its own demands upon your body; some put a strain on the legs, others put a strain on the arms. It is foolish to take part without having done at least some basic training to reduce the chance of a strain or a sprain. Your training should also include having a basic knowledge of the game, such as its rules and regulations so that you know how to participate. A player who goes onto a hockey pitch without any knowledge of the rules could be very dangerous!

- *Warm-up* – this is essential in all activities (see unit 29) to prepare you physically immediately before taking part.

- *Physical state* – you should remove all jewellery such as watches, earrings and bracelets and you may even be required to make sure that your finger nails are short (netball has a rule about this). This is also the time to make sure that you are wearing the proper clothing or equipment.

Participation

While you are actually taking part or participating in a particular sport you need to be aware of the following.

- *Fair play* – the rules of any activity also have a vital part to play and you should be aware of their role. You should always play fairly. Sticking to the rules ensures that you play safely. A high tackle in rugby, for example, is against the rules as it is potentially dangerous and could result in a serious neck or head injury.

- *Officials* – players have a responsibility to make sure that they respond positively to the officials in charge and also to respond positively to any other instructions which others, such as teachers and coaches, might give them, as these are additional safeguards regarding safety.

TASK 1

*For **two** physical activities make a list of the ways that injuries could happen through deliberate foul play.*

Equipment

Appropriate equipment is probably one of the most important factors when it comes to injury prevention and it can also be a major cause of injuries. The following points about equipment need to be considered.

- *Correctness* – the right equipment must be worn at the right time and it must be appropriate for the activity. Helmets are worn by American footballers, but it would be inappropriate for one player to wear one in a game of rugby!

Equipment must also be worn correctly. A loose strap or fitting could be dangerous to the person playing, or to an opponent.

Helmets are essential for American football

Wearing the correct sports footwear can help by giving support to the arches and cushioning the ankle joint on the impact when running or jumping. Wearing the wrong kind of footwear, such as high back shoes can cause Achilles tendon damage. The equipment must fit properly. An ill-fitting gum shield can be very dangerous, so it is best fitted by a dentist.

The equipment must only be used for protection and not in any other way. There is a rule in American football which stops players from using their helmets in a dangerous way when tackling.

■ *Condition* – all equipment must be regularly checked and kept in good order. Items such as football boot studs need to be checked to make sure that there are no sharp edges which could cut an opponent. Equipment must be checked to make sure it cannot injure opponents but it is also important that it still does its job to protect the wearer. Loose spikes in a running shoe could lead to a trip or fall if they don't grip properly.

Equipment must be regularly checked and protected. Goal posts and marker flags need to be in good condition and rugby posts should have protective coverings around them. Job officials often check things like this before a game.

Equipment used to play the game must be checked. A damaged hockey stick could break, or splinters could come from it. A worn grip on a racket can cause blisters or loss of grip and an opponent could be hit.

TASK 2

*Choose **two** physical activities and, for each one, write out a list of equipment and the necessary checks.*

Environment

This is not always something which you can control. Therefore you may have to be extra cautious. The environment can be considered in two ways.

■ *Uncontrolled environment* – this would include such things as the weather. In any outdoor activity the weather may be a factor and in some outdoor pursuits it can be potentially dangerous.

The ground conditions can be affected by the weather. Wet grounds can be slippery and dangerous as it is not possible to get a firm grip, while very dry, hard grounds can cause injuries when landing. Hard grounds can also be difficult to get a grip on if they are too dry for studs. Severe weather conditions such as hard frosts or electrical storms can mean that games should not be played, or, even abandoned once under way.

■ *Controlled environment* – these are things which you can do something about – for example, by inspecting a pitch before a match for stones or broken glass.

Spectators and crowds must be very carefully controlled. If not controlled they can be a danger to themselves and there is a chance that they can be a danger to the participants. Excited crowds invading playing areas can cause injuries and they themselves can be injured if they are too close to the playing area and get hit by a player or a ball.

TASK 3

Make a list of as many items of protective equipment as you can think of that are used in physical activities.

Causes of injury

There are many potential causes of injury and not all of them can be prevented. Mainly, injuries are:

■ internally caused

■ externally caused.

Internally caused injuries

These are injuries for which performers themselves are responsible. There are no other factors such as opponents. These injuries include the following categories.

■ *Overuse injuries* – these come about, fairly obviously, through training or performing too much. The pressures on performers are so great that there is a temptation to do far too much and many sportspeople take up regular sport at a very young age. All this puts a strain on the body and the body may not always be able to cope with it.

Performers can suffer stress fractures in bones caused through too much running, as well as tendon and muscle injuries. Cricket bowlers often sustain back and shoulder injuries caused through their bowling action, tennis players get tennis elbow (an inflammation of the elbow joint, caused by the forced straightening of the arm during play) and many soccer and hockey players get knee cartilage damage through constantly twisting and turning.

It is impossible to play these sports without putting some kind of strain on the body. What is important is that the performer does not overdo it and also that they cut down, or stop, if there is any sign of injury. Carrying on will only make it worse.

Injuries are common in many of the major team games such as hockey

- *Sudden injuries* – these are caused instantly by such things as overstretching or twisting or turning quickly. They may be caused by tiredness or fatigue. Many of these types of injuries happen quite late on in a game or a match.

Obviously, lack of a suitable warm-up can also be a cause. One more cause can be trying to do something which is either too difficult or which is clearly dangerous.

Externally caused injuries

These are caused by factors other than the performers themselves. It could be the equipment used, the playing conditions or an opponent. They can be considered under the following headings.

- *Impact injuries* – these are often injuries such as cuts, bruises and fractures. Impact can be caused by another player (many of these occur in team games where physical contact is allowed) who may be tackling or it can be the equipment used, such as goal posts, hockey sticks or soccer boots.

The playing surface is also a very common cause of these injuries. It is not only outdoor surfaces that are dangerous. Indoor surfaces can be just as hard and just as harmful.

- *Foul play/incorrect actions* – this involves other players, usually opponents. The type of injury received may be very minor or it might be serious. Potentially, the injuries can be very serious, so there are rules to prevent them.

- *Accidents* – no matter how many safety precautions are taken there will always be accidents. They occur in all physical activities, but because some sports are more dangerous than others the accidents will be more serious. Skiing is a good example of this. The aim is to move as fast as possible so a skier who falls is bound to be going quickly and the accident is likely to be serious.

Injuries are more likely in some activities than others

In some activities the activity is itself dangerous. Boxing would be an example of this. Many boxers have died as a result of a punch which was delivered quite fairly. In certain activities, performers have to be aware of the risks they take simply by participating.

- *Equipment* – a simple thing like a blister can be caused by the equipment. For example, tight fitting shoes can cause blisters, or even corns and bunions. However, the equipment does not have to be faulty to cause an injury. Running long distances can often leave performers with blisters on their feet and this cannot be avoided, no matter how specialist the running shoes are.

Often injuries are caused by damaged, ill-fitting or faulty equipment which is not doing its job properly.

TASK 4

Draw up a checklist which could be used for a particular activity, to ensure that all the equipment used is safe and suitable.

A word of warning: you should not consider yourself an expert in first aid after reading this unit. This section is designed to allow you to have an understanding and knowledge of the types of common injuries which can occur and the basic actions that can then be taken. When taking part in physical activities there is always the risk that some form of injury might occur. Many of these are only minor ones. However, you may have a responsibility to assess the level of this injury and then take the appropriate action. If in any doubt, you should contact the emergency services and let them deal with the situation.

General rules for treatment

The following rules apply in most cases where a sporting injury has occurred.

- Do not move the injured person until you are sure what the injury is. Ask the injured person to give you details of the injury and any affected areas. If for any reason the person is unconscious, or was unconscious, you must call an ambulance.

- Look at the damaged or affected areas to see if there is any sign of an injury. Cuts or wounds should be obvious but if there is any bone damage you may find a misshapen area or damage to a joint or signs of swelling.

  You can then gently touch the injured area and see if there are any signs of tenderness or further injury. If there does not seem to be too much damage ask the injured person if they are able to move the area which is injured. If they cannot move it themselves do not try to do it for them! If they can move, see how much movement there is that does not cause any discomfort.

- If you have been through all of these stages, and the injured person feels able to, then see if they can stand and move and take their own weight. They may need help to do this so you may need to support them. They should only continue to take part in the activity if they are clearly fully recovered. Any injury will be made worse by carrying on but a minor 'knock' or temporary damage should not prevent a performer from continuing.

- If at any time they are not able to carry on through these gradual stages they must get expert help straight away. There is a big difference between first aid and medical treatment.

Depending on the type of injury you are faced with there are various different things which you can do.

Head injuries

You should place the injured person in the **coma position** (see the photo opposite), lying on their side, and you must make sure that they are able to breathe, so you must check that their mouth and nose are clear.

If they are not breathing you will need to give expelled air resuscitation (see page 121) and if there is no sign of a pulse you will need to give cardiac massage (see page 122). Details of resuscitation come later in this unit.

Fractures

This is the name given to broken bones and there are three main types of fracture which you should be able to identify.

- *Simple or closed* – the most straightforward type of fracture where the bone is broken but it has not pierced the skin.

- *Open or compound* – the skin is broken so there is a wound caused by the broken bone which may even be sticking out.

The coma or recovery position

■ *Complicated* – there is serious damage to a blood vessel or a nerve. This damage could cause heavy bleeding which could be more serious than the break itself.

These are the signs you should look for when checking for fractures.

■ Has the snap of the bone been heard or felt?

■ Is there pain where the injury has occurred and is there a lack of movement in the limb?

■ Is the shape and outline of the limb different from normal? You can check against the other limb to see this.

■ Is the limb in an unnatural position? For example, a knee or foot facing the wrong way would show this.

■ Is there a lot of swelling around the injured area?

■ Can you feel some clear damage to the bone?

If, after considering all of these points, you think that there is a chance of a fracture you must be very careful not to move the injured area but to immobilize it – that is to keep it in a stable position.

You can do this by applying a splint, which is anything you can use to keep the injured person's damaged bone straight and protected. If it is a fractured leg you can splint the good leg to the bad one to give support. You could even use cricket stumps or hockey sticks! You might also need to pad the area. Clothing such as jumpers or towels would be good for this. If the damage is to an arm then you can put the arm in a sling to support and protect it.

Treating a fracture is an expert's job so as soon as you have done what you can to protect the injury and make the injured person comfortable you must get expert help and call an ambulance.

TASK 1

With a partner, take it in turns to practise placing each other in the coma position.

Dislocations

These occur at a joint, where one bone comes out of its normal position against another. There will be damage to the ligaments around the joint as well so this is quite a painful injury. The common places where this happens are:

- shoulder
- elbow
- jaw
- thumb
- fingers.

It can be very difficult to tell the difference between a dislocation and a fracture so you should treat them the same way. On no account should you attempt to put the bone back in place; this is very much a job for an expert.

Sprains

These occur where there is overstretching, or tearing, of ligaments at a joint. They are usually caused by a sudden wrench or twist and it is a very common injury at the ankle.

Again, it can be very difficult to tell this injury from a fracture or a dislocation so it should be treated the same way as a fracture. Often, the only way to tell these three injuries apart is to have an X-ray so it is always best to be cautious.

Strains

These are caused by overstretching of a muscle rather than a joint and they can also be caused by a twist or a wrench. They are quite painful and there may be some reduced or weakened movement where the injury occurred, but the symptoms would not be as serious as a sprain, dislocation or fracture.

Bandaging the area will help as this will give some support to the injury. An elastic bandage can be particularly good.

The other treatment is covered later under the soft tissue injury treatment (page 121).

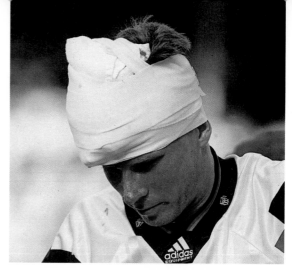

A head wound as large as this will require hospital treatment

Cuts

The technical name for any form of bleeding is a **haemorrhage**. Cuts can vary greatly in size and seriousness.

Any wound such as a cut should be gently cleaned and dressed. A plaster may be enough to cover and protect the cut. If not, it may be necessary to put on a bandage. Large or deep cuts may need hospital treatment as they may need stitching to close the wound properly.

If there is blood pumping out of a cut under pressure, there has been damage to an artery and this must be treated as very serious. An ambulance must be called immediately.

Bruises

These are extremely common and are collections of blood beneath the skin. The blood vessels have been damaged just like a cut but the skin has not been broken so the bleeding occurs beneath the skin.

The first sign of a bruise is swelling and then there will be discoloration of the area as it might go blue or purple first and then green or yellow.

A bruise should be treated by applying ice. This will reduce the swelling and relieve the pain. The ice needs to be applied quite quickly. If it is, it will limit the extent of the injury. Witch-hazel is a lotion which can be applied and which also relieves the symptoms.

Shock

There are two types of shock.

- *Primary shock* – is a feeling of faintness which can come on immediately after an emotional or traumatic event. This is only a temporary feeling and often passes quite quickly. Calming and reassuring the person will usually be enough to help them to overcome this. They may be able to take some liquid and might also need to be kept warm.

- *True shock* – is a far more serious state. It will come about after a serious injury, such as a very bad cut or fracture. The person affected will be close to collapse and it is very important that they are treated in hospital. You can calm and reassure them but an ambulance must be called.

One of the ways to treat shock is to move the person from the scene of the injury (follow all the safeguards outlined earlier). It may be necessary to decide whether to treat them for shock or their injury.

It may be their own injury or someone else's which is causing the state of shock and they have to be treated accordingly. If at all possible, the person should not be left. Instead, try to get someone else to go for help. Your support and reassurance will be vital.

Concussion

This is a sudden loss of consciousness and it is often caused by a blow to the head. It does not have to be a particularly hard blow to cause concussion. The sufferer may be unconscious for a few seconds or even for several hours. There is such a thing as **delayed concussion** which means that the person becomes unconscious up to several hours after being injured. If there is any doubt, the person must be checked in hospital. It is a set procedure now for people to be kept in hospital overnight as a precaution if there is any chance of concussion.

The signs of concussion are:

- immediate unconsciousness
- very relaxed limbs with a very weak and irregular pulse
- slow and shallow breathing
- large pupils (known as dilated)
- bleeding from the ears (this indicates a serious injury and must be dealt with as an emergency).

Like many other injuries listed here, concussion is a matter for the experts. At the scene, the important task is to spot it and get help.

Cramp

This is an involuntary contraction of a muscle and although it is quite painful it is easy to treat and to 'cure'. To do this, the sufferer needs to stretch the muscle affected as far as it will go. For example, if you get cramp in the calf you should straighten the knee and bend the foot back upwards at the ankle.

Cramp does not always stop the performer from carrying on, although serious cases can. Often it is just a slight cramp which can be put right. Remember, also, that it can be caused by loss of salt through sweating.

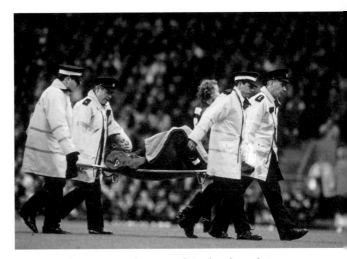

An injury during a match can result in the player being stretchered off the pitch

Skin infections

Although these are often considered to be minor, they can be very painful and uncomfortable. People who regularly take part in physical activity are very likely to suffer from them.

■ *Athlete's foot* – is a fungal infection which causes itching and broken skin on the feet, between the toes. In severe cases it causes bleeding and it is most uncomfortable. One of the causes can be not drying the feet properly. It is also highly contagious and can be passed on by sharing towels and socks. Creams and powders are available to treat it and these have to be used regularly.

■ *Verrucas* – are also known as plantar warts and are a type of wart which occurs on the feet. These are contagious and can be painful. They may need to be treated by a doctor.

■ *Blisters* – are very common and are caused by friction on the skin. This causes a break in the layers of the skin. The small gap between the layers then fills up with a fluid called serum and the blister forms in a bubble shape.

If the blister is small, it can just be left to disperse on its own or it can be covered with some sticky plaster. If the blister is very big (and therefore also very uncomfortable and painful), it may be necessary to burst it to drain the fluid. This should be done very carefully by making a small hole with a sterile needle and gently squeezing out the fluid. It is important not to let the area become infected. Severe blisters can stop a performer from carrying on in sport.

Most skin infections are only minor, but they can turn into more serious infections if they are not treated carefully. The skin is a defence barrier so performers must be very careful if it is damaged in any way.

Environmental 'injuries'

These are any disorders which can be caused by the environment and they include the following.

■ *Exposure* – can happen when a performer is in very low temperatures and the severe cold affects their body. They may not be able to keep their body temperature at the normal rate and prolonged exposure can result in death.

■ *Frostbite* – can happen if a performer is suffering from exposure where the tissue is damaged by the extreme cold and a condition called gangrene sets in. This is a decay of the tissue and is very serious. Affected areas often have to be amputated.

■ *Hypothermia* – is a rapid cooling of the body where the temperature drops quickly. If this condition occurs any wet clothing should be removed and the casualty should be covered with warm and dry clothing or blankets and medical help sought.

The main cure for all of the above is prevention. If a performer is taking part in anything where the temperatures are low they should ensure that they are dressed properly. Warm clothing is essential as a safety precaution.

■ *Heat-stroke* – is caused by very high temperatures and can lead to vomiting and uncontrollable shaking. It is caused because the body is overheating and is not able to keep the temperature down. Exposure to very high temperatures should be avoided to prevent this.

■ *Exhaustion* – can be caused by a variety of factors but it is a state of extreme fatigue. Excessive heat or cold can cause this because the body system is struggling to cope with the extremes of temperature.

Soft tissue injury treatment

Soft tissue injury is where there is an injury to ligaments or muscles. The standard treatment which can be applied to any soft tissue injury is known as the RICE treatment. RICE stands for Rest, Ice, Compression and Elevation and is described in more detail below.

- *Rest* – stop straight away and rest the injury, carrying on can make things far worse.

- *Ice* – applying ice to the injury reduces swelling and relieves some of the pain. Do not put ice on directly but use an ice pack or wrap the ice in a towel.

- *Compression* – this can be with either a bandage or some tape which will put some support and pressure to the injured area. Be very careful not to apply this too tightly and restrict the blood flow.

- *Elevation* – try to raise the injured body part as this will decrease the circulation to the area as it must work against gravity. This will also help to drain away any other fluid at the injury.

The RICE treatment should be applied to any injury to the muscles, the ligaments or the skin as it is not only a simple treatment, but also a very effective treatment.

Emergency treatments

Other treatments may need to be given to a person who is seriously injured and who has either stopped breathing or whose heart has stopped beating.

A knowledge of the following expelled air resuscitation techniques could enable you to save someone's life. These resuscitation techniques are quite easy to do if you follow the steps described.

Expelled air resuscitation

This technique is often called 'mouth-to-mouth' resuscitation. If someone has stopped breathing, it is the most effective way to get their breathing started again.

1 Before starting to treat the casualty, get someone to phone 999 for an ambulance.

2 Tilt the casualty's chin back and check that their airways are clear.

3 Carefully look/listen/feel for any signs of breathing. If there are none:

4 Take a deep breath, pinch the casualty's nostrils together with your fingers and seal your lips around their open mouth.

5 Blow into the casualty's lungs. Look along their chest to see if their chest is rising.

6 Move your mouth away and breathe out any excess air as their chest falls. Take a deep breath and blow again.

7 After two inflations, spend ten seconds checking for a pulse. If there is none then give two more inflations and check again. Do this for up to five attempts.

If you are unable to do mouth-to-mouth resuscitation, you can use mouth-to-nose as an alternative. To do this, you seal the casualty's mouth with your thumb and seal your lips around the nose.

Provided the heart is beating, continue inflations at about 12–16 per minute until the person is breathing on their own. *If there is no pulse or sign of a heartbeat, you will have to perform cardio-pulmonary resuscitation.*

TASK 2

If you have access to a resuscitation dummy, use the seven steps above to practise the resuscitation procedure.

Throughout the history of sport there has been change and improvement but these have been far more rapid in recent years. The changes have mostly come about in the two main areas of equipment and materials.

Equipment

The equipment which is available today for people taking part in sport is far more varied, safer and better designed than it was in the past. It is also constantly changing – so much so that governing bodies have to keep a check on it to make sure that it is legal and does not give anyone an unfair advantage.

The impact these changes have made can be seen in particular sports.

Racket sports

It is only comparatively recently that wooden tennis rackets were replaced by aluminium and then graphite rackets. As the material used to make the rackets was lighter it was possible to enlarge the head. Although the overall length of a modern tennis racket is the same as a wooden framed one the actual striking surface head is now much larger.

The design and efficiency of the rackets is now so advanced that players can hit the ball much harder and more accurately. This has not necessarily been a good thing.

In the 1994 Men's Tennis Final at Wimbledon only six minutes of every hour were actual action and only one rally lasted more than four strokes. This was because both of the finalists, Pete Sampras and Goran Ivanisevic, were both 'serve and volley' players who relied on hard hitting. They were greatly helped by the equipment they used.

There is even a campaign to change the rules to make the improvements in the equipment less crucial to the outcome of the game.

On a positive note, tennis courts can now be fitted with an 'electronic eye' which is placed by lines to indicate if a ball is in or out of court. Nowadays the ball is travelling so fast that it requires modern technology to track it.

Also, like many other sports, tennis is directly monitored by computers which can analyse each result and constantly update the ranking number of all the current players. This is very important because a player's computer ranking will dictate whether or not they can play in certain competitions.

Like tennis rackets, squash rackets are now mainly constructed of graphite and have larger heads. They also last longer. One of the problems with wooden rackets was that they often broke when players struck the walls as they played shots. The stronger, tougher graphite construction has reduced this.

Badminton rackets are also now mainly constructed of graphite. The size of the head has not increased greatly but there is no longer a need for racket presses. These were wooden, sprung devices which were used to stop the badminton rackets from warping and going out of shape when they were not in use.

In all racket sports there is now a variety of synthetic materials used to string the rackets. These are stronger and longer lasting and the rackets can be strung at a higher tension, enabling more power to be generated.

TASK I

Obtain and weigh some different rackets from racket events and compare the differences.

Athletics

Field events have benefited from improved equipment in several ways. The pole in the modern pole vault is now constructed from a lightweight fibreglass compound which makes

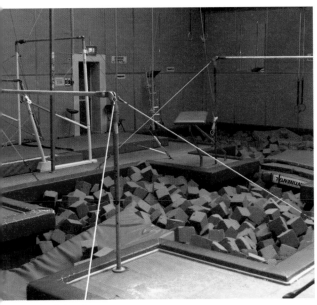

Safe landing area

it lighter, stronger and more flexible. This means the vaulters can jump much higher. To ensure safety, large, air-filled, and purpose-built landing areas have been designed which are more suitable and efficient. These can allow a jumper to land safely after coming down from a height of nearly seven metres (about 20 feet).

The high jump also now has a similar type landing area which has replaced the old sand landing area. This has been necessary due to the changes in the techniques of the jumpers. It would not be possible for high jumpers to land safely on their backs in sand so the inflatable areas have to be used.

The javelin went through many changes as more advanced materials were used in its construction. However, they became so efficient that they were dangerous. Competitors were throwing them so far that the stadiums were not big enough. Therefore they are now reduced in weight and the position of the centre of gravity has been moved, to reduce the distances they can be thrown. This was an example of technology being too effective.

Advances in timing equipment in athletics has also been a major factor. Previously, all competitors were timed by officials using hand-held stopwatches, lined up in banked seating by the start and finish lines. Now, the starting gun, starting blocks and lanes are connected to automatic electronic timing systems which give a very accurate and instant time. When a championship can depend on one-thousandth of a second this is very important.

TASK 2

Try timing a televised sporting event which has electronic timing and compare how accurate you are with the official time.

Footwear and clothing equipment has also advanced in athletics but this will be dealt with later (see pages 128–9).

Another major advance is the construction of the running surfaces. These are now artificial instead of grass, which not only allows events to go on in bad weather but also enables the athletes to get a better grip and run faster.

Cricket

There is now a full range of protective equipment available for cricket players. Protective helmets were introduced as a result of head injuries resulting from fast bowling. Other protective equipment has become much lighter and less bulky as designs and materials used have improved.

TASK 3

Make a list of all the different protective items a cricketer might use.

One major technological innovation has been the introduction of the third umpire. This is an extra official who is able to watch slow motion action replays from television cameras to help reach decisions. There is a direct radio link between the two umpires on the pitch and the third umpire in a booth and they can be advised of the decision to be made. This is something which is being closely monitored by other sports as it ensures that all decisions are as fair as possible.

Materials

A major change over recent years is the great number of synthetic materials available for use in sport.

This ranges from the light aerodynamic materials used for clothing for swimmers, speed skaters and cyclists right through to the variety of artificial surfaces used for tennis, hockey, soccer, athletics and sports halls.

Previously, it was only possible to use natural materials, such as wood or metal, cotton, wool and leather for clothing and equipment.

The developments of improved materials for playing surfaces has greatly changed the nature of some of the games. Top class hockey is now played exclusively on artificial surfaces and very rarely on grass. This allows the players to benefit far more from high levels of skill, as the ball does not move about as much as it would on a bumpy grass pitch. This has removed the element of luck which always existed as the ball can be relied upon to move predictably when a player is dribbling, passing or shooting. It also makes learning and acquiring skills easier as both beginners and the more experienced players find practising easier.

Artificial practice strips for cricket are becoming more popular for the same reason. The even and predictable bounce makes practising easier. However, the condition of a grass wicket and the way it can help different types of bowlers and batspeople is an essential part of cricket. It is therefore most unlikely that cricket will follow the example of hockey and have its top standard matches played on artificial surfaces.

Artificial pitches have helped to improve the skill levels in hockey

Two sports have already turned away from playing on artificial surfaces and are reverting back to grass. These are soccer and American football. Several soccer teams laid artificial pitches in the late 1980s and early 1990s but there was a great deal of criticism of them. In the end they were outlawed by the governing body, the Football Association, and grass pitches were reintroduced.

Although the American football authorities have not taken the step of outlawing artificial pitches, many of the teams are giving them up by choice. They found that many injuries occurred because of the surface. The grip on the surface was so good that knee and ankle injuries were occurring during tackles, when the feet could not move to absorb the impact. Many overuse and impact injuries were also occurring because the surface did not have the same amount of 'give' that a grass pitch has.

Many of the large stadiums in America are indoors so they have little choice but to keep their artificial surfaces, but there are fewer and fewer of them. Instead, the technology is concentrating on finding ways to protect the playing areas from the weather and of providing under-soil heating systems to combat snow and frosts.

Many of the materials which are being used in sport today are by-products of the 'space race' of the 1960s and 1970s. One example of this is Teflon. This was originally a tough non-stick resilient material which was developed as a low-friction surface for use in spacecraft. As a spin-off, it was used as a lining for saucepans. It is now being used to treat materials – both natural and artificial – to make them windproof and water resistant. This would be ideal for swimming costumes to reduce water resistance. Swimmers already resort to shaving off all their body hair to improve their times by thousandths of a second. More efficient costumes would be welcomed.

TASK 5

What other uses could Teflon have for sportspeople?

The Astrodome sports stadium in Houston, Texas

General developments and improvements

There have been many recent developments which sport has used in various ways. Technology is changing at such a rapid rate that there will no doubt be very many new changes to come.

Facilities

In the past basic sports facilities were provided and activities were catered for within them. This has now changed so that many facilities are purpose built specifically for certain activities.

An example is the facilities provided for gymnastics. Previously gymnasts were just accommodated within sports halls or sports arenas. Now there are facilities with recessed areas where the activities are performed above pits fitted with safety mats and there are safe landing areas below the competitors.

Centres are now being built specifically for tennis. Many of them are indoor areas where play can go on all the year round.

Many fitness gyms and clubs now make use of high tech equipment for weight training and aerobic fitness (see unit 30). Many of these machines make use of computers and computer programs so that individuals can key in their own particular details and have the machine work out the appropriate programme they should follow.

Many new sports complexes are being built as multi-purpose facilities. This means that they can easily be adapted for different activities and trends. For example, a new soccer stadium or pitch may have an athletics track around it and indoor training and sports facilities attached.

The structure of facilities has also been developed considerably to incorporate many features. The Millennium Stadium in Cardiff, Wales, is an excellent example of a new facility which has made full use of the advanced technology available.

This stadium has replaced the old national stadium in Wales and consists of a 75,000-seater stadium with a fully retractable roof. This means that the entire playing area can be covered in the event of bad weather, such as snow, frost or heavy rain. When the roof is opened, it allows natural light for playing games and matches and also allows the grass to grow naturally. The stadium also has other facilities included in the complex: a fitness and medical centre, media facilities, conference and hospitality suites, a rugby museum, a riverside walk and a public plaza which opens up to the city centre. However, facilities such as this do not come cheaply – the total cost for the stadium was £138,823,914!

One of the reasons that large sports stadiums are being upgraded, and often re-located, is to make the facilities much safer. There is a requirement for these stadiums to be all-seater to make them safer for spectators. Accidents have occurred in the past in stadiums where spectators stood rather than sat. This has sometimes led to serious injuries and even fatalities. Another trend has been to locate these stadiums more on the outskirts of towns and cities so that getting to and moving in and out of the stadiums can be more convenient and safer.

The Millennium Stadium in Cardiff

Technological advances

There are constant developments in the technology used in competitions and tournaments to ensure that results are either fair or accurately decided/measured.

Timing systems – the majority of timing systems are electronically operated using dual beam laser systems which accurately measure when performers have started and finished the event they are taking part in. The technology now means that these are accurate to hundredths of a second. There are different types for different activities.

- In athletic events, the timing devices are linked to the starting gun (and in sprint events using starting blocks they are linked to the blocks themselves) and to the finish line.

- In longer distance events, there are devices which can be put on the performers themselves. In triathlon events performers have sensors fixed to their ankles which are linked to a central computer giving constant readouts for the times they are taking over the various parts of the course.

- There are even hand-held timers which can be linked up to printers to give readouts of competitors' times. These are portable and easily moved around.

Sensor systems – systems using electronic sensors exist in many sports.

- The London Marathon introduced a system where all competitors carried a sensor attached to their running shoes which was recorded by electronic pads at different stages of the race. This was to ensure that all of the runners completed the whole course and did not cheat in any way!

- In fencing competitions, the competitors have suits that are linked to their fencing swords and which not only record hits to the body but also exactly where the hits took place.

- Sprinters have sensors installed in their starting blocks which are linked to the

Sprinters react quickly. Sensors in their starting blocks can detect false starts.

starter and can indicate if the athlete has started too quickly – the tolerance is 0.1 seconds. Anyone taking off quicker than that is deemed to have had a false start.

- Soccer referees have a sensor band fixed to the upper arm which is linked to their assistants' flags. The sensor 'pulses' when a switch is pressed on the flag to indicate off-sides or foul play.

- Research is underway to provide cricket with a device provisionally known as 'Hawkeye' that uses laser points and laser beams to track the exact trajectory of the ball. It is claimed that the umpires will be able to use a hand-held display that will give information on possible LBW decisions accurate to within 5mm!

Nassar Hussein and Alec Stewart after officially receiving their laptop computers

Cameras – developments in cameras and forms of digital recording equipment are now commonly used in many sporting events – often to check decisions made by officials.

■ Rugby league uses video playbacks to see whether or not tries were scored fairly.

■ Cricket has the 'third umpire' who sits in a booth and checks video footage to make particular decisions about possible run-outs and caught ball decisions

■ American football umpires wear what is known as the 'ump-cam', which is fixed to the peak of their cap and gives a players'-eye view of the action. (This official stands in the middle of the scrimmage.)

Information Communication Technology (ICT)

ICT developments are often used in sport and physical education. The benefits computers bring, and especially the fact that computers are now portable in laptop form, means that they are being used more and more to improve knowledge in the following ways:

■ CD-ROMs can contain theory information on a range of topics

■ Websites are up-to-date and provide interaction with such things as interactive circuit training.

ICT can also be used to improve performance in a variety of ways:

■ Laptop computers were given to members of the England cricket team in 2001 on their tour of Sri Lanka. The players were able to practise in the nets and then study their techniques with their coaches by looking at their performances using video images transmitted to the laptops.

■ Professional football clubs use 'Prozone'. This system uses up to ten sensors placed next to TV cameras around a pitch to build up a 360-degree view of a match. Pictures are downloaded, refined by an image processor, then grouped into categories – tactics, statistics, animation, or athletics (this category records things like average speed and intensity). Using the tactics menu, a coach can even judge how well his game plan has worked. The whole of the play is accurately recorded including every players' full contribution – if anything happens, at any time, in any part of the playing area, then it is recorded.

Technological teaching and training aids

More of these are becoming available and they range from application technology, such as interactive whiteboards which can be set up on sports hall walls, to specific sport devices. For instance, cyclists can make use of the 'ergocrank' which measures left and right side power independently to help measure asymmetry in pedalling style, or even to diagnose an injury.

Footwear

One of the biggest growth areas in sport has been the development and marketing of footwear.

In the UK in 1998, nearly one in every three pairs of shoes bought were sports shoes. In that year alone, there were over 45 million pairs of sports shoes sold by the main four suppliers, HiTec, Reebok, Nike and Adidas. This has meant a tremendous development in design, interest and sales from when Joseph Foster first put nails into the soles of his track shoes in 1895 to help improve his performance.

All sports shoes are now pieces of specialist equipment on which the manufacturers have spent a great deal of money in research, design and development. This is well illustrated by the Reebok range of footwear and the materials and innovations they use.

- *Hexalite* is a honeycomb structure which is 92 per cent air and absorbs 20 per cent more impact than ordinary foam, as well as being tougher and longer lasting.

- *Graphlite* is a woven fabric of graphite and glass fibres impregnated with polymer resin. This makes it as strong as steel but 45 per cent lighter than foam or rubber. It is used for arch support and cushioning

- *Instapump* is a system in which there are various chambers within the shoes which are filled up and inflated by air. These chambers are located at the critical joints of the foot and the ankle where most of the injuries occur.

Obviously, sports shoe manufacturers want to sell their products and will make various claims to do so. They now carry out research using high speed cameras, video and computerized force measuring platforms to

Images such as this have helped to create a huge market for sports shoes

check the efficiency of designs and the demands that movements put on the feet and ankles. This research has shown them that a nine-stone exerciser in a 10 minute session can produce a shock loading of 172 tonnes or the equivalent of the weight of 25 elephants on each foot.

There is little doubt that there have been great improvements in terms of safety and comfort in footwear and that the specialist shoes for different activities have led to improvements in the performers at all levels.

TASK 6

Carry out a survey within your teaching group to find out which is the most popular make and type of footwear.

Training aids

At one time, just about the only training aid a performer could have was a coach or a personal trainer. These days there are all sorts of aids which are reasonably inexpensive. Because of the varirty and more accessible prices of aids performers of any level can benefit.

Computerized machines have already been mentioned. These can measure and record heart rate, training zones and calorie expenditure while you are using them (see page 101). While they may be too expensive to have in your own home, they are readily available at fitness centres, leisure centres and sports clubs.

Alternatively, there is an extensive range of watches or wrist worn monitors available on the market which can also provide a variety of information.

An exercise trainer has a calorie burned measurement function which is calibrated after feeding in information about age, weight and sex. It can work out the calories burned off during training, set targets and store information.

Specially designed watches for marathon runners can even count your strides and calculate distances covered. They can also store up to 30 sets of data.

Some watches can take the pulse rate, **systolic** blood pressure and **diastolic** blood

Denise Lewis wearing her specially designed pentathlon suit in the 2000 Sydney Olympics

pressure and record and feed back the information.

Performance timers are also available to give information on distances travelled and time taken and they are becoming more and more advanced. There was equipment available previously to monitor and record this type of information, but it was never so convenient or as portable and easy to use.

Being able to monitor, as these watches do, is very important and valuable to anyone taking part in physical education.

The greatest change and development these aids have introduced is their size. They are now compact enough to be available to and used by anyone.

TASK 7

Within your teaching group, find out which would be the most popular training aid watch and why.

SECTION 3

Factors affecting individual performance and participation
and
Social and cultural factors affecting participation

This section looks at the way that sport and society are very closely linked. Sport has existed for hundreds of years in various forms and today the sports industry is one of the most important in society.

Sport is usually looked upon as being a positive influence and taking part is encouraged at all levels. This section looks at the ways in which various factors can encourage greater participation in sport as well as the ways in which they can improve levels of performance.

Many of the social factors identified here, such as the role of schools, the use of leisure time and the provision of facilities, are very closely linked to the content of the earlier sections referring to health, fitness and training. These physiological factors interrelate with the social factors and should not be considered as two separate areas. For instance, one of the main reasons for providing physical education within schools is to ensure that young people are taught the benefits of maintaining a healthy lifestyle, through maintaining fitness levels and considering the need for regular and suitable training. As well as this, many of these factors raise the levels of knowledge and understanding, thus improving the levels of participation and performance. An excellent example of this would be the influence of the media, which not only gives out a mass of information in its various forms but also encourages greater participation with higher levels of understanding from those who take part.

The units within this section also interrelate. Sponsorship is very closely linked not only to the media but also to international sport, the finance of sport and sports bodies and organizations. It is important to understand that many of the units in this section are prone to change at a rapid rate. Many issues, such as those relating to amateurs and professionals, sponsorship, finance, organization of sport and the media have aspects which can change almost overnight. You therefore have a responsibility to keep up-to-date with issues as they change. You may find that you have to make use of the media almost daily and many of the tasks in this section ask you to do just that!

131

It is very important, however, as without proper organization the levels of participation would not be as high as they are.

- internationally
- nationally
- regionally
- locally.

Competitive sport is different from recreational sport because it needs careful organization. It attracts people who like something which has rules and regulations. It also has to be structured so that you can progress through the various levels and stages.

An example of this is how a netball player progresses from the very basic level to the very highest level. Most players would start by playing for their school team. From there they could go on to play for their town or region. The region might be split up into a county, combined county or national region.

The Royal and Ancient Golf Club – the headquarters of golf

The next level would be to play at a national level and if you were good enough to play at this level you would have achieved international status.

That would be the route a player would take if they were able to progress right to the top at their sport, but it is not the way that the sports themselves are organized. They start at the top and work down.

TASK 1

Choose a sporting activity which is played locally to you. Chart the various levels at which it is played in your area, right up to the international team for that sport.

National governing bodies

These are the organizations which actually run the sports. They decide on:

- finance
- fixtures
- discipline
- team selection
- coaching
- promotion.

The national governing bodies do not organize this at all of the levels, but they make the rules and issue the guidelines which all the regional and local organizations have to follow.

The vast majority of people who help with the organization of sport do so as volunteers, but at the top level there are often full time, paid officials in the most responsible jobs.

TASK 2

*Find out who the national governing bodies are for **three** different sports.*

Club structure

At all levels of sport, the main organizers are clubs. No matter how big or how small they are, they all have much the same structure and organization. They all have:

■ a chairperson
■ a vice-chair
■ a secretary
■ a treasurer
■ committee members
■ members.

All those listed above the members would be the officials of the club and they would usually be elected by the members. Elections usually take place at the Annual General Meeting which is a time when all of the members meet and decide who they want to represent them, and who will do what job.

This is all decided and controlled by the club's **constitution**, which is a set of rules and guidelines for running the club. The constitution will have been discussed and accepted by the majority of the members.

Chairperson

This is the person who has overall control of meetings which take place and they may also represent the club at other meetings. This is the most senior job in the club and the chairperson is generally considered to be the one in charge.

Vice-chair

This person deputizes for the chairperson, running meetings and representing the committee when the chairperson is unable to do so. The vice-chair needs to be ready to take over at short notice.

Secretary

This person mainly deals with all of the written work, for example answering and writing letters and keeping the minutes (notes) of meetings. It is usually one of the busiest jobs, especially in a big club where there is a lot of paperwork.

Officials of a small sports club discussing club business

Treasurer

This person deals with all of the club's financial matters. She or he would generally have to control a bank account to pay bills, collect subscriptions from members and collect match fees.

Committee members

This is a selection of people who are elected by the members and they have regular meetings to make decisions on behalf of the club. There are often sub-committees for such things as team selection or, perhaps, discipline.

Members

Everyone who belongs to the club will be a member and they may pay an annual subscription to belong. You cannot have any of the other positions in the club if you are not a member.

TASK 3

Find out the structure of one of your local clubs. Try to find out who the officials are.

133

Functions of clubs

All sports clubs have a variety of functions but there are many which are common to most clubs.

- *Provision of facilities* – who provides facilities and who finances them is dealt with in more detail in unit 38, but all clubs have to have somewhere to play their sport and they often provide it and maintain it themselves.

- *Organization of competitions and competitive play* – the types of competitions and how they are organized is dealt with in unit 37, but clubs will arrange competitive play within the club, between their own members and also against other clubs.

- *Promotion of their sport* – the clubs provide the opportunity to play their particular sport and they would promote it and encourage as many people as possible to take it up.

- *Encouragement for juniors* – all clubs need to get young players involved to ensure the club will keep going and prosper in the future. Many have junior sections, organized particularly to suit young players. For instance, tennis clubs often have short tennis for juniors to prepare them for the full game when they are older.

- *Community status and involvement* – large, or even professional, clubs can play a major role in a community. Not only can they get people involved in taking part but they can also get them involved as spectators and supporters.

Local authority provision

Local authorities such as local councils have a duty to provide facilities for their area and one of the most important is sporting and leisure facilities. These usually come in two categories:

- school and educational facilities

- leisure centres.

Schools need sports facilities so that Physical Education can be taught, so there is usually an arrangement for **dual use** or **dual provision**. Dual use means that the school has priority use of the sports facilities during the day and at other times they are available for some public use. It makes more sense as the public can use the facilities rather than have them standing empty. Many people with jobs would not be

Dual use of facilities allows the public access to this school gym

able to use the facilities during the school day anyway. This is a very popular option as it means that only one facility has to be provided.

With dual provision, a leisure centre, or perhaps a sports hall, is built so that it can be used by both the school and the public. Again, the use has to be shared but it may mean that the public uses some of the facilities while the school uses others.

TASK 4

Try to find examples of dual use and dual provision facilities in your area. Make a list of the types of activities you can do there.

Sporting links

There are usually very good links between schools and clubs because most school pupils are encouraged to join clubs so that they can do more sport.

Many schools run clubs after school (these are known as **extra-curricular activities**) and this is something that has happened for many years. Many of the teams formed in the past were known as 'former pupils' because they developed from clubs which were formed after school hours and kept going even after the pupils had left school. Some of these clubs still exist today.

With the wide range of sporting activities now available it is not always possible for schools to devote enough time to all activities, so clubs are vital to give young people the opportunity to spend more time on the sports of their choice.

Clubs are also very keen to keep their standards up so they will be on the look out for young members to join them. Professional clubs, such as soccer clubs, will even send scouts (members of staff whose job it is to try and spot, and sign on, talented players) to school matches to get youngsters to join them.

It is very good for the image of the school to have their pupils playing sport at a high standard so these links are encouraged and are very strong.

If clubs can get a player involved and into the club at a young age they do not have to spend vast amounts of money on buying

Soccer clubs often have youth policies to train promising young local players

players from other clubs in the future. This is why many clubs run youth policies and run several youth teams made up of local youngsters.

TASK 5

Make a list of the strong sporting links which exist in your area between schools and clubs and professional sporting clubs.

Research which has been carried out has clearly shown that many young people lose interest in sport when they leave school and stop taking part in it. This was known as the Wolfendon Gap (named after the writer of a report) and it showed that young people did sporting activity when it was compulsory at school but then often did none at all as soon as they left.

This is why the setting up of strong links with clubs was encouraged, to encourage more to continue to take part. The situation has also been greatly improved by the increased number of facilities available. There was a time when young people could not continue with particular activities because the only facilities were in the schools and they could not use them once they had left.

TASK 6

Do a survey within your class, or group, to find out how many people are members of clubs outside of school. Find out how many will continue to be members once they have left school.

Most sport is competitive and this is often one of the main reasons people like to play it. The competition has to be organized and this may take the form of:

■ knockout

■ ladders

■ round robin

■ league.

Many competitions use a mixture of the ways listed above because the organizers must try to find the fairest possible way to run their competition.

Knockout competitions

This method is usually used when there is a very large entry to the competition because it is the quickest and easiest way to organize it.

The event is always played in rounds, so that each team plays against one other team and the winner goes through to the next round. This means that the number of teams who take part is halved in each round as the losing teams drop out. This is one of the main disadvantages of this type of competition, teams only get one chance. The second best team in the whole competition could get knocked out in the very first round and a less skilful team could get to the final.

One way of avoiding this is to have **seeded** players or teams. The Wimbledon tennis tournament uses this system. The best players, or teams, are spread out evenly in the draw for the competition so that the two top ones can only meet if they get through to the final. Of course, this depends on the committee who decides on the seeds getting the seeding order right. This is often done with the help of computers which keep a check of all the players' results and gives them a ranking position.

Another method is to have preliminary rounds to the competition where less skilled

teams play against each other first for the right to play against the top teams, or players, in the final rounds. This is often done in soccer. It happens in the World Cup (here it is played in qualifying groups) and also in the Football Association Cup (the FA Cup).

Most of the international competitions in any sport end in a knockout stage and start with a qualifying stage.

Organizing a knockout competition can appear to be very complicated because you must have rounds with possibly 128, 64, 32, 16, 8, 4 and finally 2 players or teams. You may not always have the right number of entries for the system, but the competition will not work any other way. The solution is to have a preliminary round with byes (no games played) for some of the teams or players so that you

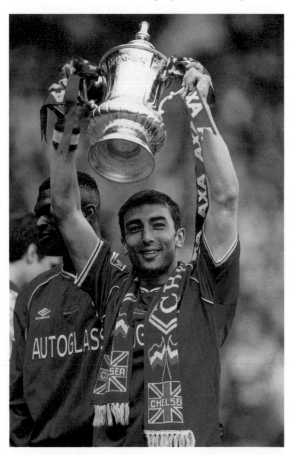

The FA Cup is one of the oldest knockout competitions

end up with the right numbers for your proper first round.

So that teams or players can have further opportunities to play when they have been knocked out in their first game, you can also organize a **plate competition**. This is another knockout competition which all the losers go on to play among themselves.

TASK 1

a   On a piece of paper work out how you would organize a knockout competition for 21 teams named A to U.

b   Organize a knockout competition for your group in one of the activities you do. Decide whether you may need to seed players, have preliminary rounds or byes, or a plate competition.

Ladders

These are more 'social competitions' as they tend to be played in clubs where there is not so much at stake for winning and losing.

All players have their names listed on a long 'ladder' and the idea is to challenge people above you on the ladder to games and then to take their place in a higher position. There are usually certain rules about how high up you can challenge someone, so the bottom player could not challenge the top one and take their place. They would have to work their way up gradually.

The top player in the club would then be at the top of the ladder and other players would be trying to improve their position. One of the main drawbacks to this system is that it does not encourage new players to join as it may take them a long time to work their way up the ladder.

TASK 2

Choose **one** activity which is played locally to you. Find a club which has a ladder competition for members taking part. What makes the ladder system of competition particularly suitable for members of this club?

Squash clubs often have a ladder competition

Round robin

In this type of competition all of those taking part play against each other. One of the drawbacks of this type of competition is that you can only do it if you have a small number of entries, otherwise it would take too long.

This system is often used for individual or pairs events such as tennis but there is usually some sort of qualifying stage for it and the round robin is used in the final stages.

One of the main advantages is that it does give all the top players a chance to play against each other and it is an attractive type of competition for spectators because all the games should be very close and of a high standard.

TASK 3

Find out about a competition in a sporting activity which is arranged on a round robin basis.

League

This is another very popular type of competition and is often considered to be the hardest to win because it takes place over a very long period of time. If sports have knockout competitions they usually have leagues as well. This is particularly the case with team games.

This method is well suited to competitions with a high number of entries because it gives them all a chance to play and it also makes sure that they play lots of games. Each team, or player, plays against the others at least once (often they play twice, once at home and once away) and they get points for winning or drawing games or matches. They do not usually get any points if they lose the game.

The team that finishes with the most points is the winner of that league. There may be several leagues, with one overall winner of the top league and a system of promotion and relegation in the other leagues. This means that if a team finishes top of their league they go up to the league above them and are promoted. Teams which finish bottom of their league go down a league (it is sometimes also called a division) and are **relegated**.

There are hundreds of leagues which take place in any country in most sports, although it is usually only the national leagues which you hear about. There will be local and regional leagues which teams or players start playing in. By the system of promotion it is possible to work up from playing in a local league right up to a national league, although it would probably take a long time.

The league usually runs for the entire length of the season for that particular sport, so a winning team has to be very consistent over a long time. They cannot usually afford to lose many matches.

Nearly all professional sport is played on a league basis because:

- fixtures can be arranged in advance and publicized

- a certain number of games are guaranteed to be played

- tickets (and season tickets) can be sold a long time in advance

- it is the most profitable system over a long period of time, in terms of finance.

TASK 4

a Find **at least five** different activities which are run as leagues in your area. Find out how many teams play in them in total and from that work out the total number of players regularly involved in the activities.

b Choose a professional sport in your area. Which league do the teams or players play in? Find out how many games they have to play and how many players would be involved in the league in total.

Tickets for league fixtures can be sold in advance to increase the chances of drawing a large crowd

Combined competitions

These are very common and they combine the other types of competition. The advantages and disadvantages of each of these are shown in the chart below.

Whatever type of competition you run there will be claims that it is unfair in one way or another, so a combination is often thought to be the fairest way. The main aims of a competition should be to:

■ have as many games as possible

■ give teams more than one chance to qualify or win

■ allow as many teams to play against each other as possible

■ allow the best team, or player, to win.

Nearly all international sport starts on a league basis, usually in regions (this may be continents or even groups of countries) and then goes on to the final stages. Teams, or players, who qualify may then play in leagues again, or even round robin competitions, before getting to the final stages.

Whatever type you decide to use, there usually always has to be a knockout stage as the ultimate final because:

■ there is more tension and excitement in head-to-head finals

■ leagues can be won and decided before all of the games are played which de-motivates players and teams

■ they are more attractive propositions to the media (television, radio and the press).

TASK 5

a For a recent major international sporting event, trace how teams, or players, had to qualify for the final stages.

b Try to find another event which has a different way of finding the winner and compare the two types of competition.

Activity	Advantages	Disadvantages
Knockout	Easy to organize for large entry. Quickest way to run a tournament.	Teams only get one chance. Best teams or players may not get to the final.
Ladder	Easy to set up and administer. Levels standards of play.	Not suitable for team games and can be off-putting for new players.
Round robin	Easy way to run a small entry competition. Everyone plays everyone.	Not suitable for a large entry. Can take a long time.
League	All teams play against each other, sometimes twice. Rewards consistent teams over a period of time.	May take a long period of time to play. If there is a large entry the leagues are divided up.

Sports facilities vary considerably but fall into two main categories.

- *Outdoor facilities* include sports pitches, water sports areas, outdoor pursuit areas and any natural features which might be used for sporting events such as cross-country courses.

- *Indoor facilities* are usually specifically built for certain sports (such as swimming pools, fitness gyms) or built to be flexible to allow a variety of sports (sports halls or leisure centres).

Outdoor facilities

These may have to be situated in certain places, especially if they need natural features such as lakes, seas or landscapes. If this is the case, the people have to travel to the facility as it is not always possible to build or locate the facility near to where people live.

For sports pitches you just need an available area, preferably of flat land, where a pitch, or pitches can be laid down, prepared and maintained. There are now more and more artificial surfaces being used (see unit 47).

For a sport which uses a natural surface, such as grass, you must have the facility outdoors, otherwise the grass will not grow. Other activities, such as cross-country, use such a large area that it would not be possible to enclose it all indoors. Land is expensive, especially in inner city areas, and many outdoor facilities are located out of towns. There is also pressure on landowners to use their land for more profitable things such as farming or property development.

There have been changes and trends in recent years to make more use of outdoor areas. Many disused quarries and gravel pits have been flooded and turned into lakes to allow for the increased interest in water-based sports such as windsurfing, jet skiing, water skiing and sailing.

TASK 1

*Investigate the outdoor facilities available in your area. Try to find **at least five** different activities which happen at different places.*

Many outdoor areas are used for what are considered to be adventurous outdoor activities –such as canoeing, climbing, mountaineering, orienteering, sailing and skiing. When making provision for this, factors such as the possible risk, access and possible damage to the environment also have to be considered.

Apart from outdoor sports stadiums, it is not easy to get spectators to many outdoor events, often due to the uncertainty of the weather. Bad weather can even result in the activities not taking place. These would certainly put a lot of people off going to watch. However, some outdoor sports such as golf attract very large numbers of spectators.

Indoor facilities

The main difference between indoor and outdoor facilities is that there is some choice of where you could locate indoor ones. However, before this is done there are a great many factors which have to be taken into consideration.

Population and expected use

There is no point in building a facility if there is no one around to use it. Because of this most of the major indoor facilities are built in areas with a large population. The cost of running a facility is very high and you would need a lot of people to use it to make it pay.

Access

People need to be able reach the facility. They may travel by road, rail or even plane (this would be important if you were hoping to hold international events in the facility). All the

Disused gravel pits are now often flooded and used for water sports

transport links need to be considered and either provided or improved.

Parking

For many local facilities the most common way of getting there is to drive. You need suitable and adequate parking space to fit everyone in.

Cost

This is not always just the cost of building the facility but also the cost of the site to build it on. The building cost will be much the same wherever it is but the price of land can vary considerably. Sometimes this will be a very important factor in the location of the facility.

Natural features

Such things as good drainage or climate may be very important when considering where to build stadiums.

Demand

The facility may be intended for a particular activity and you would have to check if there was enough demand in that particular area to justify locating the facility there.

Competition and rival facilities

There is little point in duplicating a facility if one already exists, unless the demand is so great that one facility cannot satisfy it. You may be able to build several sports halls in an area and have them all well used, but it is unlikely that including a swimming pool or ice rink with each of them would be worthwhile.

Flexibility and versatility

If the facility can be used for other things this will be an advantage. Some activities occur as trends and if the interest drops, and that is all the facility can be used for, it causes problems. This is why so many leisure centres are the main provision, because they are flexible in what they can put on and provide.

Dual use

Many school sites are dual use so that facilities are not duplicated in the area. Therefore it may be worth updating or improving existing facilities rather than building brand new ones.

TASK 2

Consider the factors above and suggest a facility you would like to see provided in your area. Say where you would want it and the reasons for locating it there.

Providers of facilities

Providers of facilities fall into two distinct categories – the private sector and the public sector.

Private sector

This covers any type of facility which is owned and run by individuals or firms or companies. They have to be run as businesses because the main aim of their owners is to make money. This type of facility includes:

■ health clubs

■ hotels, with sports facilities such as pools, fitness suites, swimming pools

■ holiday camps

■ outward bound centres

■ riding schools.

In addition, there are also many clubs which are run privately and are either owned by the members (see unit 36) or by companies. These can include some of the major facilities within the country, such as:

■ football stadiums and grounds

■ rugby grounds

■ Centres of Excellence

■ golf clubs

■ tennis clubs

■ squash clubs

■ sports stadiums (such as Crystal Palace)

■ large venues which stage major sporting events, such as the Millennium Stadium in Cardiff, Birmingham International Conference Centre, the Albert Hall.

One thing that all of these have in common is that they must be able to make money, or at least break even financially. Clubs with members are usually quite happy just to break even because their main intention is to provide facilities which can be used. They do not usually need to employ many staff as many of the jobs would be done by the members.

However, the larger companies would want to make large profits and they would probably have to spend a lot of money paying staff and for the upkeep of their facilities. Some of the soccer clubs, such as Manchester United and Tottenham Hotspur are PLCs (public limited companies) and they have shareholders. This means that they are major companies just like any others not connected with sport, and they are expected to make money and to pay some of the profits to the shareholders in dividends.

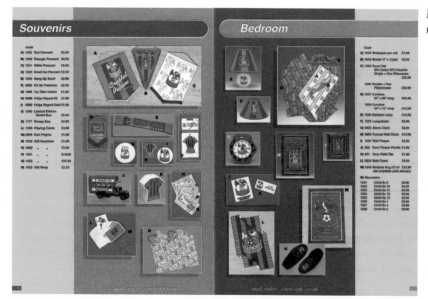

Many clubs sell a variety of merchandise to make extra money

TASK 3

a Make a list of as many small clubs in your area as you can which are owned and run by the members.

b Find **at least two** major sports facilities in your area which are privately run and find out who the owners are.

c Find a financial shares section of a newspaper and see how many limited companies connected with sport you can find, other than those mentioned above.

Public sector

Public sector facilities are owned and run by local authorities or councils. They do not run a private membership scheme. People still have to pay to use them but anyone can do so. These include places such as:

- leisure centres
- sports halls
- swimming pools
- sports pitches
- schools
- town halls.

All of these are financed from the taxes paid by local people, which are meant to provide amenities in their area. Some of the money goes on road maintenance, street lighting and a great many other things, but some also goes towards providing facilities for anyone to use.

The cost of building these facilities is very high. A swimming pool, for example, would cost several million pounds to build and hundreds of thousands of pounds a year to maintain and run. This is because of the complicated procedure needed to heat, clean and maintain the water and the pool itself. It is a fact that there is not a public swimming pool in the country that makes money.

So how do they get built and stay open? The answer is that they are subsidized by the local authority (and therefore by local taxpayers) and kept going although they are losing money. This is also how they are able to keep the cost of using the facility quite low and even to have special very low rates for some people or even free use for others.

All local authorities aim to provide facilities for people in their area, although it is a discretionary requirement, and in some places sporting and leisure facilities are given a priority.

The fact that they are able to subsidize the facilities means that they can often provide a great deal as they do not have to make money from them. There are very few privately owned swimming pools or leisure centres in the UK for this reason. The building and running costs would be too great ever to allow a profit to be made.

One problem can be that people living in rural areas do not have the same access to leisure facilities as people living in large cities or towns. Often, the facilities they have available are scaled down and if they wish to use a major facility they will have to travel quite a way to do so. Local authorities in highly populated areas often have large budgets and are therefore able to spend more money on bigger and better facilities.

TASK 4

a List some of the publicly owned facilities available in your area.

b Who is the main provider of the public facilities in your area?

c Try to find out the building cost and running cost of one of the publicly owned facilities in your area. Your local authority may be able to give you these details.

This unit looks at the ways sport is organized and looked after – without this organizational structure the amount of participation would not be so high. One of the main aims of all these organizations is to increase participation wherever possible.

Sport England

The official logo of Sport England

In 1997 the former Sports Council was split into an English Sports Council and a UK Sports Council (now known as UK Sport). There are separate sports councils for Scotland, Wales and Northern Ireland.

In March 1999 the English Sports Council was rebranded as Sport England. Its three main aims are:

- to get more people involved in sport
- to provide more places to play sport
- to present more medals through higher standards of performance in sport.

At present this new organization intends to continues with some of the initiatives and aims of its predecessor, the Sports Council as well as new programmes. These include:

Participation

Various surveys have been carried out to see how many people participate in sport. Only 10 per cent of women and 25 per cent of men take part in outdoor sport. For indoor sport it is 18 per cent of women and 33 per cent of men. Nationally, there are over 21.5 million adults and 7 million young people who participate in sport and physical recreation at least once a month. Sport England aims to increase participation through the more People programme by:

- *developing programmes* such as Active Sports, Active Schools and Active Communities
- *running campaigns* to provide information about sports and encourage non-participants to take part
- *funding development staff* to help the governing bodies for different sports and local authortities
- *organizing programmes* to promote sport through other agencies.

Facilities

The objective of Sport England's development work is to ensure correct facilities are in the correct place and are maintained at the highest standard possible. Its plan of action includes:

- *encouraging* new and improved facilities by giving advice and financial assistance (through the Sport England Lottery Fund)
- *researching and preparing* efficient and economical standard designs for sports buildings and systems
- *designing, building and testing* innovative facilities and systems, including artificial playing surfaces and the use of computers
- *identifying* good practice of design, facilities or management to be used elsewhere
- *funding research* and feasibility studies into sports requirements.

Standards of performance

To try to ensure that there is as much sporting success as possible, especially at international level, these initiatives are in place:

- *five centres of excellence:*
- Crystal Palace
- Bisham Abbey
- Lilleshall
  (all the above are multi-purpose sports centres for swimming, tennis, gymnastics, athletics, football etc.)

A cricket coaching scheme run by the National Coaching Foundation

- Plas y Brenin (mountain activities)
- Holme Pierrepont (water sports)

■ *offering support*, often financially, to governing bodies of sport for excellence programmes, improving standards, coaching, international competition, facilities and equipment

■ *funding of the National Coaching Foundation* to provide support for the development of coaching

■ *finding and encouraging* sponsors for top class sport.

Information

Sport England continues to provide information and data and promote sport:

■ through a national information centre and ten regional offices (now run by Sport England)

■ by briefing journalists, politicians, central and regional government, students and private organizations

■ by researching and publishing data on all subjects to do with sport

■ by running conferences and exhibitions to do with sport.

Finance of Sport England

Sport England is funded by the government and the money it receives goes towards developing sport at all levels. In addition, Sport England is responsible for distributing National Lottery funds that are allocated for the development of sport in England and it does this through the Sport England Lottery Fund.

To help with the efficient running of the organization there are ten regional offices throughout England. Their job is to bring together local interest, including local authorities, voluntary organizations and the regional branches of governing bodies. The developments in regional offices are backed up by secretarial and administrative staff.

TASK I

Find out information regarding the programmes Active Sports, Active Schools and Active Communities.

International Olympic Committee (IOC)

This is the governing body of the Olympic Games. Its main functions are:

- to select host cities for the summer and winter Games

- to approve the sports to be included in the Olympics

- to work with the host city, international governing bodies and international sports federations to plan the Games.

New members of the IOC are elected by the current members and a representative may be elected from any nation that has a national Olympic committee. Usually any one nation only has one representative but nations which have hosted the Games may have two.

Members used to be elected for life but any member elected since 1965 must retire at the age of 76. There is an executive board which handles many decisions and this is led by a president (who serves for eight years, but can then be re-elected for four-year terms), three vice-presidents and seven members (all these serve for four years).

British Olympic Association (BOA)

This body works closely with the IOC and promotes and organizes all the British involvement with the Olympics. Its main responsibilities are organizing and choosing teams for the Games and raising enough money to send them there.

The Olympic charter does not allow any political involvement so the BOA is constantly involved in fund-raising and this always becomes a high priority as an Olympic year approaches.

The high status of the Games means that sponsorship of the team is quite an attractive proposition for sponsoring bodies.

Central Council of Physical Recreation (CCPR)

This is one of the most important sports organizations. It was founded in 1935 and set two particular objectives:

Angling is one of the many activities promoted by the Central Council of Physical Recreation

1   to encourage as many people as possible (male and female) to participate in all forms of sport and physical recreation

2   to provide the separate governing bodies of the individual sports with a central organization to represent and promote their individual and collective interests.

These objectives are being met as the CCPR now has a membership of 209 British sporting organizations and 68 English ones. The representation varies from the National Federation of Anglers through to the British Judo Association and the Squash Racquets Association.

The CCPR is a completely voluntary, and independent, organization and it has an Executive Committee which is elected from the member governing bodies. There is a team of officers and secretarial staff who help to administer all the policies and decisions which are made.

The CCPR and UK Sport

The CCPR has very strong and close links with UK Sport. There is not a direct connection, so that the CCPR keeps its independence, but it does act as an advisory body.

When UK Sport's predecessor, the Sports Council, was first set up in 1966 (it was then also just an advisory body and did not become properly established until 1972) the CCPR helped greatly with shared knowledge and experience. In 1971 the CCPR actually made over many of its assets to the Sports Council and this included a number of national sports centres which it had established.

The governing bodies did not want to be part of the Sports Council and this is why the CCPR became a consultative body. However, the Sports Council did have a clearly defined responsibility to the CCPR and this is the agreement that was made:

'The Sports Council agrees that (so long as the CCPR is a body representing national organizations of sport and physical recreation as a whole) the Sports Council will make such resources and facilities available to the CCPR without cost to the CCPR as may be reasonably required.'

Because the membership of the CCPR is so large it has grouped the governing bodies into six separate divisions:

- games and sports
- interested organizations
- major spectator sports
- movement and dance
- outdoor pursuits
- water recreation.

Each of these divisions has the same administration organization which reports back to the main body.

Funding of the CCPR is very important because it is such a large body. Funding is through:

- donations from governing bodies
- sponsorship from industry and commerce under the 'Sponsors of Sport' scheme
- sponsorship by individuals or companies
- sale and marketing of CCPR publications and research material
- contracted financial support from UK Sport.

The CCPR has been successful in raising these amounts. In 1994 sponsors contributed £275 million and the advisory service of the CCPR raised more than £250,000 through commercial sponsorship. Services provided include:

- *representing its members' interests* – this can include media campaigns and through formal and informal contact with other organizations
- *analysis of issues* – this varies from developing women's sport, looking at competitive sport in schools, and sport and drugs
- *liaison with the government* – there are both formal and informal contacts which effectively work in both directions and this has been used for advice on sport in schools in the past
- *liaison with local authorities* – as these are the greatest providers of facilities in the country this is a very important link
- *financial management and advice* – this is a service which the member bodies find very useful. One important one is that the CCPR offers schoolchildren a scheme for full protection against sporting injuries
- *international contacts* – this includes setting up festivals and conferences
- *information service* – the CCPR produces a wide range of publications on a full range of activities.

It is not just amateur sport which has connections with the CCPR but professional sports as well. One of the CCPR's major projects recently has been the Community Sports Leaders Award Scheme. Research showed that there are many volunteers who work in sport (50 million hours a year in total) so a scheme was set up to provide a basic award which is now provided at three levels:

- preliminary
- basic expedition training
- higher (Hanson Award).

So far, there have been over 2500 courses and 35,000 leaders have qualified.

Governing bodies

Each sport has to be organized and administered separately. The main responsibilities of the governing bodies are:

- organizing local and national competitions
- selecting teams for international competitions such as the Olympic Games and the various World Championships
- keeping players and participants informed
- maintaining relationships with the media
- drafting the rules and laws of the game
- advancing the special interests of the sport.

They are also to be represented as members of the CCPR (see page 146).

TASK 2

Find out the governing body of **at least one** sport for each of the six divisions of sport represented on the CCPR (see page 147).

National Coaching Foundation (NCF)

This was originally set up in 1983 by the Sports Council with the intention of organizing coaching in all the different sports. At that time it was based at Leeds Polytechnic but it is now a nationwide organization with different centres at colleges throughout the country.

The NCF is now a totally independent body with a committee made up of members from UK Sport, the CCPR, the BOA and various other interested sports bodies.

The National Trust

The National Trust was first formed in 1895 and it was given legal status in 1907 after the National Trust Act. This gave the Trust the right to designate its land 'inalienable' which means that property and land owned by it cannot be sold or mortgaged. It will always be the property of the National Trust.

One of the successful NCF coaches at work with a young gymnast

The Trust is a charity and it is the largest landowner and conservation society in Britain. Throughout the country it owns 570,000 acres with over 140,000 acres of fell, dale, lake and forest in the Lake District alone. Access to land and property of the Trust is available to members, who pay an annual fee. However, much of the open land, moorland and coastal stretches are looked after and maintained by the Trust with free access to everyone.

Many walkers and people who enjoy outdoor activities are very grateful for the work the National Trust does because it makes all of these areas available to them for their leisure pursuits.

Countryside Commission

This was created under the Countryside Act in 1968 and replaced the National Parks Commission. It created over 160 country parks which are open and available to the public. This allows anyone who enjoys the countryside and outdoor pursuits activities access to areas they can enjoy. It also makes sure that access is free and that these areas are open to all.

The Arts Council

This was incorporated in 1945 with a special responsibility for music, drama and visual arts. More recently it has had a greater responsibility for dance. This has been important for people connected with physical education as dance has to be taught in schools to satisfy the National Curriculum.

The Arts Council of England is one of the organizations which can benefit from the National Lottery as it is one of the bodies to which funds are given.

Youth organizations

There are many youth organizations which provide a lot of sporting and leisure activities.

These mainly fall into two categories:

- youth clubs and organizations such as the National Association of Boys Clubs

- uniformed organizations such as the Guides, the Scouts and the Air Training Corps.

These organizations often promote many outdoor pursuits, providing training and expertise. Many of them run their own qualification and award schemes which provide a very good basic knowledge.

The organizations also have access to (or own) facilities which are used for various leisure activities and they often run organizations and competitions. The National Association of Boys Clubs, for example, runs many boxing tournaments.

Walkers making full use of the countryside

Competing internationally is every performer's ultimate aim. It is one of the main reasons for some people taking up sport and continuing to participate in it.

The Olympic Games

The earliest recorded Olympic Games took place in 776 BC in the stadium of Olympia, which is where the Olympics get their name. They were held in honour of the God Zeus. Even that long ago, the stadium in which the Games took place was quite impressive as there was enough room for 40,000 spectators.

These Games were held every four years and all hostilities and wars stopped while the Games took place. Typical events at that time were wrestling, boxing, running (the main event was over 200 yards), discus, javelin, long jump and chariot racing. It is interesting to note that nearly all of those events still take place today.

The Games carried on in this way for many years until the reign of Emperor Theodosius in AD 394. He thought the Games had lost their religious meaning and that the performers only took part for the riches of winning, so he stopped the Games.

The Olympics were not held again until 1500 years later when they were re-launched in 1896 in Athens, Greece. The links with the original Olympics went further than simply holding them in the same country. Many traditions were established based on the old Games. Before each Olympics a torch is lit at Olympia using the sun's rays and this torch is carried by a relay of runners to the host city's stadium to light a flame which then burns throughout the Games.

Thirteen nations entered the Games of 1896, and the total number of athletes was 285. They were all men as women were not allowed to enter.

The modern Olympics

The Olympic Games which have taken place since 1896 are referred to as the modern Olympics. They were started largely due to the efforts and determination of one man.

The spectacular opening ceremony of the Sydney Olympics

Baron Pierre de Coubertin was a French educationalist who had been very impressed with the way that sport was organized and run in England. He had made several visits and liked the way that events such as the Henley Regatta were organized. This, together with the fact that in 1875 some German archaeologists had discovered the ruins of the original stadium in Olympia, made him decide to start up a movement and reintroduce the games. So, in 1894 the International Olympic Committee was formed and it set about the task of organizing the Games for 1896.

Baron de Coubertin believed that the Olympic movement which he had founded would promote world peace and harmony. One of his famous quotes is displayed on the scoreboard at the opening of each Olympic Games as it is what he based his ideas on:

'The most important thing in the Olympic Games is not to win but to take part. Just as the most important thing in life is not the triumph but the struggle.'

The International Olympic Committee originally consisted of people chosen by De Coubertin himself but it is now a very large body with representatives from all of the participating nations. It is this committee which decides where the Games are to be held. De Coubertin decided that the Games should move all around the world and be awarded to a city rather than a country. Now, cities have to make a bid to stage the Olympic Games and the final decision can be made six years before, to give the host city time to prepare.

At one time, not many cities were prepared to host the Games because they were very expensive and usually ran at a loss. This situation changed after the 1984 Games in Los Angeles where the marketing and sponsorship of the Games resulted in a 'surplus' being made. In theory the Olympics should not run at a profit, which is why they used the word 'surplus'. Once cities – and countries – realized that there was an opportunity to promote themselves, improve facilities and standards and make money as well, the whole business of bidding for and staging the Games took on more importance.

Nearly as much fuss and expense is involved in making a bid to be the host as there is in actually staging the Games themselves.

Host countries and venues

Year	Summer	Winter
1896	Athens, Greece	Not held
1900	Paris, France	Not held
1904	St. Louis, USA	Not held
1908	London, England	Not held
1912	Stockholm, Sweden	Not held
1916	World War I, none held	
1920	Antwerp, Belgium	Not held
1924	Paris, France	Chamonix, France
1928	Amsterdam, Holland	St. Moritz
1932	Los Angeles, USA	Lake Placid
1936	Berlin, Germany	Garmisch
1940	World War II, none held	
1944	World War II, none held	
1948	London, England	St. Moritz
1952	Helsinki, Finland	Oslo, Norway
1956	Melbourne, Australia	Cortina, Italy
1960	Rome, Italy	Squaw Valley, USA
1964	Tokyo, Japan	Innsbruck, Austria
1968	Mexico City	Grenoble, France
1972	Munich, Germany	Sapporo, Japan
1976	Montreal, Canada	Innsbruck, Austria
1980	Moscow, USSR	Lake Placid, USA
1984	Los Angeles, USA	Sarayevo, Yugoslavia
1988	Seoul, S. Korea	Calgary, Canada
1992	Barcelona, Spain	Albertville, France
1994	–	Lillehammer, Norway
1996	Atlanta, USA	–
1998	–	Nagano, Japan
2000	Sydney, Australia	–
2002	–	Salt Lake City, USA
2004	Athens, Greece	–
2006	–	Turin, Italy

TASK I

Either find out which cities bid to become the hosts for the last Olympic Games to be held *or* find out which cities are bidding to be the hosts for future Olympic Games.

The recent Games and some hitches

The Olympic Games were the first major international sporting event and they are still the most important and successful of all of the events which take place. However, things have not always run smoothly and nearly all of the recent ones have been affected by problems of one sort or another. The following is a brief description of the major events which have affected the Games.

1936, Berlin

The decision to award these Games to Berlin was made in 1931, two years before Adolph Hitler and his Nazi party came to power in Germany.

One of the main beliefs of Hitler and the Nazis was that there was a master race, known as the Aryans. These people were blond and fair skinned and were true Germans. The Nazis despised the Jews and by the time of the Olympics had started to persecute them and introduce separate laws for them.

Hitler tried to use the Berlin Games to promote all of these ideas and they were used as a propaganda exercise. One of the main reasons it failed was due to the success of a black American athlete called Jesse Owens.

Jesse Owens ended up winning four gold medals in the track and field events, much to Hitler's obvious disapproval. The American team had only narrowly voted to attend the Games, because of Hitler's well known views on black athletes and Jews. The success of the many black athletes in the American team was a great embarrassment for Hitler and stopped him achieving what he had set out to do.

This was the most extreme case of political interference in any of the Olympic Games and it did make the organizers far more careful in selecting hosts in the future.

1968, Mexico City

One of the main controversies about these Games was that they were awarded to Mexico City in the first place. This was because it is situated at a very high altitude and this helps the performance of athletes who train in these conditions. It also assists athletes in the shorter, more explosive events. There was genuine concern for performers in longer events in case the rarefied atmosphere caused them difficulties.

The cost of putting on the event was also criticized. Mexico was a very poor country with poor housing and food shortages. A vast amount of money was spent on just staging the Games. The city of Tokyo, which had held the Games four years earlier, had spent $200 million and it was doubtful if Mexico could really afford the Games.

Some black American athletes gave a 'Black Power' salute during the medal ceremony, by raising a black gloved fist. The first and third runners in the 200 metres, Tommie Smith and John Carlos, plus the 400 metre relay team were sent home for doing so. The athletes took this action to highlight the way that black people were treated in America. At that time there was a great deal of prejudice against black citizens in the United States and the athletes chose this way to make their protest and make the world more aware of the problem.

Jesse Owens on his way to winning the 200 metres final at the Berlin Games in 1936

One of the Palestinian terrorists with a member of the negotiating team during the hostage crisis in 1972

There was another Black Power protest by two Americans, Vince Matthews and Wayne Collett, during a medal ceremony in the Munich Games when they failed to stand to attention. However, these Games were completely dominated by a terrorist attack on some of the athletes.

There was unrest in the Middle East and a group of Palestinian terrorists attacked members of the Israeli team. Eight terrorists attacked the Israeli quarters, killed two of the team and took nine others hostage. After a gun battle (seen throughout the world on television), all of the hostages, five terrorists and a German police officer were killed.

The security aspect of staging the Games was highlighted and was to become a major consideration for the future Games.

1976, Montreal

South Africa had been banned from the Games since 1964 (Tokyo) because of the apartheid policy which existed in that country (see unit 48). However, a rugby team from New Zealand had toured South Africa and thereby had upset most of the other African nations. The African nations threatened to boycott the Games unless the New Zealand team were banned.

New Zealand took part and the African nations stayed away, a total of 30 nations altogether did not go. This was to be the start of a long period of boycotts for various reasons.

The financial cost of these Games was very high. After the incident in Munich the security had to be greatly increased and this was on top of the enormous cost of staging the Games. The city of Montreal continued to pay off the debt of staging the Games for many years.

TASK 2

See if you can find out about any controversial events that occurred in any other major international competitions.

153

1980, Moscow

The choice of Moscow for these Games had been quite controversial because the Soviet Union did not have a very good record on human rights. However, they were one of the most successful competing countries in the history of the Olympics and had never staged it before.

To make matters worse, the Soviet Union invaded the neighbouring country of Afghanistan in late 1979 and still had an invasion force there in 1980.

It was too late to change the venue for the Games but many countries demanded that the Soviet Union withdraw its forces or they would boycott the Games.

The Soviet Union refused to withdraw its troops and many countries had to decide whether or not to send competitors. Some countries, such as the USA, refused to send any. Great Britain advised its competitors against going but did not stop them. As a result, a total of 52 nations, including the USA and Canada, boycotted and many individuals also decided not to go.

Many thought the Games were devalued because of this. The American teams were always very strong and with so many nations away the standard was not always as high as it had been.

1984, Los Angeles

As the venue is chosen six years in advance, the International Olympic Committee could not avoid America staging the Olympics immediately after it had boycotted the Moscow Games. There was a great fear that the Soviet Union would retaliate against the USA, and it did.

The Soviet Union, and fourteen other nations, boycotted the Games. The official reason they gave was concern over security arrangements. There was still ill feeling between the USA and the Soviet Union over the invasion of Afghanistan and there were threats of demonstrations in America against Soviet performers.

The first of the opening ceremony spectaculars was at Los Angeles in 1984

There is little doubt that the worry about security was a convenient excuse for the Soviet Union to get its own back and nearly all of the other countries that boycotted were influenced by this, as they were also communist countries.

Another excuse was that the Games were being over commercialized. The staging of the Games and its organization followed the American tradition of showmanship and the opening ceremony was one of the most spectacular ever seen. The whole event was sponsored by large international companies and, for the first time, the Games ran at a large profit. All of this was against what the communist countries believed in.

1988, Seoul

Seoul is in South Korea and there had been a longstanding dispute between them and the neighbouring country of North Korea. There had been a war between the two countries in 1952 and the situation in 1988 was not much better. The IOC was criticized for awarding them the Games and there was a great amount of tension, right up until the start, that the facilities would not be ready and that North Korea would interfere. The North Koreans had already demanded that they be allowed to stage some of the events.

In the end there was very little disruption and the Games were quite successful. There was another boycott by five countries, including North Korea and Cuba. It is likely that more countries would have considered boycotting but the IOC had introduced a rule that if a country boycotted the Games all their officials would be excluded and not allowed to take part in decision-making. This clearly deterred many.

Sadly, the main controversy at these Games involved positive drug tests. In all, ten athletes were banned after testing positive for performance-enhancing drugs. The most famous one was Ben Johnson. He was a Canadian sprinter who won the 100 metres in a world record time and was then stripped of his title two days later.

1992, Barcelona

After all the controversial events which had gone before, the 1992 Games were just about incident free.

A great deal of political change had occurred since the previous Games. The Eastern European communist governments had collapsed and the Soviet Union had ceased to exist. This meant that there was no longer an East and a West Germany but a unified German team. Also, the countries that had previously made up the Soviet Union all now existed in their own right and were able to compete individually. There were twelve new competing states from the former Soviet Union and some individuals, who could not be considered to be from an affiliated nation, competed under the Olympic flag.

Another 'new' face was South Africa which was allowed to return to the Olympics for the first time since 1964. The South Africans had abolished the apartheid system (see unit 48) and were entering a mixed race team.

The total number of official sports was increased to 25 with the addition of badminton and baseball, and the total number of medal events was increased by 20 to 257. There were over 12,000 athletes and officials involved in the Games.

Weightlifter Andrew Davies was one of three British competitors sent home from Barcelona in 1992 for failing a drugs test

There was still some drug controversy as three British competitors – sprinter Jason Livingstone and weightlifters Andrew Saxton and Andrew Davies – were tested positive and sent home.

One of the major changes made by the IOC in recent years was to organize the Winter Olympics to take place between the Summer Olympics. This is why the 1992 Games in Albertville, France were followed two years later by the Games in Lillehammer, Norway. They then continued on a four year cycle in between the summer Games.

With the constantly changing worldwide political situation there will almost certainly be more new member states to each of next Olympic Games. Changes were also made to allow previously professional sports players and performers to compete. The most obvious of these were tennis and basketball, introduced in 1992.

TASK 3

*What problems do you think are likely to occur at the **next** Olympic Games?*

1996, Atlanta

The Games were scheduled to run from 19 July right through to 4 August and there had been some controversy about the switching of the venue at this time of the year. Atlanta, however, had spent six years planning, constructing and organizing the largest Olympics yet.

The high temperatures and high humidity were thought to be potentially dangerous in many of the events. One of the measures the organizers took was to have fans blowing fine mists of water. This was used in many of the cross-country horse riding events.

There were 197 nations taking part and over 11,000 competitors took part in the opening ceremony alone. This meant that the ceremony lasted over four hours, and as a result it was decided to review the format for Sydney in 2000.

By day three there were problems due to the large number of media and spectators who had come along for the event. There were crushes and queues at many of the venues and the IOC criticized the organizers for repeated transportation breakdowns (performers were often late getting to events or struggled to get there at all) and for computer failures which left the media unable to report properly.

Softball was introduced to the Olympics for the first time. Another new sport to be added to the Olympic events was beach volleyball.

Atlanta also saw a great deal of attention focused on the 'Dream Team' of American professional basketball stars.

Irish swimmer Michelle Smith won her third gold medal by day six and insisted her rapid progress was not due to any performance-enhancing drugs. By 1997 Smith had been tested positive and charged, and was eventually banned in 1999. There are still moves to have her medals taken from her.

On day nine, 27 July, there was a tragedy which marred the whole event. A pipe bomb blast in Centennial Olympic Park (a nearby park which had been renamed and was a meeting point for people attending the Olympic Stadium) killed Alice Hawthorne and injured a further eleven people who were attending a concert there.

This brought new fears of terrorist attacks and although the Games continued, security was greatly increased and the park was closed for three days.

At the closing ceremony the IOC president Juan Antonio Samaranch invoked the memory of the eleven Israeli athletes who had been killed in Munich in 1972 and also asked for a minute's silence for the injured and dead from the bomb explosion earlier during the Games.

The American basketball 'Dream Team'

1998, Nagano

On 4 February the Winter Olympics got underway in Japan with estimates that over 1.2 million visitors would arrive to watch competitors from the 72 different competing nations.

The organizers had problems when one of the main events of the Games, the men's downhill, had to be postponed due to bad weather, with heavy snow and high winds.

One of the other main talking points of these Games was the use of new and improved technology in many of the events.

In the skating events the Dutch skaters used revolutionary skates with a hinged mechanism together with specially designed aerodynamically improved one-piece body suits. These were presented to the International Speedskating Union for approval just 48 hours before the events were due to take place – this meant that none of the other competitors could copy them. The Dutch skaters then went on to take the first four places in the 5000 metres race!

There were also protests from other competitors in the luge when the United States and Canadian teams protested about the boots worn by the winner, Georg Hackl. His bright yellow aerodynamically improved boots saved three-hundredths of a second off each of his runs and helped him to win gold.

Dutch speed skaters caused controversy in Nagano by revealing their new, aerodynamically improved suits just 48 hours before the first event

2000, Sydney

This was generally thought to be one of the most successful games of recent times. The Games were very well organized and presented and there was very little in the way of controversy or major incident.

Perhaps the most controversial aspect was the withdrawal of 27 athletes and 13 team officials by the Chinese team just before the Games. They also withdrew an entire rowing team after 'suspicious tests' were returned regarding drugs. The general opinion was that the Chinese had decided to pull out team members rather than risk them failing drug tests during the Games. As it was there were ten positive tests during the event with athletes from eighteen different countries being banned through positive drug tests. An Uzbekistan Olympic official also had two phials of Human Growth Hormone (HGH) seized at Sydney airport just before the Games began.

The drug testing procedures for Sydney were said to be the most advanced and effective yet used. It was claimed that the low levels of performance in many of the events (such as the marathon) were evidence that less cheating had occurred.

These Games also proved to be the most successful ones for the Great Britain team since 1920. This was thought to be largely through the vast amounts of money the National Lottery had made available to performers. A total of £53.7 million had been provided since 1997. Rowing received £9.6 million and proved to be one of the most successful, with two gold medals. One of these medallists was Steve Redgrave, who won his fifth gold medal in a row – a record for an endurance event athlete and an amazing achievement over a twenty-year period!

Other international events

In many ways most other major international events are based on the success of the Olympics. There are several other major 'Games' which take place throughout the world.

Commonwealth Games

The idea of staging some Games for all the members of what was the British Empire (countries previously governed and ruled by Great Britain) was first suggested by Astley Cooper in 1891. It was not until about 40 years later, in 1930, at Hamilton, Ontario, Canada, that the first such Games took place.

There had been similar types of events because just after the 1920 Antwerp Olympics there was an athletics match between the USA and the British Empire, and the same thing happened after the 1924 Paris Olympics.

Originally the organization which ran the games was called the British Empire Games Federation, but this was later changed to the British Commonwealth Games Federation. Any country that is a member of the Commonwealth may take part. The Games follow the format of the Olympics very closely and are also held every four years, following each Olympics by two years.

They have a reputation for being the 'friendly games' and have not been as disrupted by boycotts or scandals as the Olympics.

Venus Williams winning the 2000 women's final at Wimbledon

Pan-American Games

These were started in 1951 and took place in Buenos Aires. They are also modelled on the Olympic Games even down to a copy of the opening ceremony. They take place the year before each Olympics and any country in North or South America may take part.

Wimbledon

The Wimbledon tennis tournament is actually known as the All England Tennis Championships, but it is largely regarded as the most important tennis tournament of all. There is no official World Championship in tennis, but if there were the players would regard Wimbledon to be it.

Originally, Wimbledon was the home of the All England Croquet Club and the members decided to use the well tended croquet lawns to play tennis. In 1877 the first tennis championships were held and apart from breaks for World War I and World War II, they have been held every year since.

In 1968, the organizers took the very bold step of declaring the championship to be an open event so that both amateurs and professionals could play. This was the first major international competition to take this step and it paved the way for the breakdown of barriers in other sports.

World championships

Many different sports stage their own world championships which are now established as major international sporting events. Some of them have only begun fairly recently but it is unusual to find any major sport that does not have one.

Soccer

The world championship in soccer is usually simply called the World Cup. This is because it was one of the first world championships to be held in any of the major sports. The first World Cup was held in Uruguay in 1930. It took the ruling body of soccer, FIFA, quite a long time to get it all organized. When the six member countries met in 1904, they decided to organize

France winning the 1998 soccer World Cup final

a tournament. The principle of the cup was agreed in 1920 and the president, Jules Rimet (after whom the first World Cup trophy was named) was influential in getting it under way.

The choice of Uruguay to host the first World Cup was not unexpected. It had won the Olympic gold in 1924 and 1928, and 1930 was its centenary. The government also offered to pay all of the competing teams' expenses and build a new stadium for 100,000 spectators.

The tournament has continued to be very successful and is televised throughout the world. Its success encouraged other sports to start their own version, in the same way that the Olympics set the standards for other championships.

Cricket

Cricket was quite late organizing a world championship and this was mainly due to the nature of the game. At test level a game lasts for five days and to organize a tournament on this basis would be just about impossible. The development of the one day knockout games meant that cricket could be played in a format that could be used in a tournament.

The first Cricket World Cup was held in 1983 in England and has been played every four years since.

Rugby

The Rugby World Cup was not started until 1987 when New Zealand beat France in the first final on home territory. The second finals were held in England and the third in South Africa. Each tournament has been bigger and more successful than the last.

Specific matches and events

Some sports become international events because of interest in a particular contest, or due to nations promoting their own interests. This is often true of boxing and, in particular, many of the heavyweight contests. One problem is that there are so many versions of the world championship that it is held several times a year.

Test match series, such as those played in cricket and rugby, are considered to be international events and command a lot of attention.

The Superbowl is the climax of the American football season when the final game is played between the winners of the two conferences (that is, the two separate leagues) in America. It is billed as the World Championship but it is only open to American teams.

It seems that if the media can be involved, just about any event can be international.

TASK 4

List as many other major international sporting events as you can.

Sponsorship is now a vital part of sport. Without it many sports would not be able to provide what they do and many performers would not be able to participate at the level they do – some top-level performers would not be able to take part at all without it.

What is sponsored?

The range of sponsorship now covers individuals, teams or clubs, sports and events. It is now very rare to find any aspect of sport where there is not some form of sponsorship.

Individuals

It is not just sportspeople who take part in individual sports who are sponsored. It is increasingly common for individuals within a team to be sponsored, too. Most professional sportspeople are sponsored, often by more than one company. For example, a racing driver's overalls and car are often completely covered with sponsors' names and products. Each sponsor must pay for that space.

Individuals (such as basketball players) may have their own sponsorship for some things, while the team is also separately sponsored.

If the sportsperson is particularly successful they can be paid very large amounts of money and have companies queuing up to sign them. It can reach the stage for some that they make far more out of sponsorship deals than they do from the actual sport itself, in terms of prize money or wages.

TASK 1

Find out the main sponsors for:
a a sportsperson of your choice who plays just as an individual
b one who plays as part of a team.

Teams and clubs

At just about any level, from small local soccer teams to full international teams, there is a great deal of sponsorship. Particularly successful teams can attract a very great amount of sponsorship which can have great benefits (see pages 161–3).

Sometimes local firms and businesses sponsor local teams. This is a good system, as the local teams would not be able to attract major sponsors and small firms or businesses would not be able to afford to sponsor very big clubs.

TASK 2

Find **one** local small team, or club, which is sponsored by a small local company and **one** large local club which is sponsored by a major company.

Sports

Sometimes, the actual sport itself, or its controlling association, is sponsored. This means that all the members of the association, including all the clubs and players, benefit.

Many sports with a good image are chosen by sponsors and they are happy to help the sport nationally, not just in one area.

TASK 3

Find **two** sports which have their own sponsorship deals with firms.

Events

Events have become very popular to sponsor because sponsors are guaranteed to be associated with success and successful teams. They do not have to take the risk that an individual, or team, might fail if they take charge of the whole event and, as long as the event or competition goes smoothly, they are guaranteed to get a lot of free advertising and publicity.

All sorts of events are sponsored, from local gymnastic competitions right through to major international events such as the Olympic Games. In the case of the Olympics, the event is so big that it can attract a large number of sponsors.

Most big events are guaranteed to be a financial success because of the sponsors alone, where in the past they had to rely on making money by people attending.

TASK 4

*Find out the sponsor of a local event or competition and also the main sponsors of **at least one** major international competition.*

Types of sponsorship

Sponsorship can take many forms. It originally started in the days when there was more amateur sport (see unit 44), when it was a way of helping a sportsperson without directly giving them money, as this was not allowed. Now it takes the following forms:

Equipment

As part of a sponsorship arrangement a sportsperson is given all their equipment for their chosen sport. This equipment would obviously be manufactured by the sponsors and could range from sports shoes to rackets, even to specialist training equipment.

Clothing

This does not even have to be the actual clothing worn by the sportsperson when taking part. It can often be extra items such as sun visors or baseball caps with the manufacturer's name on. In some sports there are even rules saying how large the manufacturer's logo can be on clothing and where it may be displayed.

Accessories

Some firms are prepared to pay for their products to be worn even though they have no direct link to the sport. This is why many tennis players are sponsored to wear certain watches (which can be seen on television as the player serves) and cricketers are paid to wear sun glasses.

Transport and travel

This is often at least paid for and, in some cases, it is even provided. Car firms will provide free cars, often with drivers, for competitions and air travel companies will provide free flights. Even at lower levels, coach firms will provide free transport (or at least at a reduced cost) and local garages will provide cars and/or petrol.

Money

Actual payments of money are made and the person sponsored can choose what to spend it on. If all the other aspects are covered then this just becomes an extra income for the sportsperson.

Training

This can be sponsored in several ways. The facilities can be provided, or paid for, or paid time off work can be arranged to enable training to take place. In some sports, such as tennis, personal trainers or coaches are provided for individual players.

Entry fees and expenses

These can mount up and be quite expensive and if not paid for could put a performer off taking part.

Food

This is another very common type of sponsorship. There are many examples of butchers sponsoring field athletes who need a large protein input which they get from meat.

TASK 5

*Find **at least one** example in sport of each of the eight types of sponsorship listed above.*

Benefits for sponsors

Advertising

Sponsoring in any of the ways outlined on pages 160–1 is one of the most effective ways of advertising a product or service. It can also work out to be cheaper than many other forms of advertising, such as television, newspapers, billboards or radio. It also has the added advantage that if the event, or performer, is shown on television they get this as a bonus.

Some products are not allowed to be advertised on television (e.g. cigarettes and other tobacco products) so sponsorship can sometimes be a way around these rules.

Tax relief

The sponsors can claim for any of their sponsoring against the taxes which they have to pay. This means that it can actually save them money to sponsor certain things.

Image

Sport generates a good image like a healthy, successful lifestyle. It is good for companies and products to be associated with this image.

Research and development

By getting performers to use their products, many sponsors are able to try out new developments in materials or equipment to see how well they work.

Goodwill

Although this is closely linked with image, many sponsors are prepared to help as a gesture of goodwill without any guarantee that they will gain from it.

Improved sales

This is probably the single most important benefit to any sponsor. If they have to pay money out in some form then they will wish to get as much back as possible in terms of increased sales of their product. Successful sponsorship, it has been proved, guarantees this.

Acceptable and unacceptable sponsorship

Most sports and sports performers are always on the lookout for sponsorship. Not all forms of sponsorship are seen as acceptable however.

Tobacco companies – Because of the health risks associated with smoking, any form of sponsorship from tobacco companies could be seen to encourage smoking, particularly amongst young people. Associating tobacco with sporting activities could glamorize the image of smoking. The government has very strict guidelines which prohibit the direct advertising of tobacco products. There are moves to have all forms of advertising, including sponsorship, completely banned.

Alcoholic drinks firms – Because of problems associated with alcohol abuse, sponsorship could be seen to glamorize excessive drinking, therefore encouraging young people to drink before they are 18.

Certain legal restrictions on both smoking and drinking are another reason for considering the sponsorship of these types of companies to be unacceptable. Alcoholic drinks companies sponsor senior clubs and competitions (such as the Worthington Cup in soccer), but they are not deemed to be acceptable for any junior sporting situations.

The companies that benefit the most from associations with sport are those that make sports goods. This is why Nike, Reebok and Adidas sponsor as many sports personalities, events and sports as possible. A sponsorship deal arranged between Bolton Football Club and Reebok even resulted in Bolton's new soccer stadium being called the Reebok Stadium! The highest paid sponsored performer currently is Tiger Woods. In 2001, he had at least 12 different sponsorship deals (Nike was one of the main ones), worth a total of £36.4 million!

Many sporting personalities are paid to wear brand name sportswear

TASK 6

a Name a sport and its sponsor which are both commonly associated as having a good image.

b Name **three** sports award schemes and their sponsors.

c Name a sport which has been sponsored, resulting in an increase in interest and participation.

d Give an example of a sport where the clothing worn has been changed to suit a sponsor.

e Give an example of an event taking place at an unusual time in order to satisfy the sponsor.

Advantages and disadvantages of sponsorship

Advantages	Disadvantages
Young and promising sportspeople are able to concentrate on their sport without many of the financial worries.	The sport can lose its own identity and be dictated to by the sponsors. This can happen in the following ways:
Sports can be promoted and encouraged so that participation levels increase.	Rules can be changed at the sponsors' request. This is particularly so in the case of what it is appropriate to wear and sometimes the length of time the event is to last.
The image of the sport can be improved with a good link up to a company which has a good image.	The timing of events is often dictated by sponsors, particularly when the sport is being televised. Times are chosen to suit an international audience and this might not be in the best interest of the performer or the sport.
More money is provided for the sport to pay for administration, facilities, coaching, training and improving standards.	Less successful sports and performers do not receive any sponsorship.
Bigger and better events can be staged and organized.	A bad product image can damage a sport.
Award schemes can be paid for and advertised.	If the sponsor has to withdraw, the sport or performer may not be able to carry on.
New and minority sports can be encouraged and financed.	The sport may become over-commercialized reducing the fun aspect of taking part.
Competitions and leagues can be run, and prizes and money provided.	
Sponsors can get the many benefits listed on the opposite page.	

The media – including TV, newspapers, the Internet and radio – are extremely influential in sport. One of the greatest strengths of the media is as a source of information and a shaper of ideas and views and this can influence people to take part in sport and even to turn away from some activities.

Television

In the UK, sport has been regulated and controlled since the Television Act 1954. This gave the government power to draw up a list of protected events. These 'listed events' cannot be shown exclusively on 'pay per view' channels (i.e. cable or satellite channels where you have to pay extra to see a particular event).

The list was revised in January 1999 and the listed events were placed in two categories.

Group A

- The Olympic Games
- The FIFA World Cup Finals tournament
- The FA Cup Final
- The Scottish FA Cup Final (in Scotland)
- The Grand National
- The Derby
- The Wimbledon Tennis Finals
- The European Football Championships Finals tournament
- The Rugby League Championship Finals tournament
- The Rugby League Challenge Cup Final
- The Rugby World Cup Final

Group B

- Cricket test matches played in England
- Non-finals play in the Wimbledon tournament
- All other matches in the Rugby World Cup Finals tournament
- Five Nations Rugby tournament matches involving home countries
- The Commonwealth Games
- The World Athletics Championship
- The Cricket World Cup – the final, semi-finals, and matches involving home nation teams
- The Ryder Cup
- The Open Golf Championship

The basic difference between the two groups is that there is a legal requirement that the events listed in Group A must be made available to 'free-to-air' terrestrial television, while the Group B events can have live coverage on pay TV as long as there are satisfactory arrangements for secondary coverage (such as delayed coverage or edited highlights) by a 'free-to-air' broadcaster.

There is quite a complicated list of the amount of time that has to be allocated to these highlights as well as rules about the maximum amount of delay between the end of live coverage and the start of highlights.

Most major sporting events are extensively covered by the media

The reason for establishing and amending these lists was to make sure that the 'pay per view' TV companies were not able to buy up all of the rights to show all of the major sporting events.

The body that regulates the arrangements for the televising of sport is the Independent Television Commission (ITC).

The terrestrial television programmes are those that can be received by ordinary televisions using just an aerial and you must pay a TV licence fee to watch these programmes.

The following networks transmit throughout the UK:

■ BBC 1

■ BBC 2

■ ITV (broken down into geographic regions)

■ Channel 4

■ Channel 5.

The BBC receive money to pay for making and transmitting their programmes from the licence fee which each household with a television must pay. The other three channels are what is known as 'independent networks' and they raise all of their money through advertising revenue for adverts shown during commercial breaks.

Televised sports programmes are very popular and the figures for the three independent providers for 1998, shown below, give some idea about how much time is given over to televised sports broadcasts.

■ ITV: 10 hours 15 minutes per week

■ Channel 4: 16 hours 40 minutes per week

■ Channel 5: 23 hours 43 minutes per week

Television companies bid for the sporting events that are shown on television. This means that

Satellite television now brings a wider variety of sports coverage into the home

they have to negotiate with the individual sports (and sometimes with organizers of specific competitions) for the right to televise that activity. This has led to a lot of competition between the TV companies for the rights to show certain sports and the sports have been able to sell to the highest bidder (see page 158).

TASK 2

Name two sports (or sporting events) which have recently 'changed channels' due to higher bids being accepted.

TASK I

Check how many hours of sport are shown on BBC I and BBC 2 in any one week and compare that to the figures for ITV, Channel 4 and Channel 5.

Satellite television

Sky launched its Sky Sports service on the Astra satellite in 1991 and you could obtain its service by subscription in 1992. In August 1994, a second Sky Sports channel was launched, followed by a third one in 1996. In addition to this there is a Eurosport channel which is also broadcast as a specific British version for viewers in the U.K.

Television rights

Getting the rights to show sporting events on television is an expensive business. In 1992, BSkyB paid £304 million for the rights for Premier League soccer, with live games being transmitted only on Sky Sports and recorded highlights on BBC. ITV offered £262 million for the rights and even queried the deal in the High Court, but lost their case. In 1996, BSkyB negotiated a new deal with the Premier League for a further four-year contract to run from 1997. The rights were secured for £670 million. This is a very good example of the organizers of a particular sport (in this case the English soccer Premier league) being able to negotiate with a TV company for the rights to show their sport – and it shows the vast sums of money that are involved!

Digital television

A comparatively recent development in television broadcasting is digital television. This started development in 1991 and was first transmitted by Sky with a digital service in October 1998, followed by ONdigital in November 1998.

Kirsty Gallagher in the Sky Sports News Studio

Broadcasting using digital technology means that not only is picture quality and sound greatly increased but hundreds of channels can be broadcast, with many of them offering an 'interactive' service. This allows the viewer to choose camera angles, watch certain players, listen to different commentaries and see updated facts and statistics.

There are now 24-hour sports news programmes and Manchester United have even launched their own subscription channel. Additional sporting fixtures such as major boxing contests and special broadcasting events are also broadcast on a 'pay per view' system.

TASK 3

Find out just how many specific sports channels are currently being broadcast in all of the different forms of broadcasting.

Television and sponsorship

The relationship between TV and sponsorship can be a very complex and controversial one.

In 1994, a government committee recommended that the BBC should stop broadcasting any sporting events sponsored by tobacco companies. The ITV network had stopped this in 1987 and even has its own Code of Programme Sponsorship which clearly lays out what is – and is not – acceptable sponsorship. The code lists prohibited sponsors and advertisers – including political interest groups and tobacco products. There is also a list of restricted sponsors which includes pharmaceutical products, betting and gaming.

Certain types of programmes are not allowed to be sponsored at all. These 'unsponsorable programmes' include:

■ news – except for weather reports, sports reports or traffic and travel reports

■ business and financial reports

■ current affairs

■ news presenters – not immediately after they have appeared in an 'unsponsorable programme'.

All – or part – of other programmes may be sponsored, provided general guidelines are obeyed. The main rules are that sponsors must not be allowed any undue influence and that they must be clearly identified at the beginning and end of the programme. They must also be acceptable manufacturers or suppliers.

Sponsors themselves like the coverage because it is a form of advertising for them and they can be assured of large audiences. Some of the highest viewing figures for any programme in any year are for sporting events. The sponsors also have the benefit of being associated with something that may have a good and healthy image.

TASK 4

*Choose **two** recent sporting events broadcast on television. Name the sponsors of the television programmes that covered these events.*

Types of programmes broadcast

There is a wide variety of different ways in which television shows and promotes sport, including:

- live sporting action
- highlights programmes
- documentaries
- quiz programmes
- news bulletins
- information services (Ceefax and Teletext)
- coverage of major sporting events
- sporting magazine programmes
- educational, schools, skills programmes
- dedicated channels (such as Manchester United TV).
- interactive programmes

One of the main reasons for the large and varied amount of sporting coverage is that sport is relatively cheap to televise. Many programmes are far more expensive to produce

Live coverage can often add to the excitement and enjoyment of sports

and film and they do not have the uncertainty and drama of a live sports event.

Benefits TV brings to sport

Television clearly benefits from showing sport but it is not entirely a one-way process because sport benefits too through:

- increased popularity – many minority sports have greatly increased in popularity, and in the number of participants, due to TV coverage – for example, gymnastics nearly always has a boom period immediately following an Olympic Games after there has been extensive coverage
- increased revenue – through sponsorship and endorsements
- direct payments from television for the rights to broadcast events.

167

Conflicts between the media and sport

For the most part, the media only brings benefits to sport, but there are some occasions when there are problems as:

■ television may intrude upon an event

■ directors can even influence what we see

■ sometimes rules are changed or adapted to make sports more appealing

■ timings can be dictated by the TV companies, and the audience or crowd may have to wait until the broadcast is ready to start (on some occasions the entire starting time of the event is decided by TV)

■ use of replays both in slow motion and from various angles can undermine officials (the official in charge does not have all of these benefits and many panellists and commentators sit in judgement upon decisions)

■ if particular sports are not shown on TV, they may decline in popularity and participation in them may drop off

■ if a match or activity is shown on TV, it can discourage spectators from going along. This can lead to a loss of revenue for sports. Also, if something is being televised, it could clash with another sporting event and reduce attendance

■ the media can intrude upon a performer's privacy.

However, despite the points listed above, the benefits of televised sport almost certainly outweigh the disadvantages, otherwise it is unlikely that there would be so much sport on television.

Developments are being made all of the time and television is constantly looking at ways of improving sports coverage. Interactive television is being introduced on the digital networks where viewers can choose their own camera angles, replays and views of the action (see page 166).

The Internet can be used as a source of information about sports

TASK 5

While you are watching a televised sports event, try to work out how many different cameras are being used.

Information technology

The widespread use of computers, especially in schools, now allows far greater use of information technology.

CD-ROMs can be used as either a source of information or as interactive programmes. However, the Internet has the greatest influence as a provider of information, with literally thousands of websites allowing access to a wealth of information on sport and leisure.

TASK 6

Choose any sport, or sports-based subject. Then find out how many websites you can find on the Internet connected with that particular subject.

Radio

Most radio stations cover sport in much the same format as television. The obvious disadvantage is that they cannot broadcast pictures. However, because of this they are not regarded as rivals by TV, and particularly by the satellite companies, so they are allowed to cover all of the major sporting events. It is quite common to have these events broadcast on TV and radio at the same time.

There are even specialist radio stations that concentrate on sports coverage. Radio 5 Live is a good example of this. Its coverage is spread between news and sport and it has a very large output of live coverage of sporting events such as athletics and major championships, boxing, soccer, rugby and cricket.

Radio has advantages over TV because:

- broadcasting costs are much lower as it only requires one commentator (sometimes with an expert analyst) and the basic technology to transmit the broadcast

- radios are portable, cheap and plentiful and listeners can even tune in while driving their cars, so the potential audience is bigger.

Many sporting events are covered on radio as well as TV

The Press

The Press consists of newspapers, magazines and books. All of these can be very influential and cover sports in a variety of ways.

Newspapers

All daily newspapers have sports sections, usually at the back. Some, especially the Sunday papers, even have separate sports section supplements, which are newspapers in themselves.

They are very influential as not only do they print results, match reports, team news, rule changes and fixtures but they also comment on many major sporting issues – and especially about sporting personalities!

After a series of poor results many newspapers were very critical of the then England soccer manager, Graham Taylor. There was a campaign to get him sacked and eventually he was. The same happened to Glenn Hoddle in 1999 after he was involved in controversy. There is little doubt that the press coverage influenced this.

TASK 7

Study three different daily newspapers and find out how many sports pages are in each.

Magazines

There has been a great increase in the number of specialist sports magazines in recent years and most sports have at least one publication devoted to them. They concentrate on issues to do with those sports, or on health and fitness and often print very detailed information for readers.

Books

These can vary from novels with sporting themes to textbooks dealing with particular aspects of a sport.

Some of the most controversial books recently have been autobiographies.

Leisure time

Your leisure time is the time when you are free to do what you choose. To many people, this is the time they have after work or after school.

However, not all of this is really free time because there are various essential activities that you must fit in. You need to spend some time sleeping and eating and you may also have to spend some time travelling. Only the time left after this is available for you to take part in some sort of leisure activity.

For many people this will not be a particularly active time. They may choose to watch television, play computer games, listen to music or read. For others it might be a time to take part in sport or to do something physically active such as dancing.

One important thing about leisure time is that it is something which has been increasing. There are many reasons for this including the following.

■ *Greater automation at work and home* – there are more machines capable of doing jobs which used to take a long time. Labour-saving devices (such as automatic washing machines) leave individuals more spare time.

■ *Shorter working week* – the average working week is now considerably shorter than it was.

■ *Unemployment levels* – these are higher, some people are unable to obtain full-time work and are left with more spare time.

TASK I

Carry out a survey within your class or group to find out what the most common leisure activities are. In addition, find out how much leisure time is available to each person and work out what proportion of that person's time is spent on leisure activities.

Leisure provision

With the increase of leisure time there has been a need to provide leisure services. 'The leisure industry' is quite a recent expression and it refers to all the different provisions which are made for your leisure time.

Much of the leisure provision is made by local authorities (see unit 36). They have to accept the responsibility to provide many of the leisure services. This can range from providing a library or allotments, right through to building swimming pools or sports halls. Most local authorities provide a leisure centre in the area, usually designed to cater for as many activities as possible. It is not just local authorities that provide leisure facilities. Cinemas, discos and clubs are privately run and aim to make money out of providing for the leisure needs of their customers.

TASK 2

Find out how many leisure centres there are in your area. Then find out what sort of activities they offer and how many different types of leisure activity you can identify.

Recreation

This can mean relaxing, or amusing yourself, but the term is also commonly used to mean doing something which is active and healthy. There is no single definition which sums it up, but it is something which can be done during your leisure time. Many people consider that if your recreational time is spent being active and trying to follow a more healthy lifestyle, the time is well spent and with a purpose. The Sports Council referred to recreation as 'the purposeful use of leisure time' and most sports bodies look on recreation as being worthwhile and something to be encouraged.

Recreation and leisure

The link between these two is very strong because the providers of leisure opportunities usually try to offer recreational activities.

It is important for the providers of leisure services to be able to predict and follow trends in leisure activities. These tend to come and go and it can be difficult to provide for them. There was a large increase in squash playing in the 1970s and 1980s which resulted in a lot of squash courts being built. As interest fell, the amount they were used decreased and the owners of squash courts found that there was no real alternative use for them. Some leisure centres have even made unprofitable squash courts into table tennis rooms or snooker rooms.

Micro-scooters are a good example of a leisure trend that developed rapidly

If trends require just a small expenditure on equipment (the step aerobics boom of the early 1990s is an example), the leisure industry can cater for it, although it usually means recruiting and training staff for the particular activity which is proving to be popular.

Provision – needs and range

One of the difficulties in providing for recreation and leisure is the variety of people who have to be catered for in terms of age, ability and interest.

Due to this, providers such as local authorities have made efforts to identify what are known as 'user groups'. These usually fall into the following categories:

- mothers and young children
- retired people
- committed sportspeople
- unemployed people.

It is not possible to put on the same type of activities for all of these groups, so the provision has to be varied. The timings of provision may also have to be adjusted and frequently there are concessions made for these user groups, often in the form of reduced fees and charges.

TASK 3

Try to find out about a particular course or activity, that is aimed at each of the user groups identified above. If you cannot find one, think of a suitable activity that could be provided.

The 'leisure industry' is one of the fastest growing areas in society today. In 1999, it was estimated that £12 billion was spent on sport and related goods and services. If the trend continues as expected, more jobs and more provision must be made in the future.

It is only in comparatively recent times that there has been any such thing as a professional sportsperson and only very recently that they have been paid such large amounts of money.

Sometimes it is very difficult to tell the difference between a professional and an amateur, but these are definitions of what they should be.

■ *Amateur* – someone who takes part in sport, or an activity, as a pastime or hobby rather than for gain. They take part for enjoyment only, do not get paid and usually have a full-time job.

■ *Professional* – someone who takes part in a sport or an activity as a means of their livelihood. They get paid for taking part and do it as a full-time job.

There are also two other types of sportspeople who should be considered.

■ *Shamateurs* – these are people who claim to be amateurs but are, in fact, being paid to take part. These payments would be illegal and unofficial.

■ *Semi-professionals* – these are people who have a job and also take part in sport, for which they are legally paid. Some have full-time jobs and only take part in their sport in their spare time and others have part-time jobs and spend the rest of their time at their sport.

Not all people who take part in sport fit neatly into any of these categories and it is often very difficult, in certain sports, to tell who is what. There are very many ways around the rules.

Some sports are what is known as **open** and these allow both professionals and amateurs to compete together. If there is prize money to be won, the amateurs are not usually allowed to keep it.

TASK I

a Name a **professional** sport and one person who takes part in it.

b Name an **amateur** sport and one person who takes part in it.

c Name an **open** sport or competition and name one amateur and one professional who might compete against each other in it.

d Name a **semi-professional** sport and one person who takes part in it.

Historical background

Before the turn of the century, very few sports had professional players, although it was quite common for people who were wealthy to play sport full time. This was often the case in cricket, for example. Because they had the time and did not need to work for a living, they were able to dedicate themselves full time to their chosen sport. They were called 'true amateurs' because they received no payments or rewards for taking part other than perhaps a trophy if they won.

Cricket's influence

In cricket there were what was known as 'gentlemen' and 'players'. The gentlemen were wealthy and played for fun whereas the players were paid to play, although it was usually only a very small amount. Most cricket clubs could only afford one or two 'players' who were the paid professionals for the club, the rest of the team would be made up of 'gentlemen' and other amateurs.

Many sports have only become organized within the last hundred years or so. The first cricket test match was not until 1877, which was the first year that the Wimbledon tennis

A 'gentlemen versus players' cricket match at Lords in 1891

tournament was played. The Amateur Athletic Association was not formed until 1880 and the first soccer World Cup was not played until 1930. This has meant that many sports do not have the tradition of professionals that cricket does.

Sport first had to be properly organized, stadiums built for spectators, sponsorship obtained and media interest generated before there was enough money in many sports for professionals to be even able to exist.

All sports started as amateur, but the majority now have professionals who take part at the highest levels, as well as amateurs who play at lower levels. Most have their own rules about what is allowed and these are constantly changing.

The Olympic movement changed their rules to allow amateurs to receive prize money and appearance money and they have let professional sportspeople such as tennis players and basketball players compete in the Olympics.

One sport which did maintain a barrier between amateur and professional was rugby. Following a disagreement over whether players should be paid, a breakaway group started the game of rugby league as a professional game and changed some of the rules as well. In 1995, both rugby league and rugby union officially became professional sports.

Overcoming the rules

Sponsorship

There are many benefits which can be gained from this (see unit 41).

Trust funds

Money is paid into a fund which is not supposed to be used while the sportsperson is actually performing but is only to be used when they 'retire'.

Occupations

Some of the 'jobs' which sportspeople have are arranged specifically to allow them to take part in their sport and get a wage. They are just token positions and responsibilities. In many countries being a member of any of the uniformed services is a common one.

Scholarships

Many universities and colleges offer sports scholarships which allow almost full-time sport to be undertaken with little or no study involved.

Expenses payments

These are often far more than those actually needed and amount to a payment for taking part.

Illegal payments

This is often referred to as 'boot money' as there was a practice of putting money in players' boots at the end of a match to pay them, illegally, for performing.

Gifts

Items such as luxury cars are given as prizes or gifts. These can then be traded in for cash.

TASK 2

Try to find out about some of the 'gifts' which are available to competitors in events.

Despite what many people would like to happen, it is almost impossible to keep politics out of sport. Sport in most countries is financed, or at least monitored, from a government level and is therefore bound to be influenced.

Great Britain has a minister responsible for sport who is very influential and can advise the various sporting bodies. In some other countries, especially the old communist countries, sport was a political priority area. The state was in complete control.

The degree of control was shown when in some years, the communist countries boycotted the Olympic Games and refused to send their athletes. Their political systems meant that they could do this. In a similar situation, Britain could only advise its athletes against going and could not actually stop them from taking part.

Stewards being briefed in a modern all-seat stadium. Government action has improved safety for soccer fans

TASK I

Refer back to unit 40 and list the boycotts which occurred at different Olympic Games.

Politics assisting sport

It is often thought that politicians only influence sport in a negative way, but this is not the case. Without the backing of the government there would be far less provision in terms of facilities and funding. Past and present governments have also ensured that sport is by law, part of the range of educational subjects offered in schools.

Another positive move has been the setting up of various bodies such as UK Sport (see unit 39).

If there are major problems, then the government will act. The Taylor Enquiry, which followed the Heysall Stadium disaster and the Hillsborough disaster, was set up to find solutions to the problems of controlling crowds in stadiums and making adequate provisions for them. The results of this enquiry were welcomed and some money was made available to help with the improvements.

There is no doubt that in many communist countries the political systems raised the standards of sport. Sport was given a very high profile. The athletes and sportspeople in those countries would not have considered that the government was interfering with sport, but were more likely to think that it was giving valuable assistance.

Political issues

1920 – The Olympic Games were held in Antwerp, Belgium immediately after World War I. Germany, and its wartime allies, were not sent an invitation to take part.

1925 – The year following the Paris Olympics, the Soviet Union Communist Party made a declaration that 'sport should be used as a means of rallying the broad masses of workers and peasants around the various Party and trade union organizations through which the masses of workers and peasants are to be drawn into social and political activity'. This set the tone for the communist attitude towards sport for the next 65 years.

1936 – The Olympics in Berlin were used as a propaganda exercise by Hitler (see page 152).

1949 – A New Zealand rugby team was banned from South Africa because the team contained Maori players.

1954 – China was finally admitted to the Olympics despite it still not accepting the IOC decision to recognize Taiwan.

1956 – China withdrew from the Olympic movement and started a boycott of sports organizations and competitions.

1964 – South Africa was banned from the Olympics because of the apartheid laws (see unit 48). This led to a long period of demonstrations and boycotts throughout the 1960s and 1970s.

1970 – A state of war was declared between El Salvador and Honduras after a World Cup qualifying game. Also, the South African cricket team was asked not to tour England after a formal request from James Callaghan, the Home Secretary.

1972–88 – See unit 40 for the political events which disrupted the Olympic Games over this period.

1990 – The large communist states in Eastern Europe began to crumble and many new, smaller states were formed. The communist states' dominance of many sports started to decline.

1992 – South Africa was re-admitted to world sport after finally abandoning its apartheid policy.

2000 – British Home Secretary Jack Straw allowed American boxer Mike Tyson to enter the UK for a fight with British boxer Julien Francis. The law prohibited convicted felons from being admitted to the country and Tyson had received a prison sentence in the US for a previous rape conviction. Following appeals by the promoters of the fight, Tyson was granted permission to enter the UK as a 'special case', much to the disapproval of many civil rights groups.

2000 – Following their first round exit from the African Nations Cup, the Ivory Coast national soccer team were taken prisoner by the country's military forces! The first claim by the authorities was that they were being held 'for their own security' but another official stated that they were being held 'to teach them a sense of civic responsibility because of their indiscipline'. Many of the players held were contracted players for top European clubs and this put a question mark over players being released from their clubs to play for their countries.

TASK 2

List any recent examples you can find of politics interfering with sport.

The re-admitted South African Olympic team in 1992

175

Facilities, specific activities and organization in sport all cost money and sport therefore depends on finance. Financing (or funding) is also crucial to achieving good levels of participation as people expect good facilities and organization. The provision of facilities is dealt with in unit 37. Unit 46 looks at how money is raised or provided to allow for maximum participation.

Clubs

Throughout the country there are thousands of clubs that not only provide sporting opportunities but also finance it themselves. They do this through the following.

- *Membership fees* – every member pays a set amount each year to belong to the club. This is also sometimes known as a subscription (or subs). Members may also pay a match fee each time they play a game or match.

- *Fund raising* – most clubs have social events, sponsored events, car boot sales and any other ways they can think of to raise more money.

- *Grants* – some money comes from grants from local authorities or national bodies such as Sport England (National Lottery money).

Car boot sales are one way a small sports club can raise funds

Charities

Many sports associations are registered as charities. The main reasons for this are that they gain either exemption from tax or at least some reduction in the taxes they have to pay. In addition as a charity does not aim to make a profit, it way well be more successful in attracting grants or sponsorship.

Professional clubs

Many sports have professional clubs which are run as businesses and have to raise all of their own finance. They need to make money to pay their players and they may have to pay large sums to 'sign on' new players. They raise money from the following.

- *Spectators* – if they have a large stadium they can raise a lot of money from people paying to watch matches. Many clubs sell season tickets so supporters pay in advance for a ticket to watch all of their team's games. More recently, luxury executive boxes have been introduced. These can be bought or hired by companies, who can then invite clients they are entertaining to watch a match.

- *Merchandising* – this is the sale of goods or items associated with the club. The goods can range from coffee mugs, scarves, duplicate shirts, to programmes, posters or sports equipment. This is a very big growth area. Manchester United football club estimates that half of its annual income comes from merchandising. In 1999 the club had a financial turnover in excess of £92 million.

Some big clubs run their own 'megastores' to raise money

Governing bodies

The governing body of a sporting activity receives money and can raise money. All the clubs and individuals who belong to the particular sport have to pay a subscription, part of which goes to the governing body. This often covers such things as insurance, but there is also money which can be made available for coaching and preparation of teams.

Governing bodies can also raise money through organizing and running events, competitions and tournaments. The Lawn Tennis Association makes millions of pounds each year from the Wimbledon tennis tournament and much of this money is put back into the sport by providing coaching, facilities and promoting the sport. The Rugby Football Union also receives large sums of money from international games which is then available to be distributed.

National and local government

A great deal of money is raised each year through national and local taxes. Some of this money is spent on providing sporting facilities and financing sport. Much of the money is available through grants. To obtain a grant for a particular purpose, a sporting body has to make a specific application for money to whatever body has been appointed by the government to administer the funds.

Sponsorship

Vast amounts of money are provided for sport each year by sponsorship deals (see unit 39). Sponsorship provides money for all aspects of sport and is possibly the largest and certainly the most important single source of finance.

Gambling

The National Lottery provides millions of pounds every year for funding sport throughout the UK. As we saw on page 157, £53.7 billion was provided between 1997and the 2000 Olympics! Some sports have links with other forms of gambling. Football pools companies pay large amounts of their profits to the football authorities to enable them to use the sport as the basis of their business. Horse-racing also benefits from gambling.

The media

Many sports authorities deal directly with the media (particularly television) to negotiate fees they will pay to be allowed to cover their sport. With the introduction of satellite television there is now more competition and more money to be made. Due to increased coverage all sports can gain, not just the major ones.

Many sports performers are looked upon as 'role models', so they establish behaviour, trends and attitudes that others are likely to follow. There is therefore quite a lot of pressure on top-level performers to make sure they set good examples and are not seen to be cheating or using 'gamesmanship' – a poor sporting attitude that comes very close to cheating.

All physical activities have some sort of rules or regulations. A good sporting attitude means playing within those rules or regulations, showing good sporting etiquette (see unit 3) and being very fair even to the point where it could cost you the game.

Good sporting attitude

There have been many performers who have been referred to as 'great sportspeople', but not all showed the necessary qualities or attitudes. Most activities have ways in which you can show good attitude.

- *Soccer* – if a player is injured, you might kick the ball out of play to allow the injured person to get help. When the game is restarted, you can then throw, or kick the ball back to the team who kicked it out, so that you do not gain an unfair advantage.

- *Racket games* – there are such things as 'sling shots' or 'double hits' which a player making a shot can sense and feel, but it is almost impossible for an official or opponent to observe. You can call out to your opponent when you do this as they are foul shots. In tennis and squash, it is sometimes difficult to spot a 'bump ball' (where the ball hits the ground just before you make contact) and this can also be called.

- *Rugby* – one of the sporting traditions in rugby is to form a tunnel with your team and applaud the other team off the pitch. This should happen no matter how the match went and whether you win or lose.

Greeting and meeting your opponents is an example of good sporting attitude

- *Cricket* – a batsperson can be applauded as he or she makes their way to the wicket. The batsperson should also 'walk' when they know they have touched the ball with their bat and a fair catch has been made. They should not wait for the umpire's decision but should start to walk back to the pavilion.

TASK I

*Think of **at least one more** example of good sporting attitude for all of the activities named above. If possible try to give an actual example.*

General

Here are some examples of general good sporting attitude:

- welcoming opposition players
- congratulating opponents on good play
- shaking hands after a game, especially with the officials
- accepting the decisions of officials without arguing.

TASK 2

*Think of **two more** general examples of good sporting attitude.*

Social attitudes

The way in which society views anything has an influence on people and certainly on whether or not they decide to participate in something or take it up as a regular activity.

Sport is generally seen as a positive thing for society and in recent years it has become more 'socially acceptable' to take part in sport in various ways.

This can be seen by the following:

■ *Encouraging greater overall participation* – a good example of this is the increased popularity of running, which has made taking part in marathons something that many people now do. At one time it was unusual to see people out jogging or training but now it is far more common and acceptable. This has also been linked to a greater health and fitness awareness in society generally. Taking good care of yourself through regular and sometimes quite strenuous exercise is seen to be a good thing and something that is to be encouraged.

■ *Role models* – with more and more young people looking to their sporting heroes as role models there has been an upsurge in particular sports. Soccer is an excellent example of this with many footballers becoming youth idols – a role previously more associated with pop stars. With a sporting career seen to be healthy (and quite well paid in many cases), society sees sporting role models as good examples for young people to follow and actively encourages this.

■ *Women's involvement* – it was only comparatively recently that women were not only discouraged from taking part in sport but also actually stopped from doing so. As recently as 1980, women were not allowed to run a 3,000 metre race as it was thought to be too strenuous for them! The first 'official' women's marathon was not run until 1964 and the women's pole vault was only introduced into the Olympics at Sydney in 2000! Taking part is no longer seen as 'unladylike' and more and more women also have positions as managers and officials in sport.

■ *Growth and decline of activities* – the views of society can lead to increases in the popularity of some activities, with people trying to copy their role models by taking up that sport. However, if the view is that an activity is not suitable (boxing could be an example of this) then the participation levels in that activity could go down.

TASK 3

Make a list of some recent examples of poor sporting attitudes which have occurred in major competitions or games. Suggest some rule changes which could be introduced to stop them.

David Beckham, one of sports most famous role models

Being unfair or hostile to someone for *any* reason is not acceptable, but there are examples where it has happened in sport and in some cases it still goes on. Any kind of discrimination clearly affects people's chances of participating fully and being able to perform to their best. Discrimination has taken place in the following ways.

Racial discrimination

This can and does occur, not only because of the colour of someone's skin, but often just because of their nationality. Many countries are host to more than one race that have settled there, and there are often conflicts between the different peoples. They may even have different languages and marked out areas within a country so their access to sporting facilities may be completely different.

In this sort of situation, the racial groups are often referred to as 'sub cultures'. This has also been the case with black and Asian sports performers and athletes. In America, and in many parts of Great Britain, the minority groups have been denied access to clubs, schools and organizations because of the colour of their skin. Changes in the law were necessary and were introduced to prevent this, and there has been a great improvement.

Until quite recently it would have been most unusual to find a professional black soccer player, or international athlete or cricketer. Now it is very common as the barriers are being broken down.

Apartheid

This was an extreme example of racial discrimination which existed in South Africa. A system was introduced which put people into different classes, based entirely on the colour of their skin. This **segregation** meant that they had totally separate schools, cinemas, living areas and even transport. Obviously, sports facilities and opportunities were also separate, which meant that black and coloured people were only allowed very limited sporting opportunities.

This system finally ended in 1994 but many generations suffered because of it. The political effect of apartheid is dealt with in more detail in unit 45.

National rights

Not all nations give equal rights to their citizens. There might be discrimination against some members of a society.

In some of the Eastern European countries many potential sports performers are selected, often at a very young age, and either put into special training schools or put on specific coaching and training courses. One of the famous sprinters of the past, Valeri Bortzov, was supposed to have been selected and specifically trained, using computer technology.

In Cuba, there was a period when only eight sports were made available. This was so that they could achieve a high international status in the sports on which they concentrated, due to the choice being so limited.

These forms of selection are known as **elitism**, because not all the same opportunities are made available to all people.

Religion

Many individuals – and countries – have been victims of discrimination on religious grounds.

Many committed Christians will not compete on a Sunday, so if there is a tournament or event which takes place on that day they will not take part. Many competitors have withdrawn from Olympic events because they have taken place on Sundays.

Jews were discriminated against in Germany in the 1930s when they were treated as second-class citizens. (See page 152 for the effect this had on the 1936 Olympics held in Germany.)

In strict Muslim countries it is not permitted for women to wear certain types of clothes. For example, it would be unacceptable for women to wear athletic running clothing, or swimming costumes. Women in these countries are therefore discriminated against on religious grounds.

Hassiba Boulmerka, who won the 1500 metres Olympic gold medal in 1992, caused controversy in her own country by training and performing in shorts because cultural practice in Algeria is for a woman to keep her legs and arms covered.

TASK I

*Try to think of **three** other examples where religious beliefs clash with sport.*

Sex

Sexual discrimination, notably against women, can take many forms in sport.

- *Fewer events* – many events are held for men only and in many professional sports there are no organized women's events.

- *Less prize money* – nearly all events have less prize money for women than for men.

- *Lower profile* – events are not so well promoted or publicized.

- *Women are banned* – in the contact sports such as soccer and rugby, women are not allowed to compete against men. Show jumping is one of the few activities where women compete against men on equal terms.

TASK 2

Try to identify other forms of sexual discrimination in sport.

Social, economic and cultural

In many areas, and in whole countries, there is simply a lack of money so the people who live there have less of everything.

Even in the wealthier countries there are inner city areas which are very poor and which have few – if any – facilities. Almost certainly, the few sporting opportunities that are available will be very basic. This is why many of these areas have produced many very good boxers, basketball players and soccer players. These sports do not require expensive facilities. Golf courses, tennis clubs and swimming pools may not be available so these sports are not an option.

Certain cultural groups within an area may wish to have their chosen sports available, but they may be denied the facilities because of the cost or because it clashes with the choices of the majority culture.

Hassiba Boulmerka who suffered from religious discrimination

It would be unthinkable for most sports to take place without spectators, and many clubs rely on them. However, spectators can be both good and bad. The following are the ways in which spectators can affect sport.

Finance

Spectators usually pay to watch a game or a match and this can be a very large source of income. Some soccer clubs have attendances of between 40,000 and 50,000 for their home games and there may be between 20 and 30 of these matches each season. With some people paying in advance by buying season tickets this can bring in a very large amount of money.

The fans who attend will also probably buy scarves, shirts or hats in the club colours and this all means extra money going to the club.

This is true not only for the major soccer clubs. Many indoor sports, such as basketball, can attract several thousand spectators and the clubs would rely on them to bring in enough money to keep it going.

TASK 1

a Find out the attendance of a major sports club.
b Try to find out how much that club received in receipts.
c Find out the attendance and receipts for an international match or competition.

The money raised from spectators attending games and matches is not all profit. The club has to meet many expenses to take care of its supporters.

■ *Facilities* – these all have to be provided and they may include, toilets, food and drink, separate family enclosures and even lighting and heating.

■ *Supervision and control* – with a large number of people attending, there is a great responsibility to make sure that they are safe and well looked after. This means that clubs must employ stewards and marshals and pay for the services of the police. The fans have to be escorted, or guided, to the ground then supervised while they are there. They then have to be safely escorted out and sent on their way home. The police have to be paid to do this and it is the club's responsibility to do this. Often the police fee is one of the largest bills that any of the clubs have to pay.

TASK 2

Find out how much a particular club has to pay the police for assistance with crowd control.

Police control and supervision at a soccer match

Crowd influence

It is generally thought to be an advantage for a team to play 'at home'. This is not just because they are familiar with their home ground or court or stadium, but often because of the effect the home crowd can have upon a performance. Supporters usually cheer on their team and attempt to put off the opposition team. Many players find it very intimidating to play away when they know that the opposing fans will be very critical of them and of any mistakes they might make.

Just the crowd noise itself can be enough to unsettle one player and motivate another. The American football authorities once introduced a rule which required the home fans to keep the noise down to a particular level when the opposing team was preparing and calling their moves during the game. If the crowd was too loud a penalty was inflicted on the home team. They tried this for a year and it simply did not work. There was so much opposition to it that it was scrapped.

There can be a very thin line between what would be considered to be acceptable crowd influence and unacceptable interference and this depends upon the spectators' behaviour.

Behaviour

There are many examples of incidents which have occurred where the behaviour of the spectators has been totally unacceptable and disasters have happened.

Hooliganism is a term used to describe the behaviour of supporters who disrupt a game or match severely. Cricket matches have had crowds invading the pitch, causing the game to be abandoned. Fighting has spilt over on to the pitch during soccer matches causing play to stop. Goalposts have been broken and wickets have been destroyed by weed killer or been dug up. In extreme cases players have been attacked, or even killed.

One notorious incident involved the soccer player, Eric Cantona. After being sent off he was taunted and abused by members of the crowd

Eric Cantona attacking a fan after being taunted by the crowd

and he retaliated by jumping into the crowd and attacking a spectator.

Various changes have been introduced to try to control crowds safely. The Heysell Stadium disaster, during a European soccer final, was caused when fighting occurred between Liverpool and Juventus supporters. Italian fans were crushed by a damaged stand while they were trying to get away. In the Hillsborough disaster, fans were crushed to death when too many people were allowed into one part of the stadium. Following these two incidents, all-seated stadiums were introduced. This resulted from an enquiry led by Justice Taylor who recommended various ways that grounds could be made safer. Most grounds now keep rival fans separate and have video camera surveillance as well as membership and identity schemes. Some even ban away fans.

One of the main problems to be identified was that spectators were expected or allowed to stand in small confined areas. Therefore, upgrading and improving the stadiums has been the main aim. Now nearly all sports grounds have their capacity decreased (which affects their income), to reduce dangers and incidents of crowd disturbances. If a club or organization is not able to take care of its spectators properly and safely, it may well go out of business.

Many things can influence whether you will have an interest in sport and whether you will participate. The main influences are summarized below.

School

An Act of Parliament in 1947 made it a legal requirement for physical education (PE) to be taught in schools. There were other things which schools could opt out of teaching but physical education was made a priority.

More recently, in 1988 the Education Reform Act again stated that physical education was to be taught in all schools in England and Wales. In March 1992 the details of what should be taught as physical education were made law in the National Curriculum. All National Curriculum subjects taught in schools are governed by guidelines so that all pupils are taught a similar and balanced programme.

PE is a legal requirement in schools, but it is also an opportunity for free expert tuition

There are therefore reasons why schools provide PE and these include:

■ it is a legal requirement

■ to provide a balance in the teaching programme, as it is a practical subject

■ to improve health and fitness levels

■ to reflect the importance of sport and physical activity in society

■ to prepare young people to take part in sporting activity when they leave school.

Schools also have different ways in which they provide PE and these include:

■ timetabled PE lessons

■ extra-curricular activities (these are activities which take place after school or at lunchtimes)

■ clubs and team practice sessions

■ examination-based courses – such as GCSE Physical Education

■ sports performance awards

■ outside visits

■ links with local sports clubs

■ cross-curricular links with other subject areas

■ introducing new sports and providing equipment and facilities.

The influence of school is one of the major factors in whether young people participate in sport or not. How influential school can be in this can depend on the following:

• Attitudes of staff – in most cases PE staff are seen as positive role models as they can encourage full participation and make activities enjoyable. Also, the experience of staff combined with their particular sporting interests and expertise, often leads to students taking up and following a particular sport.

However, there are cases where a student may have a bad experience in PE lessons and the reverse can take place – they are actually put off taking part.

- Increased links with ICT and key skills – physical education is seen to be one of the best ways to cover these two additional areas of the curriculum, which can therefore increase participation opportunities.

- The opportunities to adopt different roles – not only can school encourage participation as a performer but it can also encourage students to take on other important roles such as official, observer, coach, captain, leader, organizer or even choreographer. This variety of experiences which a school can, and should, offer means that young people are well prepared to carry on taking an active part in physical activities when they leave school.

Parents

The attitude of parents is also important. If parents are very much in favour of the benefits of sport, then they will almost certainly pass this attitude on to their children. There are many cases where children of quite famous sports performers have followed their parents' examples and played sport at a high level.

It is the attitude, as much as the ability, which can be important for parents to pass on. Parents can also help and encourage in other ways.

- *Providing equipment* – for many sports certain equipment is essential to enable you to play. It may also be expensive and need a financial commitment.

- *Transport* – one of the major problems for young people is that they are not able to transport themselves. This usually means that it is left to parents to find the time and the means.

Not all parents take a positive attitude to sports activities. In some cases, even with a positive attitude, parents may not be able to afford the

Some peer groups may participate in sport – others may not

financial commitment involved. Unfortunately, it would be very difficult for any young person to succeed in taking part in sport without their parents' backing.

TASK I

*Name **at least three** sports performers currently playing who are the sons or daughters of previous performers.*

Peers

Your peers are people who are of the same age and status as you. To most young people, this would be the group of school friends, or friends with whom they most often mix.

Peers are considered to be one of the most powerful influences on any person and 'peer pressure' can be very powerful.

If a peer group likes to participate in sport and can see the advantages and benefits, it is likely that the whole group will join in. However, it is very difficult for someone to go against the group if the general attitude is negative.

TASK 2

Try to identify different peer groups who are clearly for and against participating in sport.

185

Revision guidelines

All the information in this book is relevant to the examination you will be entered for and you should have knowledge of all of it. Most of the information is theory related to the final examination paper that will be *two hours* long. The examination paper will be broken up as follows:

- **Section A: Health, Fitness and the Factors Affecting Performance** – there will be two 15-mark questions testing knowledge of this section

- **Section B: Principles of Training** – there will be two 15-mark questions testing knowledge of this section

- **Section C: Factors Affecting Individual Performance and Participation** – there will be one 20-mark question testing knowledge of this section

- **Section D: Social and Cultural Factors Affecting Participation** – there will be one 20-mark question testing knowledge of this section

There will, therefore, be a total of *six* questions on the question paper. You must remember, however, that each of these will be broken up into smaller sub-sections within the question. This means that you are unlikely to have to answer a question on one particular topic, or theory area, which is worth more than about *six* marks in total.

Not all of the content of this book will be examined in your two-hour question paper but any part of it *could* be! It is because of this that you must make sure that you have covered all of the topics. You will not have any choice about the questions you are set – you will be expected to answer all of them.

A particular word of warning – and vital information – to anyone being entered for the Games specification. You will be sitting a separate paper from the Physical Education candidates and it is very important that you are aware of what that means. If you have any question that asks you to give an example from an actual sporting situation, you *must* make sure that you choose examples from *games*! These will be listed on the question paper to give you extra help and guidance. If you do not do this, you will lose marks. If you are a candidate taking the PE paper, you are able to refer to *any physical activity* when giving your answers.

The questions you will be asked in your examination will often expect you to be able to apply the knowledge that you have. This means that not all of the questions will be simple one-word answers. They may need further explanation to show that the basic knowledge you have can be related to actual physical movements, activities or sporting situations. You must remember that this is going to be a PE exam, not a biology or human anatomy one!

Examination technique

These are some basic guidelines that you *must* consider because they can make a great difference to your ability to answer a question properly, correctly and fully.

1. **Read the question carefully**. There will not be any additional reading time, just the two hours to answer the questions. Do not just pick out key words and start answering the question. Make sure you are answering the question set, rather than the question you would have liked to have been set!

2. **Check to see if there are any examples asked for**. Often questions are worded so that you have to explain or describe something *and* give examples. These examples are often the easiest part of the question and you may be able to give them from your own experience. This is also often the way in which you can show that you are able to apply the knowledge that is asked for in the question.

3. **Check all completed questions**. Leave yourself some time at the end of the exam to check all of your answers. Better still, check each answer against the question set as soon as you have finished it. If you then realize you have not answered the question as set, you have time to change it or add a new one.

4. **Diagrams are allowed as part of your answer**, and this will be stated on the front of the examination paper. You might find that you can answer a question much more easily by drawing a diagram than you can in words. Remember though, you must *clearly label* your diagram, and your diagram must be clear. Don't expect to be able to answer every question with a diagram – be selective.

5. **Content and terminology** – you must try to get used to the specialist terminology of the subject. This means that you need to know and understand the words that are used in the exam specification (and therefore the ones which are used in this book as they match the specification) so that you are absolutely clear what they mean. Many of the words are not those you would use in everyday language – for example, *fatigue*, *somatotype* and *cardiovascular* – but they are specialist terms for PE and games. Therefore, you need to know and understand them as they will be used in exam questions. This is doubly important because if you don't know them, you will not even be able to attempt the question, nor will you be able to include the terms in any of your answers. Using the correct terminology in an answer is always easier and likely to gain you more marks than trying to describe something in your own words.

6. **Key words to the question appear in bold like this** in the exam question. They are written in bold to draw your attention to them. You must make sure that your answer refers to these words and that you have taken advantage of the help the examiner has given you.

7. **Mark allocation** – at the end of each question on the question paper there will be a number in brackets. This is the number of marks allocated to that particular question, or part of the question. The answer you give must be in line with the number of marks available for that question. More marks available means that more detail (probably applied) is required in your answer.

GOOD LUCK!

Glossary

active opposition opponents in a practice situation who are actively involved

aerobic energy energy expended over a long period of time which requires oxygen

aesthetic something performed with beauty and sensitivity, pleasing performer and spectator

agility a combination of speed and flexibility

alveoli small air sacs in the lungs where gaseous exchange takes place

amateur a sportsperson usually part-time who competes without receiving payment

amino acids substances which link together to form protein molecules

anaemia deficiency or poor quality of red corpuscles in the blood

anaerobic energy energy expended in short bursts, which does not require oxygen

androgenic anabolic steroids commonly used performance-enhancing drugs

anorexia eating disorder marked by insufficient intake of food

aorta blood vessel carrying blood away from the heart, distributing it to the body

arterioles blood vessels into which the arteries sub-divide

articular capsule a strong, fibrous tissue which surrounds a synovial joint

athlete's foot a fungus infection of the feet, usually between the toes

atria the two chambers at the top of the heart, which receive blood from the veins

atrophy wastage of a muscle marked by the muscle's loss of shape and strength

basal metabolic rate the minimum rate of energy required to keep all the life processes of the body maintained when the body is at rest

beta$_2$agonists a group of stimulants and anabolic agents which are banned (performance-enhancing drugs)

bowel common name for the lower intestine

bronchioles small tubes in the lungs into which the bronchi sub-divide

bulk size or mass of a sportsperson

calorie a unit which measures heat or energy production in the body

carbohydrate load increasing the amount of carbohydrates in the body before an endurance event

cardiovascular endurance the ability of the heart and lungs to keep operating efficiently during an endurance event

cartilage a tough form of tissue which covers and protects the ends of bones, and acts as a buffer where two bones meet at a joint

cerebellum part of the brain which controls body movement

cerebrum largest part of the brain, responsible for conscious control of the body

cholesterol a fatty deposit which can build up on the inner walls of the arteries, reducing blood flow

closed skills skills performed in an unchanging environment

coma position the position in which a casualty should be placed when first aid is needed

concentric contraction (or **dynamic contraction**) when a muscle shortens and gets fatter as it contracts

concussion a head injury which may cause a person to become unconscious

conditioned game where the rules or the way a game is played is changed during a practice session to work on a particular aspect

consistency being able to perform a skill properly, the same way each time

constitution the rules by which a club or organization runs itself

control being able to perform something in a regular and consistent way

convention an agreed rule or form of etiquette in a physical activity

co-ordination the ability to properly control your body when performing a physical action

creatine a food/nutritional supplement taken by performers to aid training and muscle development

decree a set statement or order, usually about a sports rule or regulation

dehydration rapid loss of water from the body

delayed concussion when the symptoms of concussion occur some time after the injury is received

diastolic pressure the pressure of the blood flow in the arteries when the left ventricle relaxes

dietician a person who advises on the type of diet a person should have

differentiate a way of making a physical task easier or harder to perform

drill a set way of performing a practice or skill

dual provision an agreement where by sports facilities are used by one or more types of users such as schools and the public

dual use – see **dual provision**

duodenum part of the small intestine

dynamic contraction see **concentric contraction**

dynamometer a device used to measure strength

eccentric contraction the return of a muscle to its original length and shape after a concentric contraction has shortened it

ectomorph a somatotype, or body type, where a person is relatively short with thin arms and shoulders

elitism system in which certain groups are selected for special treatment, such as special squads who receive extra training and coaching

endomorph a somatotype, or body type, basically short and rounded with short legs

endurance (or **stamina**) an ability of performers to keep going with a movement or activity for a relatively long period

etiquette a convention or unwritten rule in an activity which is not enforceable but usually followed

exhale   to breathe out

expiration   the action of the diaphragm and intercostal muscles which forces air out of the body

extra-curricular activity   an activity which takes place at a school outside of time-tabled lesson time

fainting   temporary unconsciousness or dizziness

fast twitch fibre   muscle fibres which contract very rapidly but are quickly exhausted

feedback   information a performer receives about their performance

fibrous   where fibres link together, such as fibrous joints

fitness   a variety of factors which combine to give a sportsperson an efficient body, able to cope with a high degree of physical demand

flexibility (or suppleness)   the range of movement around a joint

forced breathing   the increase of the breathing rate during physical activity

form   the level of performance the performer maintains or the good shape, position, presentation or manner of a performance

foul play   play which is against the rules or regulations of a sport

gangrene   an infection which can set in after a fracture has occurred

glucose   a type of sugar found in carbohydrates

glycogen   the form in which glucose is stored

grooved performance   the ability to repeat a skill consistently as a result of a great deal of practice

group skills   skills which are performed within a unit or group in a team

haemoglobin   the substance in the red blood cells which transports oxygen and carbon dioxide

haemorrhage   when a blood vessel breaks/followed by heavy bleeding

heart attack   when the heart muscle is starved of oxygen due to a blockage, causing severe chest pain and sometimes death

heartbeat   one contraction and one relaxation of the heart

hygiene   ways of maintaining cleanliness and health, good personal habits

ileum   lower part of the small intestine

immunization   vaccination or injection which prevents disease

impartial   being fair to both sides, essential for a referee

independence   being able to do something on your own without help or interference

individual skills   physical skills performed on your own

ingrown toe nails   toe nails growing unevenly into the skin at the sides of the nails

inhale   to breathe in

inspiration   air taken in when the diaphragm flattens and moves downwards

interaction   two or more people working or reacting with each other

intercostal muscle   muscles surrounding the ribs which assist breathing

invasion games   physical activities where teams have to get into their opponents area in order to score

isokinetic training   training using specialized machinery where resistance against muscles is variable

isometric contraction   a muscle contraction where the length of the muscle does not change

isometric training   where a muscle is held at a particular point for approximately five seconds

lactic acid system   the breakdown of carbohydrates to provide energy, usually functioning during activities lasting between one and three minutes

leukocyte   white blood cell

ligaments   strong fibrous bands which stabilize joints and control movement

linear progress   fairly level and consistent skill acquisition

lineout   in a rugby match, a restart situation on the sideline

linesman   official who checks whether the ball has stayed in play

link player   a team member who connects the units in a team game

malnutrition   a poor physical condition due to a lack of nutrition

medulla oblongata   part of the brain which controls automatic functions of the brain such as breathing, heart rate and digestion

menstruation   the monthly discharge of blood from the womb

mesomorph   a somatotype, or body type, basically a 'Y' shape, well-muscled, with wide shoulders, long arms and narrow waist

movement replication   being able to exactly copy and repeat a physical movement

muscle tone   the tension which remains in the muscles, even at rest

muscular endurance   the amount of dynamic strength in a muscle, its ability to keep working for long periods

muscular fatigue   the state of a muscle when it can no longer contract

negative acceleration   where a performer first learns a skill quite quickly and their rate of progress then slows down

nerves   a state of anxiety which can affect a performance, or another name for neurons

neurons   the basic cells of the nervous system

neutral   impartial, not taking sides

nucleus   main cell body of the nervous system

obese   extremely fat or overweight

oesophagus (or gullet)   canal from mouth to stomach, along which food passes

open skills   skills which exist in a situation that is constantly changing

open sports   sports events in which both amateurs and professionals can compete

oxygen debt   a state where the body has used more oxygen that it can supply

oxyhaemoglobin   substance which oxygen turns into after gaseous exchange

passive smoking   where someone who is a non-smoker inhales someone else's cigarette smoke

passive stretching   a flexibility exercise where a performer stretches by pushing against something

peak   physical condition in which an athlete is at the best of their ability

penalty   a punishment for breaking a rule or regulation in an activity

penalty move   a set way of making use of a penalty which has been awarded

performance-enhancing drug   a type of unlawful drug which can help to improve performance

physiology   study of the function and processes of the human body

physiotherapist   a specialist who treats someone by using exercise or massage

plate competition   a separate competition for losers in a main competition

plateau   situation in which a performer stays at the same level of skill, at least temporarily

platelet   small blood cells which help to clot the blood

pleura   membrane surrounding the lungs, which acts as a lubricant

positive acceleration   where a performer finds mastering a skill difficult at first, then improves rapidly

posture   the position in which a person holds their body

power   the combination of the maximum amount of speed with the maximum amount of strength

practice   frequent repetition of an act, skill or physical activity

prescription   a medical treatment which a doctor must authorize

professional   a full time sportsperson who gets paid for competing

psychiatrist   someone who helps people to mentally prepare or mentally cope

pulmonary artery   blood vessel which carries de-oxygenated blood from the right ventricle of the heart to the lungs

pulmonary vein   blood vessel which carries oxygenated blood from the lungs to the left atrium of the heart

pulse raisers   exercises designed to increase the heart rate

pulse rate   the rate per minute at which the heart beats

reinforcement   going over a movement or skill many times to ensure it is correct

relegated   being put down to a lower division or league in a sporting event

routine   a regular and repeated procedure often of rehearsed and set moves

saliva   a digestive juice found in the mouth which helps to digest food

scout   a person who watches, finds and recommends players for sports teams

sedentary   sitting down or being physically inactive for long periods of time

seed   one of the acknowledged top players in a competition or event

segregation   keeping people or teams apart

self-esteem   a feeling of being pleased with, proud or confident of oneself

semi-permeable   a type of membrane which allows the passage of some substances but not others

set play   a pre-arranged and practised move in a physical activity

skeletal pump   muscle action which helps the veins to pump blood around the body

skill   an ability to perform certain activities or movements with control or consistency to bring about a desired result

slow twitch fibre   red fibres in skeletal muscles which contract slowly and repeatedly for long periods

somatotype   body types (see **ectomorph, endomorph, mesomorph**)

spasm   a sudden involuntary muscular contraction

sphygmomanometer   a device for measuring blood pressure

standing broad jump   a two-footed jump forwards, starting from a squat position

static opponent   an opponent in a practice situation who does not get actively involved

station   a place or area which is part of a circuit used in circuit training

stimulus   something (such as music) which influences or assists a performance

striated muscle   (or voluntary or striped muscle) skeletal muscles of the body

stroke   sudden attack when the blood supply to the brain is cut off

sucrose   a type of sugar (e.g. white table sugar)

synovial joint   a joint which has a large range of mobility

systolic pressure   the pressure of the blood in the arteries when the left ventricle contracts

tactics   pre-arranged and rehearsed strategies or methods of play

teamwork   the ability of a team to work together as a single unit with a common aim

technique   the manner in which someone performs a skill

tendon   fibrous tissue which joins a muscle to bone

testosterone   one of the banned types of androgenic anabolic steroids

tidal volume   the amount of air breathed in and out during normal breathing

training   a method of practising or preparing for physical activity

transfer of skills   skills which are common between different physical activities and which can be performed in them

travelling   moving forwards in an activity such as trampolining. Can also be a basketball infringement

undernourished   lacking in certain nutrients

unit   a group or number of players within a team

vaccinate   an injection or inoculation with a vaccine

valve   a structure which permits the flow of blood in only one direction

vein   a thin blood vessel which transports blood

ventricles   the two bottom chambers of the heart

vertebral column   the groups of vertebrae which make up the spine

vitamin deficiency   a lack of the necessary level or intake of vitamins

vitamin supplement   a means of correcting a vitamin deficiency

VO_2   the total amount of oxygen which the body needs and takes in at any time

VO_2 maximum   the maximum amount of oxygen which the body can take in

warm-down   a period of gentle exercise after taking part in physical activity to allow the body to recover safely and return to its normal state

warm-up   a preparation period before taking part in physical activity

Index